# Appointment
# in Zambia

# Appointment in Zambia

## An African Adventure

### Sara Dunn

Matador
9 Priory Business Park,
Wistow Road, Kibworth Beauchamp,
Leicestershire. LE8 0RX
Tel: (+44) 116 279 2299
Fax: (+44) 116 279 2277
Email: books@troubador.co.uk
Web: www.troubador.co.uk/matador

ISBN 978 1780882 383

British Library Cataloguing in Publication Data.
A catalogue record for this book is available from the British Library.

Typeset in 12pt Adobe Garamond Pro by Troubador Publishing Ltd, Leicester, UK
Printed and bound in Great Britain by TJ International Ltd, Padstow, Cornwall

**Matador** is an imprint of Troubador Publishing Ltd

*To Ross*
*For the dream and for getting us there.*

# Contents

# *Prologue*

I felt catastrophe snapping at our wheels. We'd suffered a disastrous day, and the next one looked no better.

Lying side by side in the night, the moon brilliant through the windscreen, neither of us had voiced our thoughts. Worry wouldn't let me rest. I wondered if Ross had managed to drop off. I shifted position and covered my head with a tee shirt to gain darkness. The Sahara crouched in silence on the other side of the car doors like a monster waiting to consume us. With a longing to lie flat I pulled up our shared blanket against the cold which still surprised us after the oven-blast heat of day.

Impatience had brought us to this. A few more weeks of waiting for our sea passage to Cape Town would have rewarded us with the trip of our dreams and money in our pockets. Ross could be concentrating on his prospective job in Chingola. Instead we'd run up a debt of a thousand pounds and had possibly ruined our pristine Hillman Hunter into the bargain. Driving to Zambia from North Africa bore no relation to touring up from Cape Town in the South. The new job would be far from Ross's thoughts now, being replaced with simple survival on a road through purgatory. If anything happened to him we'd be truly stuck. I couldn't drive. I tortured myself with the realisation that our recklessness was astounding. A toxic mix of adventurous spirit, ignorance, impulse and naivety lured us into believing in our own invincibility and we'd heedlessly, and dangerously, ignored all the warnings! Now we'd have to dig ourselves out of this mess. Literally and without a shovel!

I shifted position again to ease my shoulders tingling from sunburn and aching from hours of scraping sand from behind and under the wheels.

'Take care when you're scraping under the car that it doesn't fall on top of you!' Ross had shouted in warning a few hours ago.

The car jack we'd been using didn't look as if it would suffer much more abuse. Perhaps he'd dream up another strategy in the morning, like he'd thought of driving over the spare wheels to escape the soft sand when nothing else had worked.

Until then we'd been confident and excited about the challenge. Particularly after the official at the Sous Prefecture assessed the car's suitability to make the Sahara crossing and declared 'bien' with a reassuring smile. It took just one day for serious misgivings and doubts to invade our ingenuous heads. One day in the 'proper' Sahara and it looked like we might have to go back. What a shameful failure it would be, falling at the first hurdle, and tomorrow we could be forced to have a rethink.

We'd met only one solitary vehicle going in the opposite direction since we joined the 'piste'. The driver had slowed and we'd had a brief exchange of, 'Bonjour. Ça va? Oui merci, et vous? Au revoir, bonne route!' before driving on. If this was an average over twelve hours, at least one person would be travelling nearby the next day. The main 'highway' into southern Algeria was not a busy one. But we'd had to leave the main track on unmarked diversions, so travellers could easily miss each other and hence that single chance per day of communication with another person and civilisation.

The Sahara measures twice the area of the Mediterranean Sea. Heat shimmer can reduce visibility to two or three hundred metres and like ships in a fog another distant vehicle might pass unseen. Our choice of 'Golden Sand' for the colour when we'd ordered the car back in April was a joke of destiny. We couldn't be camouflaged better.

I adjusted the tee shirt and looked at Ross, his face illuminated in the moonlight. An oily smudge from working under the car marked his cheek. Toilet facilities were a luxury of the better petrol stations as we travelled through France and Spain. Here it was a wipe down with a damp flannel and this evening it had been cursory. He snored gently. 'That's good,' I thought. 'At least he's getting some rest. He'll need it for another day of hard driving. If we're lucky enough to get over the river bed! We really must buy a shovel if we ever get the chance.'

I spread the tee shirt back over my eyes and tried to clear sand from my ear without success. Brushing hadn't removed the sand from my hair either.

The last six months had been a roller-coaster. The excitement of a job in Africa, choosing a new car, my twenty-first birthday, the end of four years study, and our first wedding anniversary followed each other in quick succession. Then we'd disposed of unnecessary possessions, which meant all of our furniture from our two-roomed flat, and we'd felt liberated. We'd expected news of a booking on a Union Castle Line ship to arrive any day through July and August, and the frustrating weeks of waiting became too much to bear. Yes, impatience was to blame.

Britain's new Prime Minister Edward Heath was being interviewed on television on that fateful evening only six weeks earlier.

'We could always go overland now that we have wheels,' Ross had suggested out of the blue.

I'd pulled out an old atlas and we'd traced a route down through Africa through countries still marked with their colonial names. Only two strips of water interrupted the flow of land between Edinburgh and Chingola; the English Channel and the Straits of Gibraltar. We'd played with the idea for a while. Fourteen months had passed since Neil Armstrong walked on the moon so Africa couldn't be that difficult, could it? By the time Samantha was twitching her nose in 'Bewitched' the seed had been sown and the dream became wild. A month later we boarded the ferry for Calais.

I felt something on my neck and brushed it away. It wasn't impossible for a scorpion to find its way into our cosy nest.

Another thing to worry about.

I changed position again and concentrated on blanking out the errant thoughts swirling through my mind.

# MAP I
## The Journey and Index of maps

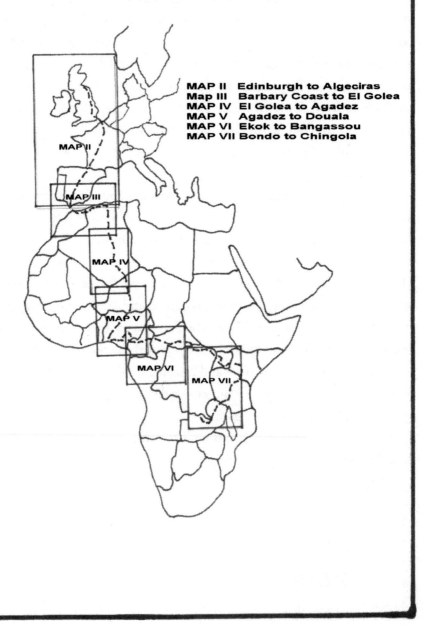

MAP II   Edinburgh to Algeciras
Map III  Barbary Coast to El Golea
MAP IV  El Golea to Agadez
MAP V   Agadez to Douala
MAP VI  Ekok to Bangassou
MAP VII Bondo to Chingola

MAP II

MAP III

MAP IV

MAP V

MAP VI

MAP VII

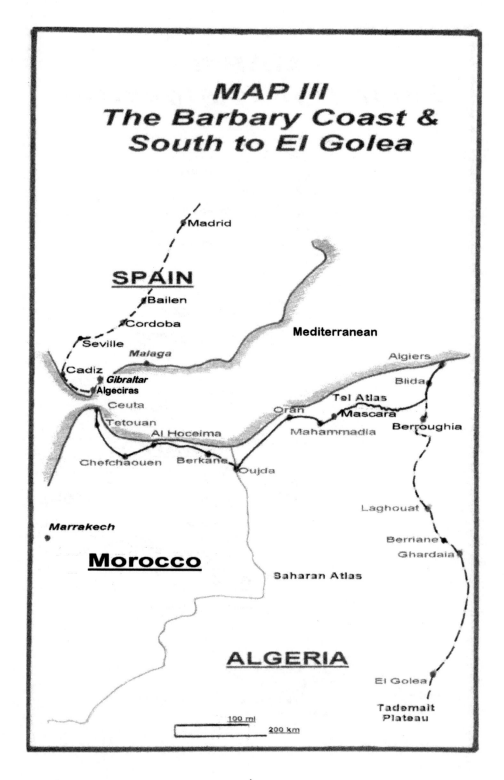

# CHAPTER ONE

## *The Barbary Coast*

13th October 1970

Across the straits of Gibraltar a faint outline of mountains spanned the horizon. Africa. The real adventure would be starting soon, and a heady mix of apprehension, excitement, fear and joy swept over us. Did we have the stamina for this? Would we survive?

To get to North Africa from Spain we had to take the Algeciras to Ceuta route. In 1969 General Franco had closed Spain's borders with Gibraltar wanting the 'Rock' for Spain. A stalemate lasted for sixteen years before the frontier would be reopened. We arrived at the port late in the evening and took a leg-stretching stroll down Calle de Cristobal Colon before driving close to the ferry terminal for the night. We wanted to be passengers on the first departure the next day.

'Do you think you are really up for such a journey?' The man in the Edinburgh AA office had asked my enthusiastic twenty-three-year-old husband back in September. After some persuasion the man disappeared into another room to consult by telephone with the London office.

'The journey is not possible.'

He returned forty minutes later with his missive explaining that due to closed borders in several North African countries and the aftermath of the Biafran war he didn't think there was a way through to Zambia, but reliable information was elusive. Clinging to his uncertainty we left undeterred and continued preparing to motor to London for the necessary papers.

Nothing could deter us. Not the smashed wing when the car was parked in Edinburgh. Not the breakdown just south of Newcastle. Not the red tape of preparations, and not when my father took me aside and suggested

1

quietly, 'You won't lose face if you change your mind.'

He'd lent us the money to take advantage of the tax-free benefit for a car intended for export. He'd also endorsed a further loan from the bank to pay for our journey.

We did not sail the next morning. Algeciras struggled to cope as the main departure point from Europe to Africa since Gibraltar was off-limits. In our search for the ticket office amongst the chaos of people and acres of vehicles a small officious Arab had spotted our hesitation.

'You want to take a boat, yes?' He wrung his hands like a pantomime Fagin and smiled through blackened teeth. 'I can help you.' Claiming familiarity with the procedure he assured us he would arrange tickets on our behalf and see us quickly and safely on to the vessel. Around us ferries belched plumes of black smoke from decrepit marine engines and a ship's horn bellowed.

We took a glance at the bustling confusion around us, a gigantic scrimmage of humanity, and considered his offer. We weakened.

'I take care of everything. You can trust me, very honest fellow. Follow me, follow me!' he ordered and grabbing Ross's arm bustled us towards a grim hut. Piles of shuffled paper lay on a table. He shouted in Arabic to a young man sitting back in a chair and they conversed for a few minutes.

'We book for you, yes? Write here your name and car details. Here. Write it here!' He jabbed a nicotine-stained finger at the paper. Ross obediently wrote it all down.

Our 'agent' then disappeared leaving us in his 'office' with the youth. Spanish failed all of us and he spoke no English.

'Give me passports and I will get your tickets now. Wait here, wait here!' The agent had returned with fresh demands.

'We'll go with you,' replied Ross firmly.

He protested but led us around buildings this way and that. 'You let me do this for you. I do many times. Other people like you they trust me to do this. You go sit in office.' He might have hoped for a good tip having seen the newness of our car. We'd gone along with his scheme for long enough but weren't about to give up our passports. We didn't lose money but we did lose time and patience. Ross dismissed him; we turned a corner and spotted the ticket office with a queue around the block. Thanks to his meddlesome performance the midday sailing was full by the time we made our reservations, so we couldn't leave until the evening.

We drove up into the hills outside Algeciras and watched the swallows swooping and gliding from sky to grass and back upwards again with whistling cries. Were they the same birds we had seen lining up in Edinburgh and London ready for their exodus? Their destination this winter would be South Africa, further than ours and we wondered who would arrive first. Lazily we contemplated the hustle of the port and passage of ships below as we sunbathed away the afternoon. Instinct told us to top up our reserves ready for a Northern winter forgetting the reality would be a tropical African summer.

The quote for transporting our car proved more than expected. The Hillman Hunter measured 14 feet 5 inches, but if it had been a couple of inches shorter in length the price would have been considerably less.

'I'll just go and remove the bumpers and that'll bring us into the lower size and price range,' announced Ross.

The disbelieving ticket officer laughed and genially agreed to the lower rate without the need to remove any bumpers. We drove into the queue looking forward to a crossing similar to the one from Dover. This was still Europe after all. If we'd looked more closely at the transport boarding with us we'd have found a clue, because battered old vans made up most of their number.

Our illusions of buying tax-free goods and passing a comfortable few hours sipping coffee in a spacious cafeteria proved to be way off the mark. It wasn't the accompanying thrum of other car engines that greeted us as we drove aboard, but the bleating of goats and the fluttering of leg-bound chickens. Untidy piles of bulging bundles occupied every corner. Instead of the anticipated freshly brewed coffee, the smell of engine oil mingled with animal excrement and human sweat accosted our nostrils. Along with several hundred hot bodies, mainly in *kaftans* and *djellabas*, we were herded down into the bowels of the vessel and considered ourselves lucky to get a makeshift seat on a ledge not too close to the smelly livestock. Our bargain tickets restricted us to this deck without even a glimpse of the beautiful bay flanked by Gibraltar on one side and Spain on the other. The ship's engine noise prevented normal conversation, so we people-watched, quickly forgetting the unfulfilled promise of a coffee.

When Spain handed over most of Morocco to the newly independent kingdom in 1956, Ceuta remained under Spanish control as an exclave. So although strictly speaking we drove off the ferry onto African soil we were effectively still in Spain. Somehow this was a disappointment to us, but not for long. We disembarked and headed off into the darkness.

The shock of culture change at the frontier hit us full on. Men and women rushed back and forth; uniformed men searched suitcases without care and left them in turmoil. Loud guttural voices suggested great urgency to our Western ears although we couldn't see any emergency. Ravaged suitcases lay on the dusty floor spilling their contents. Women frantically tried to restore order, gabbling loudly to each other in a strange tongue as they pushed scattered garments down into corners. Some women had their faces decorated with intricate henna patterns looking like tattoos. We sat tight and waited for the formalities required of us to be revealed, because all the written signs we could see bore the curls and dots of Arabic.

Since Algeciras we'd seen no other Europeans bar one or two businessmen. Far from making us feel lonely it added to the exoticism of the place. Plenty of new sights and sounds presented themselves for us to absorb and at this early stage our patience was untried and strong. A small French-speaking Moroccan came to our aid. He spoke in a loud whisper and guided us to the right counter. After a small payment for insurance the uniformed men allowed us straight through without a search.

In the no-man's land between borders a gathering of shifty-looking men sidled in from the darkness with soft leather *balgha* on their feet.

'Buy money, nice price!' they waved greasy bundles of notes in our faces. Large leather pouches stuffed with bank notes hung from their shoulders and their pestering bordered on harassment. The rates being offered sounded substantially better than the official ones making us wary but when we saw some respectable-looking men approach them we decided to do the same. A few pounds bought us two wads of greasy dog-eared Moroccan Dirham and Algerian Dinar. The bearded money-changers had given us our first impression of Moroccans, furtively dashing about in the shadows with false smarmy manners, hooded gowns and fingers dirty from over-handled notes. Feeling as if we'd entered a land of pantomime villainy we were put on our guard.

Most men in Morocco wore long hooded coats or *djellabas* in brown or white wool for the winter. While most of the women wore a *haik*, an all-encompassing white cloak which covered their heads, a few also covered their faces, a sight unfamiliar to us in 1970. Standing in the queue for our papers to be cleared, I studied these women to find clues of their reactions to us. In British fashion, the hotter the outside temperature the less I wore. In my mini-dress I felt exposed and couldn't fathom whether their quiet stares were of contempt, curiosity, or envy of my freedom. I pulled at the hem of my dress to cover more leg. Eyes alone are only half the story. The men looked too busy for these silent exchanges but as I was to learn later they were not unaware of me. Ross whistled as he does when he's waiting and restless, and a small boy started to copy him. The anonymous *haik*-clad woman sitting next to the boy administered a sharp slap to a chubby cheek and his lip wobbled but he didn't cry. My husband saw it too and stopped mid-tune. Already we both felt we had blundered in a land where we couldn't be sure of the rules and sound judgments would be obscure. The excitement of Morocco's foreignness ebbed and again we felt on guard.

At last we left Europe to enter Morocco, our first African country. It is part of the *Maghreb*, an Arabic word meaning 'place of sunset' which encompasses all of the Mediterranean coastal countries across North Africa long inhabited by Berbers. This was the Barbary Coast of old, where slave markets grew from ancient beginnings and flourished for three hundred years under Ottoman rule. Unlike others in the world they also traded European slaves acquired by pirate raids of ships or coastal towns and villages along the Mediterranean. History did nothing to reassure me.

We passed through the frontier and drove on to the port of Tétouan. All along the straight road cars reeking smoke rolled cheek by jowl with overloaded clip-clopping donkeys. Their blinkered heads bent to a life of slavery. Sometimes the warm Levanter wind which funnels through the straits of Gibraltar from the northeast blows so fiercely that this exposed road became unsafe for travel. The wind was not blowing on the evening we arrived and yellow street lamps cast luminous puddles over the scene below.

Cooking smells mixed with smoke emanated from street braziers, and long-robed figures thronged the roadside, hastening on *balgha* clad feet past rows of open stalls. Dangling light bulbs intended to draw attention to the goods on display instead had me imagining accidental fires under the loosely thatched roofs. Seeing our pale faces many held out their hands for money shouting '*Baksheesh, baksheesh!*'

Looking at the array in the bakery window our mouths watered. Round crusty *khobz*, piles of large and small unleavened flatbread, sesame sprinkled buns and cakes, honey drizzled biscuits, anise-flavoured *fekkas*, almond-stuffed *rghaif* all beckoned to be sampled, the problem was making a choice. A woman entered the shop with a tray of raw dough shapes ready for baking, and the assistant disappeared with it behind the scenes. Communal street ovens could be used by all the inhabitants of most villages if no official bakery existed. We made our selection and carried the delicious contents of the paper bags off to enjoy a wander around the town.

We had stopped to spend the night at Chefchaouen, feeling safer now that our reactions to Morocco were tempered with normal everyday life, and illogical fears of cloak and dagger scenes had stopped playing on our imaginations. The disharmony of the border towns had been replaced by something much calmer and welcoming.

Chefchaouen is in the heart of Morocco's beautiful Rif Mountains. In this pretty hillside town with the old medina buildings painted a brilliant sky blue we forgot our initial uncertainties of Morocco. Other young people had found the town before us and they walked in pairs down narrow streets exploring like us and speaking German, French, Italian, English. Carrying our goodies back up the cobbled street we caught glimpses between the houses of rugged mountains speckled with pine trees. Back at the car we ate sandwiches made with tinned sardines, and a dessert of spicy cake washed down with fresh milk. Our sandwiches for the next weeks usually consisted of tomatoes with or without canned meat or fish. Wherever we went all of these ingredients could be bought easily without much cost and made for a reasonably well-balanced meal to keep up our strength. Variety became a luxury we could not afford and with so many changes happening to us on a daily basis eating the same food day in day out brought an oddly reassuring consistency to our days.

The walk and the clear air ensured good appetites and later sound sleep claimed us tucked away in our quiet parking spot. In the darkness I changed into a yellow patterned tee shirt and leg-concealing purple bell-bottom trousers ready for the next day in a Muslim country.

## 15<sup>th</sup> October

'Difficult or dangerous section' had been marked on the map for the route we were about to tackle. The mountain road offered nearly as many potholes as tarmac covering and gave Ross no chance to admire the stunning view all around as he negotiated bend after hairpin bend. The unguarded drop to one side had me hanging onto my seat and then a jolt announced a ramp giving way to stony dirt track. Our bones rattled until another ramp returned us to tarmac and more potholes. In some parts the road had fallen away as if a giant had taken a bite out of it and left a trail of stones and dirt dribbling down the mountainside.

I yawned to make my ears pop from the altitude and overcame any vertigo by feasting my eyes on the scene laid out below showing an ever wider perspective. We rounded a bend and Ross jammed his right foot down.

The back wheels seized and the car swung at right angles with the road.

We felt the wheels skid over loose scree and helplessly wondered when they would stop. Ross kept his foot on the brake and clutched the steering wheel with closed fists, bracing himself for what might come next. My concentration snapped back from mesmerised gazing as I looked down in horror at a sheer drop with nothing to hold us back for hundreds of feet below. The car stopped inches from the vertical edge. Our hearts in our mouths we took some minutes to recover the courage to continue.

The track had disappeared and a landslide obliterated the road for the foreseeable distance ahead without any signs or barriers to give us warning. Backtracking, we found a path up the mountain made by those who had come before us, and which skirted around the impenetrable obstruction. We realised the onus was on the driver to be prepared for such unmarked hazards.

Still on the diversion we had stopped for a break and some water when two little boys in *djellabas* found us. Their dusty feet swam in scuffed shoes that might fit them in a few years time, the fronts tied with the knotted remains of laces and string. One of them wore a plastic bag on his head like a chef's hat. These bright-eyed twelve-year olds gave little concern for clothing.

'*Baksheesh, baksheesh*!' they begged holding out grubby hands. We gave them some sugar lumps and encouraged by this small success they demanded 'Cigarettes, cigarettes!'

'You are too young!' I protested.

'*Hashish, hashish*!'

Could we be hearing right? 'Hash' could be bought in student bars in Edinburgh and we had known a few undergraduates who dabbled in an undercover way. Strictly a part of the adult world in our experience, we couldn't believe what we were hearing.

'Heroin, heroin!' This final plea astounded us and recovering from our shock we looked at the cheeky youngsters. These had to be prospective dealers, not users.

We had found ourselves on a hippy trail. Hippy baby boomers from the wealthy countries of Western Europe, the United States and Australia, in fact people like us, were 'on the trail' here and in Eastern Asia to 'find themselves' and 'communicate with other cultures.'

Backpackers on their shoestring equivalent of the 'Grand Tour' lived on a few dinars a day, grew their hair, dressed in local clothes, and lived with the ideals of peace and love. Many found this peace with the help of marijuana, or *hashish* as it was called here. Newly liberated by widespread use of 'the Pill' they enjoyed the benefit of 'Free love' without its traditional responsibilities. Others sought 'enlightenment' and dabbled in new religions or exotic old ones; and some set up communes creating an alternative way of life to their own usually middle class upbringing.

'Marrakech Express', a Crosby Stills and Nash hit from the Hippy era related a train journey through Morocco from Casablanca with this personal search in mind singing of how they *'Had to get away to see what we could find.'* No one worried too much about enigmatic phrases like *'I found the garden in your hair.'* We tried to sing it as we drove along but only managed the chorus which became repetitive so we soon gave up for more familiar songs.

Slightly miffed at being grouped with these dreamers, especially with our smart new car, we gave the boys a Dirham each and left. All along the road similar boys offered us *hashish* to buy, holding up small paper bags, and some of them practically threw themselves at the car in an effort to make a sale. They spent their days standing by the roadside waiting for prospective buyers and the possibility of rich rewards, at least for their employers.

Eating an early lunch high in the mountains we looked out over the valleys at lush green plantations. Years later we discovered we had been driving past the biggest cannabis-producing area of the world.

On the downward slopes of the mountains unhealthy noises emanated from underneath us. Ross stopped the car and peered underneath.

'I think the rear suspension could be in trouble. This vehicle isn't built for the abuse we've given it on these roads.' He stood up and wiped his hands. 'This could be serious; we'll have to get it checked out as soon as we can.'

I dug out the workshop manual from the jumble on the back seat.

*Suspension knocks or rattles:*
*If the knocking comes from the rear end it may not be the suspension system but*
*the drive shaft joints that are at fault.*
*Suspension squeaks:*
*Bounce the car…Lubricate…Failure to cure the squeaks calls for expert*
*investigation as other points may be the cause, and the cure is not so easy.*

Afraid to make things worse he drove with painful caution. At a garage in Al Hoceima they peered into it and under it, rocking it violently, banging the shock absorbers, adjusting valves, checking wires and other mysteries while we waited.

'Okay, I've tightened things up and you can go now,' said the mechanic handing back the keys.

Ross looked uneasy because little if anything appeared to have been done. Not able to believe in the clean bill of health he vowed to get a second opinion. Having an 'expert' looking at it had at least convinced him that nothing major could be wrong and in spite of lingering doubts we set off at reasonable speeds again.

The disaster back on the A1 had left its mark. Our journey from Edinburgh to London, surely the most straightforward part of our trip, should have warned us off our project. Past Newcastle we had bowled along the dual carriageway at seventy miles an hour enjoying new car comfort. A loud thump from under the chassis shook us out of complacency. In the mirror Ross saw a lump of metal bouncing down the carriageway behind us. His left foot depressed the clutch and nothing happened. He took his other foot off the accelerator and pumped the brake until we could pull safely on to the hard shoulder. Then he strode back to retrieve the errant part while I watched other drivers racing southwards to their destinations mindless of our predicament. We'd driven only one hundred and thirty miles from Edinburgh, our longest journey in the car to date.

Leaving Ross peering into the engine with a torch lodged in his mouth to free both hands, I set off for help. The telephone boxes at the roadside were out of order, and I panted up the steep bank of a cutting to knock on a farmer's door, jingling some ready change to pay for the call.

'It's the slave cylinder of the clutch,' announced the AA rep an hour later. 'I've done this job for ten years and I've never come across anything like it before. It's a bizarre fault in a brand new car!'

It was fully dark by the time he towed us to the nearest garage. We spent the night with a surprised uncle and aunt who lived close to our unhappy breakdown.

After a head-shaking mechanic repaired the clutch we continued downcast but without incident to London. This inauspicious start to a long journey could have been seen as a sign, but we refused to acknowledge it. We had clocked up less than six hundred miles and already our new car had a replacement wing and clutch repair.

All through Spain Ross had become almost paranoid about strange noises from the car, fearful of breakdowns in places too distant for recovery. He felt it was vital to leave the safety of Europe with even the smallest mechanical disorders fixed and to be as prepared as possible for the rigours ahead.

Twenty-five miles from Seville we heard another loud thump, this time from under the bonnet. It wasn't paranoia. The fan belt had snapped and we sat at the side of the road for an hour waiting for the engine to cool before Ross could fit the spare one.

'Have you got any tights in your bag?' Ross had asked mysteriously.

'I think I might have one pair,' I'd replied puzzled. 'I wasn't expecting to need them in Africa.'

'They might come in handy as a temporary measure if we run out of spare fan belts. We'll need to buy plenty more spares if this is all the time they last. Perhaps it's the heat.' He'd examined the shredded remains of the old fan belt, tensioned the replacement into position and closed the bonnet. There followed hours of searching out a car-spares shop which would be open at *Fiesta* time.

'It says R547 or RH789,' I'd read aloud, holding the manual open at the page marked 'specifications'. Ross squatted in front of an array of fan-belts, the frayed one in his hand, searching for the right code. The one we needed was not available and he was trying to work out which would be the nearest equivalent. He'd picked out four and we took them to the desk to pay, crossing our fingers that they would see us through. It turned out to be the only fan-belt replacement we ever needed.

I turned the metal catch on the triangular quarter-light and pushed it to let in air while Ross flipped the switch marked 'Blower'. It was hotter than Edinburgh in a heat wave. We were back at the Moroccan coast in the Spanish-built holiday town of Al Hoceima. Blue and white houses stretched down to the sparkling Mediterranean. To refuel we first had to buy petrol coupons at the bank. Feeling safely stocked up after the palaver we ventured into a bazaar intending to 'window shop' and experience a flavour of what Morocco had to offer. They gave us a warm welcome in a small carpet boutique, with nearly every rug and kilim in the store rolled out for us to admire.

'Yes they are very beautiful, but we can't afford to buy a rug,' we protested.

'Don't worry you just look!' replied the swarthy owner rolling out another gorgeous creation. 'These ones are prayer mats. What colours do you like?'

We sat amidst the woollen piles and sipped hot, sweet, mint tea. He instructed young men to hold up rug after rug for our admiration, and we smiled and nodded, stroked and listened.

'I show you some very special carpets now,' he blustered, and his son rolled out a densely patterned prayer-rug in blues and golds. 'It is made from the finest wool and has very many threads woven very, very closely together, look here... and look at the back also, it is so fine the pattern is really clear.'

The pattern depicted intertwined trees and birds making our eyes flit from detail to detail.

'This is the tree of life. Around the edge is a pattern which tells me where it was made. Look here. Each pattern has a meaning also.' Its imperfections increased the fascination, proving it to be hand-made and affirming only Allah to be perfect.

'We must go to get some food,' I said, hoping to present a getaway ploy. He was not about to let us go so easily. Ross stayed captive while one of the owner's sons took me to buy bread and fruit at a shop we wouldn't have found on our own down the backstreets. I found fixed prices much lower than we had paid for the same goods in Chefchaouen. This favour was a part of the sales pitch and of course kept us in his clutches. Three hours later we stepped back into the squalor of the street worn down by long conversations and bartering, with a pair of laced sandals and a thin striped kilim. The merchant's long-term marketing paid off because we have had a soft spot for Oriental carpets ever since, although it was many years before we actually bought one.

We had parked the car beside a garden full of productive trees. Huge red pomegranates decorated one tall, dense bush; a few ripe lemons graced another; a third was studded with mandarins; and three more with promises of almond, cherry and peach completed the fruit selection. Both men and women raked ripe olives from the six remaining trees, letting small black ovals fall on to cloths spread out on the ground below the branches. The workers filled huge baskets ready to transport their bounty to the communal olive mill along with empty containers into which the thick green liquid would be decanted. Traditional terra-cotta jugs and jars had been rejected in favour of lighter but ugly plastic. This harvest would supply a large family with enough olive oil for a year, and it would be ready to start using in a few months, the time it took to mature.

'You should go to the beaches, they are very beautiful here and very popular with Eenglish like you. That is where they all go to stay, and you will like it very much.' The friendly young man spoke English with confidence, guaranteeing him a job in the growing Moroccan tourist industry.

But this was not what we had in mind, and regardless of beautiful beaches we single-mindedly continued east towards Algeria. Such single-mindedness would deprive us of countless sights along our way which would not have been much of a detour. France and Spain had flashed past with hardly a pause. Paris, the chateaux of the Loire, Madrid and Seville would have to wait. Like blinkered donkeys we refused to spare the time, money and energy for such distractions. So we missed ancient ruins, museums, Foreign Legion Forts, waterfalls, national parks, cathedrals and mosques as we pressed on with our journey.

We left Al Hoceima with another impression of Moroccans. They showed us great warmth and many approached us to chat easily if they spoke French or English. We left at dusk with our backs to a brilliant red sunset and Algiers still a long way to go. Ross kept driving until eleven before stopping before Berkane.

## 16th October

Just one week after motoring past Kentish apple orchards towards Dover we now followed a long straight road flanked by miles of orange groves. Stall after stall of fruit sellers lined the route. We couldn't spare the time and effort for sightseeing, but sampling local produce was another matter. Another melon and a kilo of almost sickly-sweet black grapes tempted us, and we luxuriated in their full ripe taste. The insipid-tasting expensive fruit that found its way into Scottish greengrocers could not compare to this succulence. Day after day and meal after meal of sandwiches could be endured with such treats and gave us what we considered affordable luxuries to make up for our other deprivations.

'There are strange noises coming from the wheels, can you hear it?'

We were pushing further east and Ross had become one with our lifeline the car, developing sensitivity to the slightest discord in its performance. My untuned ear and ignorance of engineering offered no help, and for the whole trip he bore the burden of responsibility for detecting warning signals and nursing our vehicle through the heavy demands we were to make of a standard saloon car. Most of these noises proved to be benign, and I resorted to diverting conversations to lighter subjects in an effort to distract him from an obsessive awareness of every click and rattle. If we'd had a radio I could have turned it up to drown out the worrisome groans and creaks.

We searched the streets of Oujda for a mechanic to find the cause of wheel noises. The task proved easier than we thought, and he aligned both front wheels then checked the rest of the car. Unfortunately he spotted an oil leak from the gear-box bearing, and to make matters worse damaged the offending bearing during its removal. So we sat bored and frustrated while a gopher looked all around town for a suitable spare. He came back empty-handed.

The mechanic then put the old bearing on the earthen floor of the garage, hit it hard with a few strokes of his hammer, blew the dust off, wiped it with a rag and refitted it. I sought the wisdom of the Rootes Owner's Instruction booklet.

### Gearbox Lubrication
*The gearbox unit is 'filled for life' and no oil changes would normally be necessary...*

The incipient leak became considerably worse after his ministrations. Across three countries up until Lagos we were condemned to spend fifteen minutes on a daily basis checking and topping up the gear box with Shell Super Motor Oil 100. To this day I can still recognise the not unpleasant vegetable smell of gear-box oil, an unusual skill for a woman.

Algeria greeted us with a dry and rocky landscape which soon became a fertile valley as farms flashed past the windows. At the frontier we completed several forms and discovered possession of Algerian money outside the country was illegal. We kept quiet about our stash realising that the favourable rate of exchange for our money near Ceuta must have been on the black market, as we'd guessed at the time.

Algeria gained its independence from France in 1962 after the eight-year Guerre d'Algérie. This decolonisation war involved guerrilla warfare, terrorism against civilians, and use of torture on both sides.

The mercenary Foreign Legion as well as the regular French army fought against the Arabs. For one hundred and thirty years the Legion's headquarters had been at Sidi Bel Abbes south of Oran, with Algeria at the centre of most of their operations. Recruits had mostly been German, but also other nationalities and few questions were asked of applicants resulting in a sizeable criminal element. In Germany certain offences could be commuted at this time by a term in the Foreign Legion, which accounted for their greater numbers. Few British joined up. In spite of this we found ourselves tarred with the same brush as the French and generally not made to feel welcome except by a few individuals.

The heater stayed permanently in the off position now even in the cooler evenings, and both quarter-lights let in a pleasant breeze. We played the guessing game of what crops grew in the fields. They looked so different from the ones back home at this time of the year. The early evening call to prayer echoed over houses and fields from a tall minaret. Darkness fell and a sickle moon shone above bright stars.

Passing through the port of Oran, Algeria's second largest city, drivers had their own rules, and several times we had to swerve to avoid a collision.

'He just cut straight out in front of me from that junction back there!' shouted Ross, indignant and tired.

'They must have a different highway code here,' I said.

'Sheer ignorance more likely!' he grumbled.

It was time to stop for the day.

## 17th October

We passed Mascara, a name coming from the Arabic 'Mother of Soldiers' and appropriate for the former location of one of The Foreign Legion training centres. New recruits travelled by ship from Marseilles to be broken into military ways by the cream of the French Military Academies. French officers ruled with an iron fist and put their motley charges through a gruelling training that had become legendary. In Strasbourg, Lyon and Paris the initiates would sign over their lives for five years. During the early 1960s over four hundred of them arrived in Algeria every month. Since the end of the Algerian war they had decamped to mainland France.

After Mohammadia all kinds of fruit, vegetables, and trinkets appeared for sale in roadside stalls. Amongst the bric-a-brac stood ornately framed pictures of Nasser, the Egyptian president, who had a huge following since the 1950s. He had helped Algeria to gain its independence. Nasser initiated revolutionary changes all over the Arab world and forty years later in 2011 he is still seen as a symbol of Arab dignity and freedom. We saw fewer smiles and friendly waves after leaving Morocco, but beggars were less and the roads in better condition.

Serpentine lanes of the Casbah in Algiers led down to the Mediterranean sea. Islands where a Carthaginian trading-post had been established in the fourth century BC bathed in sunlight off the coast. Remains of the citadel, old mosques and Ottoman-style palaces told centuries of Algiers' history, and cloaked figures could have come from an illustrated New Testament. They flitted between shadowy buildings down twisting alleyways the width of a laden donkey. Dust clouds coloured our glimpses of the city a dingy sepia to reinforce the atmosphere of timelessness. Only incessantly beeping traffic let us know it was the twentieth century.

We had made a special journey to Algiers because our AA book told us we needed permission from l'Office National de Tourisme or O.N.A.T, before crossing the Sahara. We concluded the best place for this would be the capital.

The city traffic bewildered us with its relentless chaos. Drivers used their horns as they would their voices, telling each other to move on, expressing impatience or anger, or simply announcing their presence. The universally male drivers resorted to fist-waving and shouting without restraint. We'd never seen anything like it. Gridlock was never far away whichever road we took.

'This is unbelievable. There really doesn't seem to be any concept of the

Highway Code, unless it's different here.' Ross reiterated my incredulity from the day before.

Illustrated notices about parking restrictions could be seen everywhere and understood even by non Arabic readers, but drivers parked just about anywhere knowing they would not be penalised by an inefficient administration. Unmarked streets and signs only in Arabic confused our search further and the O.N.A.T seemed to elude us with our inadequate map. After many stops for directions and frustration with one-way traffic we tracked it down, and like everyone else we parked where we could in an undesignated place.

The square grey building run by bureaucrats held many departments and it took us a further ten minutes to find the right one. At the desk an uninterested clerk knew little about crossing the Sahara and suggested we should ask again at Laghouat. He dismissed us with the same careless abruptness reminiscent of the London Consulates and Embassies where we'd spent hours queuing for visas and entry permits. Never having imagined that a town like Laghouat so far south would have a tourist office, we felt stupid at having jumped to the wrong conclusion and left the dismal building.

Dejected about a difficult and wasted journey we wandered back out onto the crowded streets. If the post office had letters from our parents for us in *poste restante* the journey would still have been worthwhile.

*Poste restante* was a way of getting letters from our families without us having a fixed address. We could send letters home, but there was no other feasible way for them to write back. Communication by telephone would be too difficult and costly. Knowing our route, our parents sent letters to post offices in larger towns where they would be held for two weeks until we called for them. No mail awaited us in Algiers.

The city heat smacked us outside the building momentarily confusing our sense of direction. We headed back along the crowded pavement breathing dust amidst a cacophony of car horns when we noticed a man with a hooked nose approaching us. He had a look of urgency about him and thinking he wanted to say something important we slowed our steps.

Ignoring Ross he approached me and reached out bony fingers to stroke my arm below the cap-sleeve of my cotton shirt. My assailant murmured something guttural in his harsh-sounding language, his dark hand travelling up and down my pale arm. He was smaller than me and at least twenty years my senior but leered lasciviously like a teenage boy with a soft-porn magazine. I recoiled and threw him a filthy look while suppressing a furious urge to lash out violently. Other Algerian citizens pushed past us wanting no involvement in the culture clash.

Uncharacteristically impotent under the heavy atmosphere of a foreign culture, Ross took my other arm and steered us both through the crowds. Repulsed and demeaned I clung to him for protection, wanting to depart this sleazy place where men undressed you with their eyes. I kept my head down to let my light hair fall across my face, afraid to look up into more prurient gazes. How could arms be erogenous zones? No one had warned me about this strange Moslem world.

The paradox of excessive modesty alongside open lechery continued to torment me throughout Algeria and I vowed to wear more clothes, never mind the heat. Keeping cool and the need to follow a dress code battled it out in my subconscious. My limited wardrobe catered for a hot British summer, a style considered blatantly suggestive and contemptible in Algeria. Fortunately most people simply ignored us and we mainly came across the problem in large towns, perhaps where men could be anonymous. I tried to keep close to Ross for protection and avoided eye contact with the opposite sex. This deterred unwelcome advances, but he couldn't always be right by my side.

❧

Huge storms clouds gathered above reflecting our mood. We battled our way back to Blida for provisions and sat in the car eating sandwiches while rain pelted down on the windscreen. The ridiculous sight of an old battered van tearing up and down in the downpour cheered us up. The back doors lay open to reveal five musicians in ankle-length white shirts sitting on wooden chairs. They tried to concentrate on playing traditional string, wind, and percussion instruments. The lilting tones of Arabian music blasted out of a loud-speaker on the roof. Struggling to keep their balance in the moving vehicle, they all but fell off their seats when it swerved around a corner. Like true musicians the band played on and to our untrained ears never missed a note. It baffled us why the driver should be in such haste going up and down the same street. Food and laughter brought our spirits back and the black clouds lifted.

# CHAPTER TWO

## *Heading Due South*

The road past Berroughia wound up the mountain, and dense mist obliterated visibility for brief unexpected stretches. Confusing signs sent us in the wrong direction and we found ourselves on a rough unmade road. We wasted half an hour and precious petrol up the blind alley. The road we should have taken appeared to be still under construction, which explained why we missed it the first time. Once heading on the right course the road works soon opened out into a decent highway again.

At the top of the climb an apparently barren landscape stretched out before us. The car had laboured to take the hills and seemed to have lost power.

'I hope that last lot of petrol was okay,' said Ross looking worried. 'If it's been mixed with something dodgy it could damage the engine.'

Another visit to a garage was in prospect. We still had not reached the challenging parts of our journey to really test the car and these problems chipped away at our confidence. A punctured tyre also needed attention.

We decided to find a place for the night at Laghouat, get a decent sleep and a proper wash. Sleeping in the car started in France, the first night of many to keep expenses to a minimum. With seats reclined as much as the contents on the back seat would allow, rolled up clothing became pillows and we used a double wool blanket over us for covering. It had been a wedding present and still had a luxurious newness with its satin edge brushing our faces. Ross had stuffed some clothes into the well between our seats, but even a chaste goodnight cuddle was uncomfortable with our new arrangements. Resigned we sank back to embrace slumber. It helped to have been up since before dawn on that first day. The discomfort of being unable to lie flat or turn over properly mattered nothing against our weariness and sleep claimed us.

Having spent nearly twenty-four hours a day in the car since London, our personal hygiene routine had been minimal. It involved surreptitious wipe-downs with a flannel dipped in tepid water. The time was right for a morale-booster.

Laghouat is an important oasis for administration, trade, and the military, and can trace its history back to the eleventh century. Like most towns in Algeria it has a dark past stretching from before the Ottoman conquest in the eighteenth century through colonial French control. More violent clashes happened in the recent war of independence. Suffering had been a way of life to generations of these poor people.

During World War Two a prisoner-of-war camp in Laghouat was run by the Vichy French. It held British prisoners whose ship had been torpedoed in the Mediterranean and survivors described conditions as vicious. They had little food or water and depended on the German Red Cross for supplies. When these ended severe hunger took hold. Disciplinary measures owed more to the middle-ages than to the Geneva Convention and punishments were both cruel and arbitrary. Prisoners reported whippings for the smallest offences.

The only hotel listed by our outdated AA book had four stars meaning it was not in our league, but we soon found several others clearly below their rigorous standards. The one we found looked squalid from the outside and in need of a lick of paint, but after a room inspection and knowing it would cost us less than ten shillings each, we thought it an improvement on the car for one night. The man in charge of this hostelry had not been to charm school and ogled me with a smirk while fawning in a sycophantic way to Ross. Under the stars we climbed an open-sided stone stair outside the building to get to our room. Inside we found two single beds, a table and two chairs. A wash-hand basin with cold water and no plug stood behind a locally-woven striped cotton curtain. Although basic, its cleanliness reassured us, as did a double lock on the door. It would effectively keep out the caretaker amongst others.

I did some vital washing and draped it over the chairs and curtain rail to dry overnight. We made good use of the space and rearranged our bags to make their contents more accessible. After more than a week of living every day and night in the car we had a better idea of useful storage and what to place ready to hand.

Sheets but no blankets covered the two beds, so we pushed them together and took down the curtain for a bedcover. It was inadequate for the cold night but a mixture of laziness and fatigue prevented us from creeping down to the car in the dark to get our own warm blanket. The danger of falling ten feet off the wall-less stairs kept me in the building and the vile landlord also stopped me from wanting to use the communal toilet. We'd learned to avoid public lavatories including those in Europe.

'Why don't you go in the sink?' said Ross. 'That's what I'll be doing.'

'That's all very well for you to say,' I answered, 'but I'm not built like you!'

'Just be careful not to break it off its mountings,' he laughed, 'here, stand on this chair and don't put your full weight down.'

I had the choice of meeting the lecherous landlord and any other undesirables, or suffering this new indignity. I chose the latter.

Revelling in the comfort of lying flat even with a hint of bed-springs sticking through the flimsy mattress, we looked up past streaky walls to where stars twinkled through high windows devoid of glass. It hadn't been the most romantic start to the evening, but in the moonlight we made up for all our bed-free nights.

## 18<sup>th</sup> October

We'd misjudged the area. The region from the coast to the Tell Atlas is fertile in spite of its barren appearance, and good for growing grain. During French rule its productivity increased substantially by the sinking of artesian wells where only water was needed to make crops grow. Wheat, barley and oats were the main cereals and enough vegetables and fruits, especially citrus, grew to allow for export. Algeria was the principal producer of oats in Africa and also exported figs, dates, esparto grass, and cork. The mullah woke us with the call to prayer and a busy town came to life.

Laghouat's many market stalls entertained us all morning. We found food prices higher than in Morocco but shopping took less time as haggling was not an option. I felt the heat of the road through my plastic flip-flops and revelled in the warmth of southern sunshine. We wandered into the covered meat section. Grey 'fresh' meat lay in a vile slimy mass, and two huge black bulls' heads hung on butcher's hooks complete with horns, dripping blood on to the ground. In a basket underneath we noticed a selection of 'feet'. Our sandwiches and water diet suddenly seemed more appealing.

While we ate our lunch of bread and tomatoes in the car, a crowd of children gathered round to stare. Eating in public was evidently not normal practice and we felt like animals in a zoo. Town children wore shoddy clothes and usually ran around barefoot, but the offspring of nomadic herdsmen had even less. Later we came across these penniless unfortunates deep in the Sahara and wondered at their ability to survive. To address their poverty, the Algerian agricultural revolution began with a national policy to settle nomadic populations. This along with education would also make the nomads easier for the government to control. Here in Laghouat UNESCO had set up the first primary boarding schools in 1967 with the government's blessing. They wanted equality of access to schools for all children, but mainly those from poor nomadic families. Existing schools in rural Algeria were being deserted for a large part of the school year as the nomads took their children with them to follow the family's goat and sheep herds in search of fresh pastures. Setting up these boarding schools three years before our arrival was the first stage of a revolution to end centuries of traditional life.

Ross decided to have a look under the bonnet. A loose connection from the distributor meant we'd been running on three cylinders, explaining the engine's lack of power. It had probably been knocked out of place on the bumpy track we found ourselves on when we took a wrong turning. Another problem had been solved, and we knew to check for it in the future. Ross visibly relaxed after he established a reconnection and his usual confidence returned.

Outside Laghouat we consulted the gendarmerie about permission to cross the desert, but our communications skills needed honing because misunderstandings arose and after considerable explanations we found that our journey would be plain sailing to El-Golea, where we should contact the 'Baira' or 'Prefecture'. They also told us we'd find a bank at Ghardaia, another indication of our AA information booklet being outdated.

Driving onwards south of the town we found ourselves in the land of our imaginings. Laden camels travelled alongside the road planting their wide hooves with a steady rhythmic plod. Sand stretched as far as we could see to both sides of the ribbon of tarmac. Camel drivers carried whips and kept dozens of roped animals moving with shouts and whistles.

Revived by a good night's sleep, confidence in the car restored, and enjoying our progress we sang *'It's a long and a dusty road,'* a popular sixties song by Tom Paxton as we drove along

We only knew the first verse, so it became repetitive, and sometimes we'd sing other songs, but always returned to this one which seemed particularly apt for our situation. Thinking we'd just started our journey across the Sahara and enjoying the adventure, we had little idea of what lay ahead. In fact we had not reached the Sahara proper and would not do so for many miles.

South of the Tell Atlas mountains is a steppe landscape ending with the Saharan Atlas and the biggest hot desert in the world starts south of the mountain range. The Hoggar route which we were following to cross the desert passes over the Ahaggar Mountains in central Sahara, southern Algeria. These mountains are found nearly a thousand miles south of Algiers and just west of Tamanrasset, one of a few desert towns on our route.

A constant breeze cooled our skin under the hot sun when we stopped for a break. Other travellers stared at us enjoying the sunshine, but we limited our exposure and to date managed to avoid being burnt. The heat seeping into our bones eased our joints stiff from sitting for hours on end. 'Mad Dogs and Englishmen go out in the midday sun,' sprang to mind.

Later as we drove down an almost empty road we saw mirages shimmering in the empty landscape. They looked so convincing that we nearly took out the Brownie camera to take one of our rare black and white pictures. Appearing to be about two hundred yards away they gave the impression of an oasis with palm trees bending over the water, their fronds swept by the wind. But as we approached full of expectation at around fifty yards they would evaporate into a heat haze. Another vision we assumed to be a mirage turned out to be real with hundreds of date-laden palm trees set around a lake.

We drove into this apparition to find a traffic-free town. The dirt track twisted around the green palm grove set right at the edge of the desert. Few reminders of the 20th Century were evident in Berriane and the buildings and people could have belonged to biblical times. We felt as if we'd stepped into a film set for Aladdin.

Berbers have inhabited this part of North Africa since history began. The M'zab area of central Algeria is home to the Mozabites, Berbers who found refuge from persecution and came here nearly a thousand years ago. In the 7th century they'd broken away from mainstream Islam which made them unpopular and a threat to other Moslems. As outcasts in the desert they became skilled at managing water resources by building underground irrigation works to extend the fertile areas of oases, the main one being Ghardaia. Most Mozabites are Ibadi Moslems, following a very fundamentalist form of Islam. Unbelievers, sinners and those destined for Hell are shunned by the Mozabites and this belief cuts them off from much of normal society. They speak Zenata, a dialect of the Berber language for which there is no surviving written form. These 'true believers' have their women wearing a *haik* which only allows them to use one eye, the ultimate modesty.

Entering Ghardaia in mid-afternoon, trade eked out the remains of the day in a large market place. Never tired of looking at the wares, we whiled away two hours stretching our legs as we wandered from stall to stall. Women sat on the ground behind sad-looking vegetables piled in small pyramids on a cloth in front of them. Camels exuded terrible breath between yellowed teeth and complained noisily as they looked down their noses. Raw meat darkened in the afternoon sun and the seller waved a switch over it to chase away swarms of flies. The smell of flesh hung thick in the air and loud bartering gave way to hushed curiosity when we passed by. As obvious unbelievers and therefore bound for hell, we had a cool reception.

We had imagined that dates would be practically free in an oasis, and prices which compared unfavourably with those at home surprised us. Countless grades confused our choice and we wondered how quality was measured, something I had never thought to apply to dates. As we made our selection a small boy watched us with wide dark eyes. His hair had been shaved because of ringworm, and he stood in vest and shorts staring as children do at our strangeness. The ghost-like figure that could be his mother pulled him away with a sharp tug when she saw him. Awareness must have been difficult with only one eye and the effect worse than being blinkered. Back to our shopping, we blindly purchased a bagful of dates and left with five cents of Algerian money.

These proud people managed their scant resources well but we noticed many with deformities, especially around the eyes. Squints, styes or inflammations were a common sight and beggars whose eyes had a milky blindness not unusual. The cause could be obvious. Small children sat in the dust, their faces smeared with dirt and snot with flies crawling around their eyes and mouths. If they swept the flies away they only returned a few seconds later so as toddlers they soon learned not to bother. They looked at us with scrunched up expressions resigned to the filthy insects crawling over their faces. Outside a general store a young man with twisted legs and dressed in rags sat on a wheeled platform begging for money. He pursued possible benefactors with speedy aggression along the concrete veranda, and claimed our meagre five cents with obvious disappointment.

We still couldn't get accustomed to seeing women in their white tent-like garb.

'I like it that way,' said a chatty man we met in a petrol station. 'I am the only one who can see my wife. No other men ever see her and my friends do not know if my wife is very beautiful or not, so they don't get jealous. It is better that way.'

It was true. The only giveaway was the elegance of a walk, the angle of a head, and the glimpse of an ankle or well-heeled shoe. On the practical side their skin and hair were protected from the harsh elements of wind and sun, as I had discovered. Travelling with the windows open for coolness my hair had become a dry tangle that broke into split ends when I tried to tame it with a comb. The skin on my face, arms and legs had developed dry patches in quite a short time and I'd taken to applying cream twice a day, far more often than I'd ever done in Edinburgh.

We hid our smiles at a small boy wearing nothing but a short white vest as he walked behind his mother, invisible but for one eye. I longed to take a photo but Ross shook his head.

'It would be intrusive and might stir up bad feeling.'

In the mountain regions wives of poor husbands had a tough life. Used as beasts of burden they bent double under huge loads of firewood trudging along the roadside. We saw a man riding a donkey while his unfortunate wife held on to its tail, clutching an uncomfortable bundle to her back.

Women never drank alcohol even if their husbands broke the Moslem code, and nor would they be seen eating in public. They belonged in the home and in 1970 only twenty per cent of young women were literate. In Morocco the statistics were even lower.

Just before sunset we took the car out of Ghardaia to look for useful cast-off metal. Ross wanted to find some protection from boulders or ramps on unsurfaced roads. He was looking for something to attach to the front registration plate.

'Our ground clearance isn't very good,' he explained. 'If we could find the right piece of metal to hang roughly fifteen centimetres above the ground it could act as a warning. We'd hear the scraping and be able to stop or at least slow down. That could prevent serious damage to the oil sump and engine.'

We discovered a large dump of promising bits and pieces at the side of the road, unearthed and claimed an appropriate piece of metal, and stashed it on top of our accumulated possessions on the back seat. It would double as a solid base for driving over soft sand if necessary. A large flat piece of wood joined it as a useful support for the car jack on sandy ground and would prove to be well worth the car space it took up, as the workshop manual advised: -

*Jacking-up the car:*
*Before attempting to jack-up the car, satisfy yourself that it is standing on firm and level ground. Make sure the handbrake is fully applied and use bricks or wooden blocks to chock the wheels that are not being raised.*

## 19th October

Back in Ghardaia early we found a mechanic to see about recurrent wheel noises. Ross watched the proceedings at the garage while I went to change some travellers' cheques eventually succeeding at the third bank I came to. The chemist came next for stocking up on water-purifying tablets. We'd started using them in southern Spain, but they made the water taste as though it had been taken from a swimming pool. The helpful pharmacist had to-hand a list of first-aid items recommended by the O.N.A.T tourist organisation for crossing the Sahara. We must have been well-prepared already because we'd covered the majority of items on the list. The chemist regarded some items on the list as superfluous including the antidote for scorpion venom which we'd bought in London. It had been a panic purchase on the day we left, along with anti-snake venom and a thousand aspirin tablets in two large bottles from the Piccadilly branch of Boots. We planned to use the latter for trade and impromptu gifts. I emerged from the shop with anti-tetanus vaccine and a box of throat pastilles.

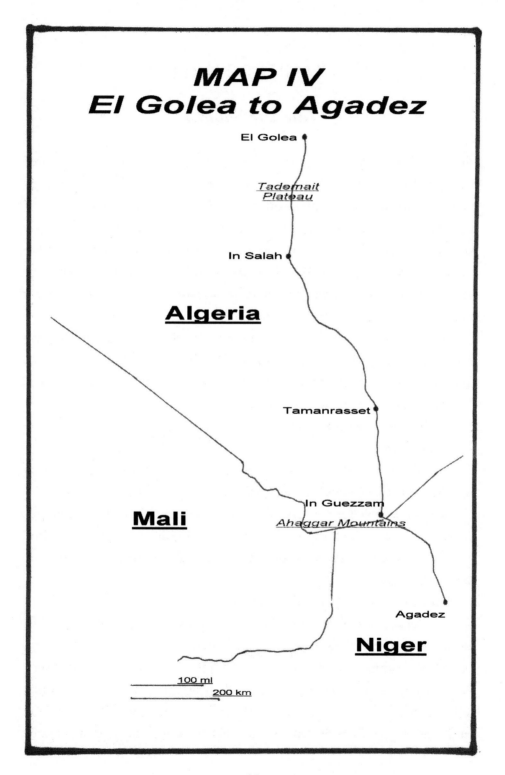

**MAP IV**
**El Golea to Agadez**

El Golea

Tademait
Plateau

In Salah

**Algeria**

Tamanrasset

In Guezzam

Ahaggar Mountains

**Mali**

Agadez

**Niger**

100 ml

200 km

# CHAPTER THREE

## *Into the Sahara*

We couldn't wait for our first taste of the real Sahara. Within an estimated twenty miles from El Golea a hand-painted sign saying *Déviation* vaguely pointed south-west and sent us off the road on a diversion. Not a hint of road works, land variation or other travellers gave us a clue to the reason. We paused for a toilet break. Just in case unseen eyes were watching or were to suddenly appear I opened the two doors on my side for maximum privacy while Ross went behind the car. These breaks would become rarer with our progression as mild dehydration took hold.

The faint dusty tracks of others led us over flat stony ground for two hours without any further signs, and no other vehicles to reassure us. As we drove vertical shapes shimmering from afar caught my eye and I pointed. We both peered into the hazy distance.

'Could that be people do you think?' I suggested.

We got closer.

'I think they're ostriches,' said Ross. 'What do you call a gathering of ostriches? A flock? A pack? It's definitely not a flight!'

Here was a topic for conversation at last. We'd been joined at the hip for twelve days, said everything there was to say already, and without stimuli from other people or the view outside the capsule of the car long silences had grown longer.

'A colony? A bevy? A brood?' I suggested.

The tracks brought us nearer and hearing us the giant birds panicked and started to run in their dozens. We laughed delighted with their company. Instead of heading away from the car the ostriches kept apace for several miles keeping to a parallel line twenty yards away. Tiny heads on long skinny necks stretched forward as if to reach an imaginary finish line first and handsome wing feathers fluffed out wide, like ball gowns held up by flustered matrons. Sturdy clockwork legs eventually took them veering off into what looked like an arid pasture. I turned around to watch them still running in panic long after we'd passed.

More silent hours stretched through the sun-drenched height of the day. To our southeast we could just make out what looked like a mirage of shimmering water surrounded by swaying palms. A wakening energy stirred us out of lassitude and we kept our eyes on it deciding to go for a closer look. An escape from the hot car would be welcome, but fabled imaginary oases could play tricks and uncertainty teased us. The tracks we'd been following continued due south and we took a risk going off in search of a vision, but the closer we got the more solid the apparition became. Heaving a sigh of relief we drove into El Golea glad to have trusted our instincts to leave the tracks. We'd not seen another vehicle since taking the diversion and had travelled over a tedious 160 miles.

The oasis town is located at the gateway to the Sahara where records of all vehicles setting off on the Hoggar route are kept. Certain recommended standards had to be demonstrated before permission could be granted to cross the next dangerous part of the Sahara. Our main worry was ground-clearance.

Being hard-pushed for money half of our household effects took up much of the car space. We had sent our unbreakable belongings in a container for shipment to Zambia before our plans had changed. Assuming a gentle sea passage we had packed everything breakable or fragile into the boot and the back seat. In this way we saved on insurance and a larger container. We saw no real reason to change the arrangement before we left Edinburgh. Thus a four foot mirror, an electric sewing machine, all our glassware and crockery, a fan heater, breakable ornaments, and other such homely items travelled in the car with us. If we lost our way in the Sahara the mirror at least might come in handy to reflect the sun and draw attention to our position.

Much more important luggage joined this assemblage in London. Ross added five jerry cans; a set of tools; a first-aid box; three five-gallon plastic containers for drinking- water; a reasonable collection of car spares; maps; a small selection of tinned foods to be replenished as we travelled; and three spare wheels tied on to the roof-rack. The jerry cans would hold twenty five gallons of petrol to cover all eventualities, and the water containers when full would see us across the Sahara between towns. But the weight we carried forced the car body closer to the ground.

Arriving late in the afternoon we wasted no time and went straight to see about permission from the 'Sous Prefecture'. We'd read the list of requirements in our AA and O.N.A.T literature and done all we could barring an improvement of the car's ground clearance in its heavily laden state. Unnerved by the uncertainty of how strict they would be we knew there was a possibility of having to retrace our tracks. That thought was unbearable and not wanting to tempt fate had avoided discussing it.

The official walked around the car in his white shirt and long black trousers, a dapper vestige of the colonial regime, ticking boxes on the form attached to his clip-board. His hair had been plastered over to one side with hair-cream. The minimum ground clearance was thirteen centimetres and he took out a measure from his back pocket. We had repacked everything to redistribute the weight favourably, and left our petrol and water supplies low. He measured the distance, scratched his head and measured it again, then wrote a note on his pad. We waited. Forty minutes later after much deliberation and a thorough examination of the petrol and water capacity, the engine and wheels he wiped his hands on a rag and nodded his head. Our doubts evaporated when he announced 'Bien,' with a smile, and felt this to be an endorsement of the car's suitability.

Resolution coursed back through our veins from his vote of confidence and we examined the prospect ahead. Our responsibility would be to report into the 'Sous Prefecture' of every town on our route, and if we failed to do so others going the same way in either direction would be looking out for us. The official would not specify how long we'd have to be missing before word would be given to other travellers, but this would be all we could hope for if we landed in trouble.

We had imagined a rather more robust safety net to be in place. In the Scottish Highlands, the largest uninhabited space in the UK, mountain rescue teams and the RAF would soon be called in for missing walkers and climbers. And yet the whole of the Highlands representing a mere blob on the map compared to the span we would be travelling just between one town and the next.

In the town we filled up the water containers with our quota of ten gallons from a public tap at the side of the road. As water gushed into the white plastic void we noticed a tight circle of teenage boys at the roadside poking something with a stick. Curious to see the victim we leaned over their crouching forms. A black scorpion about seven centimetres long (if its tail was straightened) crawled in the dirt poised for attack from the torment it was receiving. As it lashed its tail at the stick, the boys laughed, leaping up from time to time to keep their bare feet out of its reach.

Four of the thirty different varieties of scorpion in the Sahara are lethal to humans. Temporary paralysis, cardiac arrest, convulsions or respiratory failure can result from their venomous sting and in some species it's as toxic as a cobra's. This one was most likely an Emperor Scorpion, given its colour, and wasn't particularly dangerous but could still give a painful sting.

Moslems believe that scorpions always return to where they were found and cannot be frightened away. Houses are very carefully cleaned, especially in corners and dark places, and in some North African countries *Isawi* dervishes or holy men took evening tours of the cities as the scorpions emerged from their hiding places. They would lure the creatures with fire and grab them with tongs for disposal. I thought of all the dark scorpion-friendly nooks and crannies in and under the car. We usually stopped about the same time as they'd be starting their night prowls so perhaps our vaccine might come in handy after all. I shuddered in the afternoon heat.

We didn't hang about to test these theories, and drove off briskly to shake off any unwelcome hitch-hiking insects. After the car-inspection we had just enough time before sunset to change the back wheels to the 'Town and Country' tyres we thought more suitable for driving on sand. We soon had them fitted but the three spares had to be tied back onto the roof-rack in the dark.

As we fastened the ropes Thierry, a Frenchman, approached us. He was hitch-hiking to the Ivory Coast for a teaching assignment, and hoped to pay for a lift on a lorry or all-terrain vehicle like a Land Rover to take him across the desert. We didn't qualify for the direction or the vehicle, quite apart from having no room for another passenger but we enjoyed talking to a fellow adventurer. Characters like this cropped up from time to time as we headed south. The Sahara was a huge magnet for unusual ventures by the bold, the romantic, the drop-out or the loner.

We climbed back into our ordinary saloon car and left El Golea for the usual out-of-town sleeping place with a full petrol tank, correct tyre pressures, water, and food. But the minute we'd parked Ross remembered that he'd wanted the wheel alignment to be re-checked before heading off into the wilderness. The wheels had taken so many knocks the chances were high they would need a realignment. We wanted an early getaway the next day so back-tracked to find a garage in town rather than waiting until morning

The garage owner worked slowly but got the job done, and after sorting out the bill he invited us into the garage for tea.

Ahmed was in his mid-forties and claimed to have worked all day and night, only getting four hours sleep. This explained his slow pace. Looking weary, with shadows under his eyes he shared his tea, biscuits, peanuts, and dates with us. He took great care to ensure the mint and tea-leaves were infused to perfection then crammed in some misshapen lumps of sugar and replaced the teapot lid. As we waited for the brew we admired a 'Desert Rose,' a rock with crystal groups forming a rose-like shape, which was being used as a paper-weight. In arid desert regions it contained trapped sand particles and hummed if it got wet, which presumably didn't happen very often in the desert. To show us, Ahmed wet it at a tap and we all listened to the faint hum.

Ahmed showed us his identification booklet about himself, his wives and his children. Enough space had been allowed for details of four wives, plus their divorces, and fifteen children. The wives and children had no ID of their own. He had married twice, having divorced one wife, and boasted three children.

'Who now carried the ID of the divorced wife?' I wondered.

Perhaps it had been returned to her father.

'This is my wife,' he said fondly showing us a photo of wife number two, a dark-eyed beauty with a white veil draped over thick tumbling locks. 'And this is my son, Omar.' A third photo appeared. 'Here are my two daughters,' he smiled affectionately.

We admired the pictures and asked the ages of his children. When we left he gave us his card, a locally-grown orange, the 'Desert Rose' we now regretted admiring, and a rather severe photo of himself. We fought a losing battle trying to refuse these gifts, or give him payment for his kindness. He wouldn't want cigarettes because he didn't smoke (or drink). Finally he accepted an intricately decorated red tin tray which had been a wedding present, and a silver-plated teaspoon. The latter was one of a collection of spoons that Ross had won in school athletics competitions and was enamelled with the Heriot's crest. Our motley collection of possessions carried in the boot had proved to be useful for the first time instead of a burden!

## 20<sup>th</sup> October

The hardest day of our short lives lay ahead and we had our suspicions from the start. Contrary to my childhood imaginings the Sahara desert is not covered in beautiful rolling sand-dunes or *erg*. There are also gravel plains (*reg*), dry valleys (*wadis*), and salt flats. But mostly it is made up of stony plateaux called *hamadas* which account for seventy per cent of the Sahara's surface. They would provide our landscape for most of the remaining Algerian 'soil' we had to cross. Niger would prove a different experience.

The 'piste' loomed up ahead to mark the start of a truly challenging part of our journey. The metalled road ended spectacularly.

'Travelling on laterite roads is a knack,' the London AA man had explained. 'They quickly become corrugated by traffic. To stop bumping up and down you have to take the car to an ideal speed of around thirty to forty miles an hour to float over the top of the corrugations and then you can travel more comfortably.'

The first section of the track we would be following rose on a stony incline that in no way matched the description we'd been given. Heavy trucks had churned the ground to get purchase on the slope, throwing up stones and deepening the furrows. Already we felt we had the wrong vehicle and wondered at being given permission to travel. Even with good ground clearance the stony rutted surface ahead would give any vehicle a challenge. Ross stopped the car and we sat silently looking at it.

'I can't risk taking the car up that,' he said. 'The lowest part of the engine is the sump and if a stone hit it badly enough all the oil would drain away. We'd be finished!'

With this sobering thought we decided to clear a reasonable path up the hundred yard hill.

'But we can't do that for the hundreds of miles of Sahara still to be negotiated,' I thought to myself. Ross had applied himself to the task so I joined him, throwing stones aside and filling in gaps with others.

'One step at a time,' I told myself firmly, we had been given permission by the Sous Prefecture official after all.

Back in the car we tried again, but still the loose stones and corrugations made the car and everything in it judder as we ploughed onwards. In later years we travelled widely in Africa and elsewhere, but never came across corrugations like these again.

'I can't take this much longer, I'm going to try the floating theory so hang on to your seat!' Ross wiped the sweat off his forehead with the back of his hand.

With the engine revving we bumped violently over the stony ridges at speed but never arrived at the 'floating' stage and our nerves soon gave out. We felt ill both from the shake-up and the realisation that neither we nor the car could survive much more punishment. At last we reached the top of the hill hoping for a smoother ride but still the car juddered over the corrugations. My head spun from the heat, the shaking, and from racking my brains for a solution. For the first time since leaving London I had serious doubts about what we were doing, but knew it was too late for these thoughts to be spoken and regretted the disregard I'd shown for all the warnings. A few minutes later we stopped for a rest and a rethink. Ross investigated another noise coming from beneath us and found the rear-suspension bump stop had broken loose and looked irreparable. As protection for the underside of the car, two six inch cubes of rubber are vulcanised on to a steel plate, which in turn is welded to the chassis. If the rear axle is forced upwards from driving over rough ground, it hits these rubber blocks instead of the chassis, which could rupture with the impact.

Our poor new car! He decided to stick it back on immediately with epoxy resin and hope for the best.

As he busied himself with the repair I assessed the damage inside the car. The glove compartment had flown open breaking the catch so that it could no longer be closed without turning the key in the lock. We used it to store all sorts of odds and ends including our first aid supplies. They had been rattled and shaken so much that pens dismantled and lids fell off containers. I opened the clinical thermometer casing to find the mercury had burst the glass; not only from the vibrations but from the temperature too. Our first taste of unpaved roads did not bode well for the thousands more we still had to travel.

This was the Tademait plateau, a 'hamada' covering the area between El-Golea and In Salah. Flat, dull, stony desert stretched forever all around us. Not a creature, building or vehicle disturbed its arid eternity. We were completely alone. A few scrubby bushes provided a scattering of growth and they would also soon disappear.

Boulders lined the side of the 'piste' but we could see vehicle tracks in the dust at the side of the road which suggested that others had chosen a different ride. Ross shoved three smaller boulders away from the roadside to make a passageway for the car. He cautiously steered the car onto a better surface off-road. We enjoyed a couple of miles in less discomfort but as soon as the tension in my shoulders loosened the car sank into soft ground. 'Sand ladders' would have been useful if we had them. We had yet to find out about these, and we didn't even have a shovel to dig ourselves out. If it had been on the O.N.A.T list we'd have bought one, but it was futile to blame them and we were kicking ourselves for not guessing this new obstacle. Unfazed we soon found other resources. Rummaging through our belongings in the boot I pulled out two large Tupperware containers.

'We could use these for digging couldn't we?' I asked.

'I think we might have to,' laughed Ross.

Although they could have done with being more rigid, they became our makeshift shovels throughout the Sahara crossing and would see plenty of hard use unmentioned at Tupperware parties.

After this unexpected new hazard we returned to the less comfortable safety of the piste for a while, but Ross was soon ready to risk another attempt at following the vehicle tracks. We studied the land as he drove looking for telltale signs of soft sand.

'The soft sand seems to look paler in colour, don't you think?' I asked.

We peered over the black vinyl trim of the dashboard studying the desert floor as we went. Ross avoided the paler patches and we got into a rhythm of watching and weaving to make headway at a maximum speed of twenty five miles per hour until we arrived at a dry river bed.

At some time this river had been a torrent because it measured half a metre deep and thirty metres wide. When rainstorms hit they would be frightening. Sand as soft as talcum powder lined the dry bed and as I stood on it I sank up to my ankles laughing at the sensation.

'Watch out it could be quicksand,' shouted Ross.

I leapt on to the bank in fright, fearful of being swallowed up. There seemed to be nowhere suitable to cross. Bumping along the edge we explored the river bank by car, then on foot until we found a shallower section of the bank to drive down on to the dry bed. The texture at the edges felt more solid but a stick poked into the sand on the river bottom sank every time into softness. Bent double and walking backwards, we excavated a ramp down to the river bed with our plastic boxes. Ross walked back along the sand approaching the river bank and located the firmest patches of ground. He marked a trail through them with small stones and pieces of dried-out grass whose growth survived along the bank. He planned to accelerate for fifty metres following the track to the river's edge and building up enough speed in the process to span the squishy barrier. Hopefully this would carry the car to the opposite bank with its own momentum.

I stood aside ready to push if needed and he started the engine. Accelerating furiously and managing to reach forty five miles an hour the car and driver shot across the ramp only to plunge straight into the sandy middle as if it was water. Pushing would only have made things worse. The household goods and clothing stored behind our seats catapulted to the front. The wheels on the roof-rack broke their bindings and went flying. The battery had been wrenched from its mountings and lay at a drunken angle beside the engine, and the car sat immersed in sand only five metres from the near bank.

There was nothing for it but to go back. I denied myself the luxury of tears. We jacked-up the back wheels one at a time and since sand seeped above the bodywork we first had to clear it away with the now ingrained Tupperware containers. The piece of wood found on the dump outside Ghardaia came in handy for supporting the jack on soft ground and we set to work. With the jack supporting the car's weight and the wheel clear of sand we could dig below it and place what stones we could find under the first back wheel to provide a solid base. The metal strip we'd found at the same time was also placed behind the wheels and we wished we'd picked up more for our self-made mini-track.

'Take care when you're scraping under the car that it doesn't fall on top of you!' warned Ross.

We expected much from the slender pillar jack which had come with the car. It held the weight of half the vehicle on top of its fragile metal frame on a base that was none too solid.

***Working underneath the car:*** *(said the workshop manual)*
*It cannot be over-emphasised that no jack on its own is adequate for supporting*
*the car when working underneath. If you are going to work under the car some*
*extra means of support must be provided to avoid the very real danger of death or*
*injury. Really heavy baulks of timber or large, square blocks of hard stone may*
*provide adequate support but piles of bricks, breeze blocks or light sections of*
*wood are not safe.*

We scoured the sand away from the wheels and as more of the weight shifted
on to the jack, golden metal creaked in warning. Our heads sprang up to watch
in horrified anticipation then the movement settled and our arms and heads
went back under the bodywork to scrape some more. The dangerous work
wasn't finished. We repeated this procedure with the other wheel and then dug
away enough of the sand behind the car to lay a small stony track. Our clothes
stiffened with evaporating sweat and the silent sun deafened our brains.

An hour later with the battery secured back in place and the wheels on
the roof-rack tied back down, we gulped some more water and took a deep
breath. I leant my weight against the front of the car ready to push while
Ross started the engine and engaged reverse gear. The wheels spun but only
to force our laboriously laid stony track under the sand. Stuck fast again we
realised our pathetic track was futile and we'd have to put more than stones
under the wheels.

'FUCK! FUCK! FUCK!' yelled Ross still in the driver's seat, banging his
head on the steering wheel with each expletive.

I walked slowly to the car listening to his outburst, found the packet of
Players Number Six and lit two cigarettes, handing one to him wordlessly.
We flicked ash into the giant ashtray that was the Sahara, both of us
desperately trying to think of a better solution.

'We could use the spare wheels to drive across,' suggested Ross bouncing
back from his despair five minutes later and climbing out to untie the ropes
on the roof rack. 'We won't progress very fast but at least they'll provide a
firm base.'

All over again sand had to be hollowed out beneath the back wheels and we laid the spares in the hollows. The sun never lost its ferocity. Ross reversed as far as he could using the spare wheels as a platform, but it was never more than a few extra inches before we were back in the sand's clutches. So a little over a wheel's diameter at a time we repeated the whole procedure until at dusk we finally succeeded in making our way back out of the river bed centimetre by tortured centimetre. In all we'd spent five hours of exhausting, dirty work in baking conditions without making any progress in our journey and we still had the river bed to negotiate the next morning. Our first day off the unpaved road had been a trial from first thing in the morning to this potentially disastrous obstacle which would continue to dog us the following day.

Sitting in the dark car that night we made plans for further attempts in the same vein. The work in prospect looked enough to keep a team of navvies busy for a day. The two of us with our Tupperware were not looking forward to tackling it. I felt catastrophe snapping at our wheels.

## 21st October

We rose with the sun to start work in the coolest part of the day but as we dejectedly stepped out to begin, a lorry came trundling towards us. This was the first vehicle we'd seen since leaving the paved road, and what joy!! The driver and his mate attached our rope between the front of our car and a hook at the back of their truck and in no time had towed us over the insurmountable obstacle of the river bed. Words could not express our gratitude and we left the bad memory behind as we mustered fresh determination for whatever the next challenge might be.

Conversation became barren like our surroundings. We battled with thoughts we daren't speak, neither wanting to acknowledge our vulnerability. If we could stay positive things would be alright. But with the riverbed effectively blocking the way behind us it would be even harder to go back. Our situation became a private war, with us against adversity and tensions only came from outside our relationship. We had the same focus, goal, fears and aspirations and knew if we didn't present a united front we'd be courting trouble. So, mutually dependent, we never risked falling out. Difficult moments could be resolved in cigarette puffing instead of bickering.

Even further from civilisation and still heading south we saw lines of tracks alongside the road as before. Ross decided to continue his strategy of alternating these with the official road when the surface looked smoother. At last his satisfactory compromise let us make some progress and our sunken spirits dared to raise a little hope. We rolled along for several hours in complete silence recovering from the lows of the day before and as we both later admitted, said a few prayers.

Through the haze gentle hills rose up to the east of us and after a few minutes the outline of a building sitting astride the topmost hill became clear. We left the road to investigate. 'Fort Miribel' said a battered sign.

'This has to be worth a photo,' I said, 'where's the camera?'

Ross dug out our old Brownie Instamatic bargain-basement camera with its tiny amount of remaining film. Black and white film was cheaper than colour, and budget constraints prevented us from buying more. We walked up to the nineteenth-century solid walls and tried to peer through a barricaded doorway. A tiny glimpse of an open interior with arches was enough to conjure up images of French troops fighting off marauding Tuaregs with swords and muskets. It kept our minds and conversation buoyant for a couple of hours.

The bumps got noticeably worse and another puncture forced us to stop. The routine of wheel-changing now had us mechanically stepping out, collecting the jack and the slab of wood which we'd learned to keep at the top of the boot contents, and releasing a spare wheel from the roof-rack. Along the deserted road another car approached from the south and the driver slowed to see why we'd stopped. His bull head was swathed in a turban and sturdy legs in baggy Arabian trousers leapt out as he came to greet us. A wide-eyed boy gazed out at us from the battered Citroën Dyane. A tuft of white-blond hair had escaped from his smaller turban.

'Bonjour,' we chorused.

'Hello, you are English, yes?' A strong handshake matched the rest of him.

'Scottish,' Ross gave his standard reply still hoping for some advantage from the *Auld Alliance* in a country with French connections.

Wilhelm Kahn, a German, was travelling north with his six-year old son to Ghardaia.

'Your tyres are too coarse,' he remarked crossing his arms and leaning back authoritatively, his desert boots firmly planted on the sand. 'Smooth ones are much better for sand. And you should carry sand-ladders.'

'What are they?' We asked.

Sand ladders were ladder-like strips of metal, he explained, which could be placed in front of or behind the wheels to allow them to grip the surface of the metal and 'climb' out of trouble. They could straddle soft patches of sand allowing the wheels to grip something solid for a few feet. Then he described how our thick tyres would spin and dig a hole to make the car sink deeper into the sand, whereas smooth worn ones could skim the surface. Ross and I exchanged knowing looks as we remembered the antics of the day before.

During our preparations I had checked the Hillman Hunter Workshop Manual for clues to things we might need. It revealed the type of 'winter tyres' recommended for 'snow, mud or soft ground,' but no mention of tropical conditions. Ross had procured two extra wheels in London with 'Town and Country' tyres thinking their chunky construction would be good in sand. Wilhelm was recommending the opposite.

We leaned against the hot golden metal of the car to chat awhile and I regarded his modest vehicle. Its ground clearance looked much better than ours, an uncomplicated basic engine would allow for easy repairs, and a light load meant less likelihood of sinking into sand.

'I vas in ze Foreign Legion during ze Algerian war, ya? Und I have come back vith my son to see how things are now. It vas hard and ve soldiers had a tough time, but I have some good memories of zose days.'

Too soon he strode back to rescue the boy from the heat of his stationary car then this breath of fresh air breezed off in a dust cloud. For miles we found no other distractions for our minds to ponder amongst the endless stones and sand. Questions we wished we'd asked the knowledgeable desert veteran crowded our thoughts. My imagination played out scenes of Legionnaires singing their hearts out to their signature slow march. Heads topped with white kepis would be gleaming in the sun, red epaulettes flamboyant against the colourless desert landscape and they would be harmonising with deep baritone voices.

Poles had been planted all along the piste similar to those we'd seen in the North of Scotland to indicate the road's location under snow drifts. We supposed they could do the same job for drifting sand dunes. A monotonous outlook allowed Ross to concentrate fully on the land surface and aim for the least stony parts of the piste to avoid damaging the underside of the car. To relieve the boredom of a dull landscape someone had piled up boulders to look like people or animals with arms, and ears. We laughed at the joke and passed some time imagining who'd arranged the stones and what they'd been doing here. The likelihood would be French military conscripts as they laboured over constructing the road we travelled.

It was late afternoon and getting cooler when we reached a steep winding descent from the plateau. After hours of mind-numbing stony flat ground the startling mountains and crags enthralled us, and we followed a long perilous track down, wary of skidding on loose stones and the car flying over the edge. On the level again Ross steered the car into a hot dry valley. We'd entered a very different landscape, much sandier than the hamada we'd been travelling. Out of the Chichili wind which traversed southern Algeria, the temperature soared. Eeriness engulfed us in the stillness of the *wadi*, spreading an uneasiness which had nothing to do with the threat of becoming stuck in the sand again. Soon we passed a group of three bleached camel skeletons. We drove on.

Still hoping to reach In Salah before dark, an innocent-looking track turned into a sand dune with large jagged stones lurking under the surface. At the end of a testing day we felt like the proverbial camel with a broken back and the three skeletons came to mind. But the air had cooled and we somehow found the wherewithal to step out and tackle our next disaster.

I scraped away sand from behind the back wheels and stood back to let Ross reverse as far as he could. Then I scraped some more. It was much the same story as before and with patience the car returned to solid ground again. I fell into my car seat hot, disagreeable and tired; all I wanted to do was curl up and sleep away this nightmare. Then Ross pushed the lever under the front bumper, released the catch and raised the bonnet. I lost sight of him.

'Come and look at this,' he groaned.

I dragged myself back out of the car, not wanting to know. He was looking with disbelief into the engine compartment.

Horrors!

Sand had penetrated every corner, the battery had been wrenched from its mounting again and the water bag for the windscreen spray had disappeared. Ross bent over the engine examining various parts.

'If sand gets into the air intake,' he shook his head helplessly, 'or into the oil,' more head shaking, 'or into the engine…' he paused and looked up at me. 'We'd be finished,' he ended quietly.

His near whisper frightened me far more than the noisy ranting he'd shouted earlier. My head swam.

'We only have one spare air filter and this could happen twenty more times.' He went on. 'I don't know what to do.'

We did the best we could to sweep off the sand; Ross checked connections and leads and then moved the car to stonier ground for the night. Neither of us dared speak while the brief flamboyant sunset failed to work its usual magic. We hadn't seen a living soul for hours.

### 22nd October

A grim prospect awaited us for a second morning. We changed the wheels back to those with less chunky tyres, following Wilhelm's advice. Then Ross mustered up the courage to re-examine the engine in the cooler morning temperature and with a cooler head. The battery mountings could no longer do their job so he decided to relocate the battery to a safer place inside the car between my feet. This involved disconnecting the wires, chipping a hole through from the engine to the foot-well of the car, and reconnecting the wires to the battery. This act felt like vandalism on a car not yet four months old, and my comfort would be compromised even more.

I found our solitary air filter in the boot and Ross replaced the dirty one. He took the cover off the old one, brushed out the inside, tapped the filter to knock out the dust, blew into it, reassembled it and set it aside in case we were forced to use it again. With the benefit of a good night's sleep he then had the brainwave of covering the air-intake with a tissue secured by an elastic band in order to keep the air-filter in reasonable condition. The additional budget filter could be renewed twice daily until we got out of the desert and did not seem to affect the cooling system adversely. In addition to this new rigmarole he swapped the filters and repeated the brushing, knocking and blowing procedure every few days to minimise the possibility of engine damage from sand particles.

The problem was serious. Some twelve years later Mark Thatcher, later to be knighted, failed to finish the Paris to Dakar rally. Newspapers reported one of his problems to be a lack of compression in his car engine. His air filter had allegedly been destroyed by sand which subsequently got into the engine and ground the cylinders and valves beyond use.

At the approach to In Salah a smooth bitumen road took us into the town. The name *In Salah* means 'good well,' although the water is known for its rather unpleasant, salty taste. It had been a trading town in the past dealing in slaves, ivory and gold from the south in exchange for European goods from the north. Arriving at eight o'clock we sought out a petrol supply before doing anything else. Our tank didn't yet register empty but we felt we should maximise our capacity for safety's sake.

Only 'essence' was on offer and up until then we'd always used 'super,' a higher octane so we hoped for the best when we asked for a full tank and a top-up for the jerry cans.

Next we found a public water supply and again topped up our containers to their fullest capacity. If the local water did not taste too good we wouldn't notice because the water-purifying tablets which we'd been using made it taste horrible anyway.

After three days away from civilisation we enjoyed the comforting reassurance of the small town. Looking for a shovel and sand-ladders we made enquiries. My translation for the latter was inadequate, and my pocket dictionary no help because I couldn't make myself understood. We could borrow a shovel and had several offers, but none was for sale. We gave up our search as the smell from a bakery drew us in. We treated ourselves to delicious oven-hot bread and a bottle of lemonade from a nearby stall, and then headed to the Sous Prefecture to report we were still alive and not lost.

The smooth 'graded' road of the town ended and by ten o'clock we were back on corrugated 'piste'. Our first problem came quickly since Tamanrasset wasn't sign-posted. We hadn't really expected a sign but we'd arrived at a fork in the road. The better option seemed to be the one pointing due south. Five miles along the track a flimsy wooden notice told us it was the right one.

'Perhaps today would be kinder to us,' I hoped silently, but soon we came to more sand in the road like the night before. We sat and looked at it wondering what to do, and then opted for a risky off-track detour to try branching round it. Crossing fingers didn't help and we slowly stopped in soft sand. The sun's rays were rising to grill-heat, and all our efforts to get out were in vain.

An hour later we were sitting overheated, tired and ratty in our car seats when a lorry drew up beside us. With a nod for a greeting and without any explanation or requests on our part, the two men set about the task of towing us out and we were soon freed from the sand's clutches. They suggested we try the road again before they left us and it came as no surprise when the sand sucked all the motion out of our wheels again. They gave us another tow out.

'Yesterday we did the same for a German car and an English vehicle,' remarked the Arab driver in French.

'We met a German,' said Ross 'but didn't see the English, I wonder what happened to them?'

I translated.

'Perhaps they followed some tracks far from the road,' he ventured with a shrug and a gaze out into wilderness.

A picture of some poor Brits alone and stranded flashed into my mind. Leaving the track was a risk we had avoided taking for fear of getting lost. We'd also lose the chance to meet other travellers who could help us out of difficulties. Even when not in trouble it was reassuring and good to share experiences as any information could be useful.

We thanked them and carried on but two hundred metres further on the car sank again into sand and by this time it was midday with our saviours having disappeared out of sight through a shimmer of heat. Resigned to the inevitable we took out our Tupperware to clear a path out. Before we'd finished another Algerian truck passed going in our direction and they soon completed our escape from the sandy predicament. They advised us to leave the road and make a wide detour around it which we'd been scared to do after our last mishap. They offered to lead us, and knowing that we could follow them and indicate if we ran into trouble we accepted with gratitude. The ground proved to be much firmer and we followed the lorry until we couldn't take the strain any more. Following fifty yards behind them meant 'eat my dust,' and with our windows open to catch the breeze for coolness we could hardly breathe, our eyes smarted and our nostrils clogged up. Closing the windows with the fan on full pelt felt like being baked alive, so we backed up a bit without losing sight of them, washed away the dust with swigs of water and enjoyed a cleaner air-intake. When the piste became clear of windswept sand for a good distance ahead, Ross overtook them and we waved to our saviours in gratitude.

The heat of the day could be measured by the frequency of the engine overheating in spite of the extra water-cooler in our export-edition car. At its worst midday ferocity it forced us to stop every half-hour. A cool swim or a long chilled drink would have been heaven. Hours passed by in a haze of dehydration making me fuzzy-headed. Clarity came with enforced drinking of warm treated water, but never did we crave that stuff.

Leaving the windows open had been the best way to get some impression of coolness into the car. Off the surfaced roads this brought an influx of fine sand making hair stiff, getting into every corner of our possessions, and becoming ingrained in the recently pristine car interior. The dashboard would never look the same. We stopped at dusk because driving in the dark made it difficult to judge the land surface and we didn't like the sound of clonks and clanks coming from below. The other side of the rear axle stopper had become loose.

23<sup>rd</sup> October

In the cool of the morning Ross spent two hours repairing the car with me standing by as assistant. I held the Workshop Manual and read aloud: -

*Bonnet Rattles: These may be due to free play at the front catch.*

'Is that all it says?' said Ross.

The bonnet had loosened and some of the rivets holding the hinges had sheared. Ours was obviously not a common problem with normal use. We'd been doing something more akin to stock-car racing.

The wheels had moved on the roof-rack rubbing another hole in the paintwork. I checked the little blue book of 'Owners Instructions'.

*If a roof rack is fitted the total weight carried must*
*never exceed 100lb (45kg).*

'We're carrying less then that,' said Ross. 'The wheels will weigh about eighty to ninety pounds altogether. But it doesn't allow for 'shock loading' from all the corrugations and jolts. That makes the equivalent load far greater, which is why there's rubbing. You can't really measure 'shock loading' but we've certainly suffered enough bumps and jolts!'

I abandoned the books which didn't seem to hold much relevance to our situation. Ross had fixed one rear-suspension bump stop a few days earlier and now the other one was loose from constant pounding by the back axle. He pulled it off then fixed it back in place with epoxy resin. At eight o'clock he'd finished and we started on our way, hopeful that Ross had already discovered all the things which could go wrong. At least the bonnet didn't rattle quite as much as before.

We managed to stir ourselves into a few renders of '*It's a long and a dusty road,*' and drove until midday. The temperature gauge indicated an overheated engine and we were forced to stop. A rare small tree just over a metre high became our next stopping point. We made best use of the little shade it offered and hung the blanket over the open bonnet in the hope of shading the engine from relentless sun rays. Waiting for the heat to dissipate left us with no escape because at midday the car could offer no shadow. Inside it was like an oven, and underneath it would be worse, albeit in shadow. My pale complexion had not been tested beyond the summer temperatures of northern Europe and I made a makeshift head-covering with a tee shirt but left my arms bare. In the cooling breeze I was fooled into complacency as we watched lizards darting around the rocks. After half an hour the engine had hardly cooled at all but we set off regardless. That evening my skin burned where it had been exposed at midday and I slept restlessly in the cold night. Two days later a cluster of bubbling blisters covered my upper arms, hardening to thick dry itchy crusts.

We drove on for an hour and stopped again but this time Ross parked the car into a stiff breeze. No accommodating shadows could be found in the barren stony landscape which still stretched forever without interruption. The breeze made little difference and just seemed to bring more heat all the quicker. Like a hairdryer on top heat it created the opposite of the wind-chill factor. Ross went back to tracking lizards, while I covered my head again with a tee shirt and sat on the ground just trying to breathe. Finding the energy to even think was a challenge and conversation between us had virtually stopped, we were both sapped.

The climax of heat waned as it always did. At about three o'clock we made a move, and ten miles further on a gazelle leapt past us in the opposite direction.

'Where on earth did that come from?' I laughed, pleasantly surprised by this apparition.

It considerably raised our spirits and gave us a safe subject for conversation which wouldn't drag our lagging morale further down than it was already. We wondered what the creature could eat to sustain itself in the wilderness and maintain such beauty.

Later we passed a tiny village, the first since leaving In Salah. The inhabitants looked the most poverty-stricken people we'd ever seen. They sat listlessly in long, coarse, raggedy, brown clothes and survived in grass-houses in the heart of the desert with the help of a few goats and camels. We guessed they were nomads. Like the gazelle they scraped an existence from nothing, and their children bright-eyed, tangle-haired and mischievous chased one another round in the dust on tough bare feet. Their fine brown hair stuck up in unkempt tufts as if it had never seen a comb. The village offered nothing for us so we kept on going.

An hour later in complete wilderness we spotted a figure running towards us. His tattered clothes flapped around him in the wind. The old man waved his arms as he ran and everything about him spoke urgency. Ross applied the brakes.

'Avez-vous de l'eau s'il vous plait?' He asked us, panting from his exertions. He wanted water for himself and his sons who were watching the animals. With a tall staff in his hand he appeared as I'd imagined John the Baptist to look with a long straggly beard, matted hair and a wild desperate look in his eyes. It would be unthinkable to refuse him and reserve our dwindling supplies in case of emergency, so we filled his container and also gave him some bread. A stilted conversation followed but little information exchanged, his French being virtually incomprehensible to my ears. Manic eyes shifted to left and right as he nodded in thanks and watched us drive away slowly trying not to cover him in a dust cloud. He waved as though we were old friends.

This left us little water to get to Tamanrasset but according to one solitary sign-post we only had sixty miles to go. We trusted the rogue sign without question. Nearly two hours of good day-light remained and we congratulated ourselves on our progress. The fierce heat of the day receded. This and the memory of people surviving in dire poverty had cured our self-pity and inertia. But two and a half hours later after travelling at a steady sixty miles per hour Tamanrasset had not materialised. Darkness was falling, we'd run out of water and to make things worse we got a puncture with a large dent appearing on one of the rear wheel rims. Ross became silent, obviously battling with demons.

By this time I knew the ropes when it came to punctures, so I got out of the car to fix this one, giving Ross the break he desperately needed. Under normal conditions the noise from a bump or rut severe enough to dent the wheel rim would have made him stop the car immediately to look for wheel damage. But here the constant pelting from stones and rocks had become the norm, and damage to the car an inescapable fact. For someone who had revelled in an unblemished new car only a few weeks ago, it must have been torture.

# CHAPTER FOUR

## *Tamanrasset*

We reached the elusive 'Tam' in darkness after twelve hours of driving interrupted only by short breaks to cool the engine. For nearly two days we'd travelled three hundred miles at an average of sixteen miles an hour and considered this to be good-going considering the difficulties we'd had. It had been the distance between Edinburgh and London's northern suburbs, but without motorways, petrol stations, shops, houses, or anything more than a few dried-up blades of grass. We'd met a gazelle and some nomads on the second day and just a handful of drivers over the whole distance.

The rambling town offered wide dimly-lit streets and an assortment of low mud buildings with small windows. Dust was a part of desert existence and shrouded everything, but here was life! Another dose of civilisation would be welcome and seeing a roughly-marked sign we limped into a café for a cold drink. The chance to enjoy some company beckoned.

Chergui Sliman, the café owner, gave us a warm welcome with handshakes in the French fashion and gestured for us to sit outside. The undefined space outside the coarse walls of the café merged with the street, and we sat down on a bench beside a rough wooden table above which hung a paraffin lamp. A rough covering of woven palm leaves had been erected to keep the worst of the sun's rays off daytime customers. He served us hot mint tea in small glasses and came to join us bringing the teapot for refills. I had to revive my translation skills to work both ways between him and Ross and struggled to keep up after the exigencies of the day. Long days on the road had dulled my senses and I found it frustrating not to find the right words. Although I joined in from time to time, translation was proving enough of a challenge without trying to make conversation as well. The other two were determined to communicate. My inadequacies while fumbling through a pocket dictionary encouraged other ways to exchange information which they soon discovered and managed with gestures. My tea glass was not allowed to empty and on finding that Ross preferred coffee, a jar of instant appeared with a bowl of sugar, a ready-punctured tin of evaporated milk and a cup. Finger marks circled the rim of the sugar bowl, and the ingrained cup had seen better days. The table had been given a cursory wipe with a grey dishcloth to aggravate a multitude of flies briefly before they continued their nuisance. Happily unaware of the low standard he had set Chergui talked with animation and seemed genuinely delighted to be entertaining us travellers. He invited us to have a meal with him and two of his friends the following evening. It would be at a nearby house, and couscous, the national dish, was on the menu.

Conversation flowed at a lively pace and we asked if he served meals. Soon a basic omelette and chips appeared on scruffy plates. It made a change from sandwiches and we felt recovery seeping through our bodies with the simple nourishment. Ross paid, we shook hands again with a promise to return and Chergui went to serve other customers. We tried to remember the last time we had eaten a hot meal and realised that it was two weeks earlier at our farewell supper in London.

It was that evening when we'd sat down with my parents and grandmother for a celebration farewell dinner. After a glass of Cyprus sherry something very British was called for. So we tucked into steak and kidney pie with potatoes, fresh runner beans and carrots, followed by apple crumble and custard, with a jug of cream for the special occasion. By the time the pudding was over, my grandmother could not contain her feelings any longer. She stood up with a pile of dishes, and set them down again with a bang.

For the last two weeks she'd said nothing untoward to us about our plans. We'd been out of the house for most of the time when they would have had plenty of opportunities to air concerns and anxieties between the three of them, but we'd been too busy to worry about anyone other than ourselves. The build-up of frustration made her explode with anger and Ross was the main target.

'We thought all our troubles were over when you got married, but now you are taking Sara to darkest Africa, and subjecting her to all that danger.'

We shifted in our seats and everyone looked uncomfortable as she paused for breath, looking at me sternly before glaring at Ross.

'You shouldn't be doing this dangerous journey through the unknown. There will be black men waiting behind trees to jump out and get her ...'

All the bad stories related to her by cousins in Rhodesia came tumbling out. On and on she went, and soon turned to me for more scolding, venting her fury until she ran out of steam. We had, of course, reached the point of no return, so there was nothing to do about her diatribe except feebly try to defend ourselves, but she never really forgave Ross for taking me to Africa along this dangerous route. We all went to bed on a low note.

### 24th October

Drinking tea again in the café Chergui introduced us to Yousef, a garage mechanic having his breakfast. We joined him and arranged to have the wheel rim fixed. The car also needed to be thoroughly checked over after the hammering it got on our way here. This would all take several hours so we drifted around town for a while and posted some letters.

Ever since we entered Algeria and crossed into an extreme Moslem world we had not spoken to a woman without her being shrouded in a *haik*. Being a convent girl I was well versed in female modesty, and was unfazed by nun-like habits. Facial covering was another matter, and it seemed to me akin to obliteration, a denial of existence. We saw these shrouded figures in towns, following at a respectable distance behind a man, or themselves followed by a child. All of our contact with Algerians was with men, in garages, shops, and markets. A woman's touch was sadly lacking and I missed that softening of surroundings to make for comfort.

'When in Rome do as the Romans,' I thought, but short of donning a *haik* this wasn't feasible. I therefore tried to keep a low profile and let Ross deal with things as much as possible.

I discovered recently the story about an Assyrian king who decreed centuries ago that all women should be veiled except for slaves and prostitutes who would be punished for doing so. Peasant women didn't follow the rule either, so wearing the veil became a status symbol because no self-respecting woman wanted to look like one of the lower orders.

We found Tamanrasset to be a friendly place but two invitations on the same day proved very different experiences.

Showers were available at *le camping* so we ventured off to have a look before committing ourselves. On the way there a small angular man came out of his house, greeted us with a handshake in the French manner, and invited us in to have some tea, which we did, not wanting to give offence. His French was hard for me to understand and we weren't at ease in his bachelor house sitting stiffly on wooden chairs and trying to think of conversation, but he seemed to mean well. His name was Hassan and he offered us a shower, a bed and an evening meal.

The shower was very tempting but with only one room we didn't like the idea of spending the night. We decided to go back and ask our new friends whether to accept, and to get soap and towels from the car. Chergui did not know the man and said it was up to us to decide. We took a chance and went back, desperate to rid ourselves of gritty sand which had found its way into every crevice of our bodies.

Hassan welcomed us again and ushered us back into the stark room while he attended to heating up the water. Stilted conversation ensued but soon the water was hot enough and Ross decided to go in the shower first. As soon as he left the room Hassan drew his chair closer to mine. He said something I didn't understand and then mimed a kiss. Ross had just had time to lather himself with soap when I called out

'You won't be too long will you?'

'Why, what's the matter?'

'It's okay but things aren't going too well.'

He immediately stopped the shower and still wet and lathered with soap put his clothes straight on. I hadn't meant to panic him this much and had felt really uncomfortable rather than threatened. I explained what had happened when Ross returned to join us, and he glowered at Hassan.

'What shall we do now?' I asked.

The atmosphere in the room had become really uncomfortable and I wanted to escape.

'There's no reason why you can't still take a shower now that we're here. I'll keep an eye on Hassan.'

I found the cubicle and checked for privacy before undressing and stepping into curtain-free coolness of the bare concrete surrounds. The luxury of a shower in the desert was not the enjoyable experience it should have been after what had happened and I wanted to leave as soon as we could. I towelled off and did the best I could to tidy my wet hair without a mirror then re-entered the silent room. Ross was giving off body language that echoed around the walls. He sat straight-backed with his arms folded, his knees apart and feet planted firmly on the floor. Hassan sat fixed in this stare in his own house looking abashed, his head bowed.

'Merci pour la douche.' I mumbled.

And he nodded smiling sheepishly. We left him in his empty house and stepped into the daytime dazzle. Soapy remains glinted through Ross's hair.

The huge cultural divide between the accepted customs of Moslems and Christians with regard to their women had caught us all out. We still couldn't believe his behaviour and Hassan probably couldn't believe ours either. None of us attempted to explain ourselves or lay the blame, there wasn't any point.

I was at least clean, dry and refreshed but Ross made me suffer with him as he bemoaned his incomplete wash. We headed for the camp-site to do laundry, each busy with our thoughts. Here we found a thigh-challenging hole-in-the ground toilet with a violent flush. The absence of body contact with anything is supposed to be more hygienic, but the experience feels the opposite since it is impossible to avoid odoriferous fumes in that position, especially as a woman. Unless you are quick on your feet after pulling the chain you end up with wet shoes and when wearing flip-flops it isn't pleasant. There were also a couple of showers here but as the place was communal and there were no doors or curtains to the lavatory or showers, we preferred our usual arrangements for finding privacy. The camp-site was deserted and we assumed it to be off-season. We did our washing in a deep concrete tub and took it back to drape over some small bushes near the car. Most of it dried in twenty minutes.

Late in the afternoon we met Omar, Chergui's cousin, and found ourselves with another invitation. This man didn't engender doubts in our minds, so undeterred by our recent experience we went with him.

He lived in a much grander house compared to others we'd seen in the town, boasting ten rooms. We entered to a smell of beeswax and his charming wife Khalida, without a veil, welcomed us with big smiles to put us at ease, but she didn't speak. She was pretty with thick curly black hair, and brought us mint tea and plain biscuits on a metal tray. This the second private house we'd been in on our journey made a comforting change from the masculine world of garages, shops, and bachelor rooms for that matter. Ross played dominoes and draughts with Khalida's father who owned the house, while I enjoyed the comfort of the large room and translated from time to time. Small windows kept out the sun's glare to give a shady coolness. A large French dresser stood against one wall and we sat on comfortable upholstered chairs with wooden occasional tables alongside each chair. I supposed that the dresser at least must have been transported here by lorry, being too bulky for a camel's load. A thick striped runner ran the length of the room between the hall and kitchen doors. I found reassurance in this civilised house in the middle of the Sahara, and felt safer within its confines than I had since entering North Africa. Perhaps this was how most women felt and why they only ventured out when the necessity arose.

We pitched up at Chergui's café at seven o'clock in the evening to admonishments. He'd expected us back sooner and being worried had been roaming the countryside in his Land Rover thinking we might be lost. Touched by his solicitousness we apologised for our thoughtlessness and soon he became his cheery self again. He reminded us of the meal he had promised.

We entered a dimly lit room where Gabir and Yousef were already seated at the table. They stood to shake our hands firmly. Yousef was the garage mechanic who we'd already met, being one of a predominant breed on our journey. Gabir had a small business in town and the three of them clearly enjoyed the company of strangers.

We gathered around a large table for lentil soup with noodles followed by couscous with camel stew. The latter was heavily spiced and we were apprehensive. The others could hardly wait to tuck in, so under their watchful eyes we loaded our plates and pretended to eat with relish in an effort to show appreciation.

'What would you like to drink?' asked Chergui.

'Just water would be fine, thank you,' we replied not wanting to stretch his generosity further. He assured us that it was *eau potable* when he saw us scrutinising the fingered jug in which it arrived. Ross had reached for the bottle of water purifying tablets and was about to administer some to the water in our glasses. Chergui looked indignant.

'This is artesian water purified through metres and metres of sand. It is the purest water in the Sahara. It doesn't need further treatment.' He proclaimed.

We had made it our policy since we embarked at Calais not to drink any water unless we treated it for ourselves. It would have been insulting to contradict Chergui's assertions, so we drank it as it came.

The men talked, and I translated as well as I could. The conversation moved to travel and we spoke of our difficulties with the piste and with soft sand. We asked about the next section we planned to cross. They didn't mince their words. The 560 miles to Agadez would be almost impossible in our car since wind- blown sand accumulated on the road at this time of year. They advised that the only safe way to do the journey would be to travel in front of a truck. If we got into difficulty the lorry crew would help us out. Even for sturdier vehicles than ours it was normal practice to travel in convoy from Tamanrasset to Agadez, the next town. Chergui expected his brother Sassi Sliman to be passing through Tam the next day in his truck so we could go with him.

Still digesting this information, we left them late to find a private spot out of town. Omar had invited us to spend the night at their house. The comfort of a bed and prospect of lying flat between sheets sounded like luxury. It was a tempting invitation and would probably have been fine but we'd politely refused after our earlier experience and fears of misunderstandings.

25ᵗʰ October

Rising at dawn we found that everyone else had already been up for at least half an hour. The time to be active in the desert is in the cool of the morning or the evening, and there was a bustle about the town not evident during the day. The burgeoning heat that would soon be evident had to be managed at a slow pace. This gives newly arrived and less-informed visitors the false impression of the inhabitants being lethargic and lazy.

We embarked on our business of changing a traveller's cheque at the *Douanes* and collecting the wheel from the garage. Sand-ladders and a shovel were our next quest.

'Salut,' said Pierre, a young Frenchman who was also waiting at the customs. 'What is your nationality?'

'Scottish' Ross replied.

Pierre and Gaston had teemed up with Claire, an American girl who had been sick for the last three days since they arrived in Tam and looked miserable. They were waiting to hitch a lift in the same lorry that we hoped would accompany us into Niger over the next stretch.

I didn't feel very well myself so Ross and I went for a stroll to see if I could shake it off.

Twenty minutes later it hit me full force. We'd arrived at the end of a residential street and I had to stop. The sun's heat had risen to a simmer and shade was elusive. My head spun. Water flooded my mouth. My body heaved. Relief came as I was violently and uncontrollably sick in the dust of the street. Mortified at this display we sought somewhere a bit more discreet under a tree, and then it hit me again. I stopped caring. This time it was even more shameful as I lost control of my bladder at the same time. My paroxysms had taken me past concern for what others thought. Ross had to bear the brunt of that, and a fleeting doubt went through my mind. Helpless and weak I moaned to him

'Don't leave me!'

And stalwart that he is, he stood by me, administering a hankie. It couldn't have been worse, the only redeeming feature being that the sun was getting higher in the sky and most people were in the shelter of their homes out of the heat. What would they think of me now, a brazen young woman flaunting her hair and face, not to mention arms and ankles, then putting on this display? I wished for the anonymity of a *haik*.

We concluded that *l'eau potable* we had drunk with the meal at the café may have been from an artesian well but its purity was questionable. It was likely to be the source of Claire's similar problem. We should have tactfully insisted on using our tablets or asked for lemonade. Everyone sympathised and I made it somehow through the rest of the day.

A lorry had arrived and was leaving in two days for Agadez so we went with Chergui to meet Farid the driver. He agreed to keep an eye on us for a small fee and looked happy for us to tag along.

### 26th October

A Tuareg was standing by the car when we woke. A traditional five-metre veil was wrapped around his face, indigo-blue dye had stained his skin in patches and I wondered if all his body was affected by matching robes. Tuaregs in this area had put up fierce resistance to French colonialisation, but their broadswords were no match for superior French weaponry and after massacres on both sides they admitted defeat. Their nomadic existence was being compromised and this one was looking to tourism for an alternative livelihood.

He must have been waiting for us to open our eyes and bleary with sleep we had a short stilted conversation with him. Getting my head around speaking French first thing in the morning was not appealing and he got no encouragement. In spite of long silences he just stood there watching us with his head in the window. He handed us an embroidered kettle holder crafted by a Tuareg woman which we accepted, and gave him some cigarettes in exchange. We made our excuses and left.

It wasn't the first time our privacy had been invaded. Before Madrid and further south than we had been before, we'd parked under oak trees to spend our second night in the car. We awoke startled. My heart thumped. I'd been dreaming about the Spanish civil war and the scenario outside made me struggle between dream and reality as men passed close by the car shouting and whistling with shot-guns slung over their shoulders. Torches flashed onto us dazzling our sleep-sodden eyes, and curious faces bent close to look. A large van was parked in front, a smaller one behind us, and two men revved their engines in their search for spaces. Four hounds sniffed the ground with frantic noses and their ears dangling. The camouflaged torch bearers called them to heel and they set off down a forest path. My watch said five fifteen, long before the first glimmer of dawn would break through the dark trees in our hitherto peaceful spot. The men disappeared into the trees for their day of hunting, voices fading into the surrounding pine trees. As they tramped along the path past evergreen oaks, sheltering birds awoke startled and whistled warnings. Peace returned allowing us to drop our heads back on to the headrests and slide into dreamless sleep for another hour before sunrise. We thought we'd chosen a good stopping place.

Word must have got round because later another Tuareg approached us wanting to exchange a silver pendant for one of our blankets. This was not what we considered a fair exchange! The blanket was a wedding present from my grandmother, pure wool and the colour would go well with traditional Tuareg blue robes. It was at the top of our pile of belongings on the back seat and we relied on its warmth for the cold desert nights.

By late morning I still felt wretched and craved a quiet room to hide in. Even in the shade the car would be like an oven, so I blindly followed Ross's lead and we went in search of a doctor. The surgery's door was locked and the doctor out of town. We were sent to a convent for assistance; a safe haven for sickness in an emergency. Sitting under a fan in the cool room

Sister Marie-Louise treated me with a kindness that was a therapy in itself. She gave me a single pill with instructions to sip water regularly and avoid all solid food until I felt better.

'What would you like to buy?' asked the postman Mustafa.

'Tomatoes and fruit,' Ross replied. He still had to eat even if I wasn't interested. I felt a little stronger and had agreed to accompany him to the market, preferring that to being left alone in a hot car. A shovel and sand-ladders were still on our shopping list too, but continued to elude us. The market-trader couldn't understand us and Mustafa, seeing our difficulties, had come to our rescue. He helped us to negotiate for a bag of tomatoes and a *pasteque* or watermelon.

'This is the best fruit for quenching thirst,' advised Omar. 'But you must not eat too much of it or you will get belly ache!' He held his middle to demonstrate.

My body told me to have nothing to do with it, but at any other time I'd have relished the succulent fruit. It was so big and heavy that Ross bought a quarter section, and still wondered if he would manage to get through it. We had only come across yellow Honeydew melons up until then.

Omar invited us to his house again for tea later, but discovering I hadn't been well insisted we went there immediately so that I could rest. This was an offer made in heaven and I felt almost human again after lying down in cool airy surroundings for an hour giving the little white pill a chance to take effect. I awoke in a room darkened by the shutters and looked around at the furnishings. Rugs decorated the polished concrete floor, and a few pieces of wooden furniture had been placed around the room. A woven rug decorated one wall, and framed pictures hung on the others showing scenes of waterfalls and towns. The woman's touch I'd been pining for was obvious and soon Khalida tiptoed in carrying a tray with a glass of water which she had specially boiled for me. 'Merci,' I croaked my throat dry with sleep. Although she only spoke Arabic she nodded and smiled. I got up and followed her down a polished corridor over more rugs and past an antique wooden chest into the room where Ross was sitting. The remains of a chess game lay on a low table between him and Khalida's father. We stayed until an hour after sunset, talking and listening to the radio that the elderly man had brought in. Khalida didn't sit with us, but came in to offer drinks and biscuits. She looked self-conscious in front of the men, perhaps because she wasn't wearing a veil and Ross was a stranger.

Omar tuned the radio to BBC world service for our benefit. The news was being broadcast and much of it concerned Zambia and President Kaunda, who was chairman of the Organisation of African Unity at the time and bringing in major reforms. We had a glimpse of what to expect over the next three years.

I felt revived when we left and headed back to spend the evening at the café. Khalida's father had invited us to return for the night and this time we accepted.


'Bonsoir' said Chergui and his friend Gabir. Having black skin and sub-Saharan features I wondered how he came to live amongst Arabs. It seemed unlikely he'd come to the desert for economic reasons, and I imagined him to be a descendant of slaves, victims of the raids and trade of past centuries.

Pierre and Gaston were already into their first beer and we joined the group for the rest of the evening. A tall dark stranger approached us. The Tuareg in his best traditional robes stood beside Chergui and spoke to him in Arabic. They both looked at me and Chergui pointed to Ross. A serious conversation then followed in guttural tones, with Chergui shaking his head and the Tuareg continuing, insistent. Gabir started to laugh.

What's the joke?' asked Gaston.

'He has offered Ross seven camels in exchange for Sara,' said Chergui, waving his hand to dismiss the idea.

We all laughed. The Tuareg stood regal, serious and immobile.

'That would help you do the rest of the desert crossing,' laughed Pierre.

'What a good idea!' joked Ross. 'Tell him five camels and a Land Rover!'

I translated what had been said into French, and Chergui translated it into Arabic. The stranger nodded at Ross and held out his hand to seal their business deal. He had watched the laughing and joking but hadn't been a part of it. Ross stood up and reached to shake the dark hand and continue the joke. The Tuareg showed a small smile and glanced in my direction. Chergui leapt to his feet grabbing Ross's arm.

'Non! Non!' The joke had run its course and straightaway sobered, Ross sat down.

The Tuareg lingered having lengthy discussions with Chergui, still casting brief looks at me and Ross. As they talked I had a good look at this near-miss suitor. He was tall, strong and rather stern-looking, but handsome in an Arabic way. I imagined his veil to hide a neatly trimmed beard. Dark blue robes hung around his tall form and a matching swathe of cloth wound thickly around his head. Rows of braid adorned his lower sleeves and coat front, and a flash of bright metal betrayed a sword partly obscured in the folds of fabric. Would I have been destined for a harem? I wondered. Some female companionship would be welcome I thought looking round at our gathering. Alluring visions of endless grooming beside fountains, and attar of roses scenting the air in a rich man's palace came to mind. And of course the sex! Hmmm. I reconsidered the Tuareg in his smart blue robes. Unless of course he was just an emissary? I suppose I was quite marketable being young, tall and slim with long blonde hair, and he may have intended to sell me on for a profit. Or was it a set-up? It certainly seemed real enough to both of us at the time. It is supposed to be every woman's fantasy to be whisked away in the desert by one such as him. Ross would have had difficulty explaining himself to my father.

The Tuareg hung around for a while and then left us. The conversation moved on too and I mentioned we'd seen a gazelle a few days earlier.

'You'd like to see a gazelle?' asked Chergui. 'I have one as a pet here in my house. Come and look. It's very young.'

We followed him into his house and walked through a series of gloomy rooms.

'Wait here,' said Chergui and disappeared behind a locked door with Gabir. Sounds of scuffling ensued, then the door opened and we crept in. The tiny courtyard was partially covered at one end where Gabir was crouching over a struggling young gazelle trying to hold it still. Its eyes shone bright with fear. Chergui motioned for us to close the door which we did just in time as it broke loose and charged at the mud walls, kicking and rearing.

'What happened to its mother?' I asked dodging to one side.

'She is dead,' replied Chergui without explanation as he helped Gabir to take a better hold of the crazed creature.

I didn't want to inquire too closely on the cause of death, and wondered how long the gazelle would remain a 'pet' once it had fattened up. Chergui locked the door of the little animal's prison with the sound of thuds and crashes following us back to the table. The little stubs of its horns were not enough to allow an escape.

We returned to enjoy a comfortable last night in Tam at Omar and Khalida's house and found only Omar still awake. We crept into a dark room with two narrow beds. My dreams were the stuff of Arabian Nights.

In the morning we had hoped for a last thorough wash before the next long drive but the water had been cut off so it would have to wait until the next town and the next country.

# CHAPTER FIVE

## *Convoy to Niger*

### 27th October

We said *au revoir* to the friends we had made during our few days in Tam, although meeting them again would be unlikely and *adieu* would have been more apt. To notify the authorities of our intentions we headed straight for the *Douanes*. Six pale-faced hitchhikers loitered in the shade of the building hoping for a lift on top of the lorry's cargo. Among them we saw Pierre, Gaston and Claire but it looked doubtful they'd find a place as it was already oversubscribed. We wished them good luck and as we drove off Pierre crossed the road to approach the driver of a Mercedes high-lift truck.

'Now that's a good vehicle for the Sahara,' said Ross looking longingly at the chunky machine.

'It has fantastic ground clearance of at least three times more than ours. It's been cleverly designed to have drive shafts raised above the wheel centres by a system of gears. Our worries would be over with that, I wonder what they cost?'

'A fortune probably!' I replied.

As a small truck, the Mercedes looked bigger and better than the Range Rover which had been newly released in July, and that was twice the price of our Hillman Hunter. Even with the benefit of hindsight we could never have afforded either vehicle.

No one could tell us when Farid the driver would set off so we decided to press on ahead which would allow us to take reasonable rests for engine cooling before he caught up with us. The road was marked pink on our map, meaning it was unsurfaced, but the section leading for about twenty miles out of town was a great improvement on much of the *piste* which had gone before and forever the optimists we expected it to last longer than the reality. Away from the comforting safety of the town we rolled along steadily for hours, getting used to heading off into featureless landscape again. We managed a few renditions of 'It's a long and a dusty road,' until the heat and dust made silence a preference for dry throats. Keeping our eyes on the hazy horizon kept our focus, and it wasn't until we stopped and looked back at acres of nothingness that feelings of vulnerable solitude chipped away at our confidence. Knowing Farid would be following became our security blanket, and I turned my head for occasional checks hoping for the sight of his lorry. The engine needed to cool several times and with the strong wind it took less than twenty minutes each time. On one of our stops I felt fully recovered from my sickness and decided to sample the *pasteque* but found only a sticky mass of alcoholic fruit, pips and newspaper. We wondered what chance the pips ever had of growing as I dumped the damp bundle on to dusty ground. Probably zero unless a freak rainstorm came that way. The butter had turned quite rancid so that was dumped too. Being ill in Tamanrasset had made me neglect our food supplies.

The insecurity of seeing no sign of Farid started to niggle in the hottest time of the day. I found myself making more and more frequent checks.

'He couldn't have missed us could he?' I asked aloud, no longer able to suppress my anxieties.

'God, I hope not,' said Ross, 'we've never strayed far from the original track, but I must say I thought he'd have come by now.'

A few clouds dampened the intensity of the sun's rays making the heat more bearable and on we drove. By five o'clock we had made very good progress.

'I reckon we must be only sixty miles from In Guezzam by now,' said Ross.

In Guezzam was the frontier town at the border with Niger. This was an estimate as there were no signposts, and no landmarks other than the tracks we followed. But as soon as Ross spoke we hit a bad sand patch. We set to and freed the car then stopped on solid ground to wait for the lorry.

The wind had dropped as we climbed out of our car seats into the relative cool of the evening air. Without the familiar rumble of the vehicle we stood feeling the silent enormity that was the Sahara. Flat stony ground full of nothingness lay dead around us. We saw for miles in every direction and there was nothing to see. Our own shallow tracks betrayed the only hint of life. A vast sky capped the sterile void and we joined the still silence in our awe. Long-legged shadows joined us for company and clarity came to our thoughts as we breathed air that refreshed at last. We had never seen the sun so huge and scarlet as it prepared to set. Then a tiny miracle flew down from the sky.

Cautious at first it made its assessment at a few yards distance. Braver it hopped around us for a bit.

'Hello. Where did you come from?'

Our gratitude for a focus had us scurrying around for water, pouring it into a lid for an offering. I found some crumbs of bread and added them for a meal. We stood back a few feet and watched. The little sparrow-sized bird hopped to the lid and drank long and deep. He pecked at the crumbs. His thanks came as a brief chirruped song and he drank again. We would like to have hung on to our visitor in this lonely place but too soon he ruffled and preened his feathers ready for the next lap of his journey before darkness fell completely. Deathly quiet cloaked us when he'd gone.

Magic returned when the stars came out and the Milky Way splashed over a dark domed ceiling. Every few minutes a star shot in a brilliant brief display.

'Did you see that one?'

'Where?'

'It's gone.'

'Look there's one over there!'

'Fantastic! Wow, there's another one above us!'

'And two at once over to our right, look!'

I made wishes on every one and the next few weeks would determine if they would come true. We watched the show until we lost count.

The small niggling worry that Farid wouldn't find us was overtaken by sky watching until the cold forced us back to our reclining seats to wrap ourselves up for the colder night to come.

Inside the car we could worry without distraction about the lorry not seeing us in the dark. We didn't know how long we had to wait and wouldn't dare to leave even the sidelights on. A dead battery in the Sahara would kill us with it.

Lorry drivers in the desert set off at dusk for comfortable travel, we discovered later. Their experience lets them read every shadow cast from the headlights to judge the ground surface. Ross slept while I kept a lookout for headlights on the horizon with the agreement to waken him after two hours to change shift. If I saw the slightest glimmer I would reach over to the controls and shine our headlights to indicate our whereabouts. We'd stopped close to the tracks of other vehicles, but there was no real way of knowing if they were the right ones, or if we'd unwittingly veered off on a diversion blindly following the wrong trail. Even on the right path the tracks of other vehicles spread for over fifty yards, so Farid would not exactly bump into us and our car colour of 'Golden Sand' wouldn't help. Try as I might to concentrate, watching for a glimmer in a dark void became tantamount to counting sheep and soon I fell asleep. At eleven I awoke guilty and with a sickly worry running through me. I could have missed our lifeline. Falling asleep 'on duty' invited disaster and could mean the ultimate for both of us. I would have to live and possibly die with this on my conscience.

Blinking away these thoughts I vowed to concentrate better and start my watch anew. Now fully awake I looked around in the moonlight. About twenty yards away was a beautiful lump of heavy machinery. Farid had seen us and stopped for the rest of the night. I smiled to myself in relief and fell back asleep.

## 27th October

We woke to see a travellers' camp next to the lorry. A dozen people drew their robes close around themselves still chilled from the night. They had built a fire and we strolled over to investigate, our shadows long again but to the reverse side of the night before. They were making morning tea.

Breakfast over, the women piled everything into cloths and gathered up the corners to knot them securely for travel. They looked like bundles themselves with their robes ballooning in the wind as they climbed high up atop the date cargo. Hands reached for hands and feet fumbled for a foothold. The 1970s equivalent of the camel train was faster but just as lumpy. The men followed in agile leaps, someone smacked the roof of the cab to tell the driver they were all settled in place ready and with a puff of exhaust smoke our mini-caravan started to roll.

A short chat with the driver revealed that the next stretch up to the frontier would be tricky so we should stay behind him. He weaved a convoluted path for us to follow, avoiding the worst patches of soft surface. His prediction was soon proved right and every fifteen minutes or so the sand claimed our wheels, but each time a cheerful band of men came down from their perch to give us a push. This ready solution felt like instant gratification after our frustrating efforts on the approach to Tam. At midday in searing heat and apparently wearing the same clothes as for the cold night, they all descended again with their bundles and set about cooking dinner grabbing what shade they could from the vehicle's bulk.

Two men prepared a fire in a hollow in the sand out of the wind. They used wood and charcoal from one of their bundles, and squatting next to it soon had the coals glowing red hot. A woman took out an enamel bowl and mixed millet flour and salt with some water to prepare *taguella*. She kneaded it well and pressed the dough into a flat circle then handed it to one of the men. He had made a flattish surface on the glowing charcoal so that the disc of dough could be placed carefully on top. He then sprinkled hot sand and charcoal from around the edges of the fire to cover it. About twenty minutes later, although no watch was consulted, he poked it with a stick. Apparently satisfied he then turned over the semi-cooked cake and again covered it with sand and charcoal from the edge of the fire.

Meanwhile women had spread cloths on the sand ready for the picnic, and laid out small bowls. After another twenty minutes the *taguella* was taken out of the fire with the stick and dusted off. One woman dipped her fingers into a small bowl of water and flicked the liquid over the dough, while another tore the bread into pieces for sharing. They squatted with right hands outstretched to take pieces of the hot bread with dried tomatoes and onions, and a bean mixture set out in a bowl. In less than two hours they achieved a cooked meal from scratch and cleared everything away until the next time. Comfortable desert-living could evidently be enjoyed with the right skills and knowledge.

An hour later we reached In Guezzam in a gusty haze. Thirty years before Michael Palin wrote his book 'Sahara' we saw none of the car wrecks he describes on the approach to the town. It was easy to understand how it could happen. Again we blessed the lorry.

A sandstorm had blown up making it the most God-forsaken place we had seen so far. A couple of primitive mud houses and some tortured trees could be made out among the flying particles. This was a precursor of the Harmattan, the dry and dusty wind that blows south from the end of November to mid-March. Visibility was equivalent to a heavy Scottish mist but with sand stinging our faces, making us wish for Arab clothes and head covers. As the silica granules flew with the wind men and women covered their heads and faces in scarves or shawls and huddled with their backs against the gale to prevent a sand-blasting. How sensible and logical to have portable protection against the sun and sand of the desert. The practicality of Islamic dress again made sense.

Ross parked the car facing away from the wind and sheltered in its safety to sit out the storm. We both fell asleep. Three hours later the wind had dropped to manageable proportions. Luckily the sandstorm hadn't been one to last several days. While we slept the flat ground between two scant buildings had metamorphosed. Drifts of sand piled up against walls, and where people had huddled down, conical hills had formed behind their backs. A large mound had formed behind the car where it did minimum damage. The people started to emerge peeling back the face-coverings from their clothing which doubled as shelter, and shook out the folds. A great deal of spitting followed.

We joined a small crowd in a sheltered spot to wait our turn at the customs to enter Niger. A little boy and his sister approached us.

'*Halloa*,' said the boy. His sister stood behind him studying us, a dusty flowered dress hanging off one shoulder. I guessed she must have been sheltering under her mother's robes during the sandstorm.

'Hello,' I replied smiling.

'*Halloa*,' said the boy again holding out his hand.

'Hello,' said Ross and reached out to shake his hand. They ran away giggling. They returned within minutes and the same interchange started up again until it dawned on me that *halloa* meant sweets. I dug around in the car to find some sugar lumps which they grabbed and took straight to their mother – there was no question of eating anything without her say-so. They wanted to come back but she stopped them.

Our journey could continue and we queued behind others at a metal table in a concrete block building for the next stamp in our passports.

Everyone had clearance and climbed on top of the date cargo, covering their heads and hunkering down again to keep out of the wind and sun. They looked like part of the merchandise. We followed the lorry into our fifth country. The wind flurries of In Guezzam became a memory and the landscape changed subtly to look less stony. Still all around us, the view stretched flatly for miles to a circular horizon. Our wheels seized up in the sand six more times and our gang of tireless helpers continued to set us free. In the late afternoon the driver stopped again, climbed stiffly down from his cab and stretching his shoulders came over to speak to Ross. He wanted to rest until nightfall when he planned to continue his journey, and suggested that we go ahead on our own. He assured us that the land ahead should be firmer, and that he would look out for us on his way. We left them brewing up their next pot of tea and giving a friendly wave, we set off into the wilderness alone again.

The Hoggar Route had been built by the French military and road maintenance involved grading away shifting sands between lines of poles until the track was uncovered, much as snow ploughs do in British winters. Since independence in 1962 this maintenance had faltered. Many of the poles had simply disappeared and of the remainder most had been completely covered to leave no land marks, signposts, or anything of substance to guide us. The compass became our life-line.

'Goodbye, have a safe trip,' my father had pressed a compass into my hand on our morning of departure. He had come up with something we'd missed.

'It's for the Sahara and anywhere else you might need it.'

'Let's hope we never do,' I had laughed innocently.

Farid had encouraged us to go on alone knowing our frequent stops since the border were partly due to the lorry going too slowly. Our car needed to skim over the surface to prevent it from sinking into soft sand. Keeping up speed and selecting our path over the pale brown ground became an art, and generally kept us out of trouble. Ross drove for most of the time in second or third gears to keep the wheels spinning. This exacerbated the problem of engine overheating and made fuel consumption soar. What at first appeared to be a solid carpet of sand we learned had subtle variations of colour and substance indicating the differences between powder soft and harder material. The going was hard compared to blindly following Farid, especially when the road kept disappearing, and the landscape had changed to be less stony. Rolls of tumbleweed blew past us and we thought that small melons rolling in their wake had dropped off a lorry, then realised that they were gourds managing to survive against the odds in this part of the desert.

We progressed to a section where we could see the main track clearly, and sometimes we drove on it, sometimes took the ground to the side when it looked more solid. Straggly patches of tough grass emerged, and plant life started to appear out of unlikely terrain. That part of the Sahara behind us, the extreme desert that would not even support a blade of grass, was receding and evidence of human life began to appear because vegetation meant food for goats. The track began to take forks every few miles, but without signposts so each time we had to choose which track to take. The compass helped us to select the more southerly one every time for lack of any better criteria. Sometimes the road and all signs of vehicle tracks just disappeared completely so I pointed my finger south as I watched the compass needle while Ross drove in that direction and negotiated the variances in ground surface.

At dusk we passed four barefoot children and a donkey, wandering apparently in the middle of nowhere. We hadn't noticed any dwellings. They stopped to stand and stare at us, and we exchanged waves and smiles but didn't dare stop. The surface around us looked unreliable and shortly after the children had become specks on the horizon a moment's lack of concentration let the soft sand claim our back wheels. As we busied ourselves with clearing them using the usual Tupperware container and bare hands, a voice said

'Bonsoir'

I jumped, startled, and we turned round to see two camels and a stately-looking Arab sitting on one of them. We hadn't heard a sound.

The young man sat regally erect in white robes quite unlike the usual Tuareg blue. In easily-understandable French he asked where we were going and if we needed help. He'd been studying in Paris at the Sorbonne and had come home for a break to see his family. Even his camels looked aristocratic. They were cleaner and lighter in colour then any we'd seen before, but his mount still made rude and raucous grunts when he motioned for it to sit down and allow him to walk towards us and shake our hands. He tried to help us free the wheels but without success, and then invited us to go back home with him on his camels. We hesitated, Ross more adventurous than me, but we didn't accept. Farid would worry if he found our abandoned car. Translation between this prince-like figure and Ross had found me tongue-tied due to tiredness. How often since have we wondered what it would have been like? We hadn't seen any houses for hours so had no idea were he might have taken us, but such an adventure would be one too far for my waning strength. He re-mounted and with a flick of the reins turned his camels homeward.

'*Bonne route*,' he shouted to us as he adjusted flowing robes over the saddle. His camels plodded softly away.

At nine o'clock Farid's lorry arrived. The crew pushed us out and saved us yet again to drive another thirty miles. We stopped beside a lonely signpost for an artesian well, the first sign we'd seen since In Guezzam. *Eau Potable*, it declared and we could just make out an arrow under the sun-bleached writing pointing vaguely east. We didn't see any sign of a well and having reasonable water supplies didn't feel the need to pursue the search. Even this small reminder of civilisation gave us some feeling of security for another night in the desert. The ground was firm and it was time to stop for the night. Farid left us alone again and drove his lorry into the darkness.

## 28th October

Knowing we would soon reach the next town encouraged us over the first stretch of road which offered new challenges. Although the track at first appeared well-marked and solid, deep troughs travelled its length. By taking runs at it to go from one patch of firm ground to the next Ross got us through except for the car being stuck once. The cool of the morning had helped his concentration.

Farid had warned us that nocturnal insect-eating animals were responsible for these burrows, and I didn't have the vocabulary for their name so our imaginations suggested porcupines, aardvarks, armadillos… Whatever they were, they made our drive to Agadez harder than it needed to be.

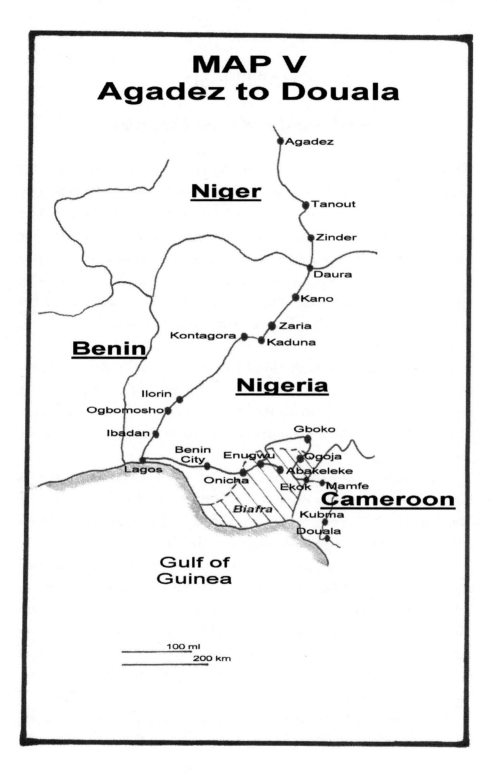

**MAP V**
**Agadez to Douala**

Agadez

**Niger**

Tanout

Zinder

Daura

Kano

Zaria

Kontagora    Kaduna

**Benin**

**Nigeria**

Ilorin

Ogbomosho

Gboko

Ibadan

Benin
City    Enugwu    Ogoja

Lagos    Onicha    Abakeleke

Ekok    Mamfe

*Biafra*    **Cameroon**

Kubma

Douala

**Gulf of**
**Guinea**

100 ml
200 km

# CHAPTER SIX

## *Sand, Sand and Food Fantasies*

We passed Farid's lorry soon afterwards, waved to everyone for the last time and made good time to Agadez on our own. On good ground it seemed easy without an escort and gave us back a false confidence. We perceived an escape from the silent threat of the desert and civilisation beckoned. The mesmerizing grandeur, calm and loneliness of open barrenness were forgotten in the hubbub of the bustling town and we fooled ourselves into thinking the toughest part had passed. We entered the city with a population of less than five thousand. It hadn't changed in over a hundred years.

Tuareg smiths manufacture the famous silver crosses of Agadez. Each tribe has its own variation which usually takes the name of a village. Tuaregs believe that wearing or carrying the crosses would bring God's protection. The true Agadez Cross and a variant design called the Iferouane Cross are the best known.

The French Armed Forces who occupied Niger for decades before its independence had badges designed for each company, usually with some variation of the Tuareg cross. Drago, the famous military badge-manufacturer in Paris, made many of over four hundred different crosses.

Agadez had seen huge growth as a trade town from the sixteenth Century onwards due to its central location for trans-Saharan traffic. Caravans of laden camels would wend their way from Kano and Timbuktu in West Africa, the North African oases of Ghat and Ghadames, and from Tripoli on the Mediterranean shore. Much of this trade had been taken over by lorries in 1970, but two major caravans still travel in November and March from Agadez to Blima to trade salt.

These twice yearly *Azalai* are made by the Tuareg tribe, and we would love to have seen them set off but we had arrived a few weeks too early for the spectacle. At the start of the colonial period in the 1920's the *Azalai* would sometimes stretch for twenty miles with 10,000 camels.

Salt is mined by the Kanuri tribe who cut solid blocks of it from underground in the Teneré desert around Agadez. It is then processed in evaporation ponds which benefit from the full blast of daytime Saharan sunshine.

We soon had a monetary problem in the ancient town. It wasn't possible to exchange travellers' cheques at the customs as we'd done in Algeria, in fact the customs officer had never heard of them and he only wanted to stamp our *carnet* for the car. Banks had not found their way here but a helpful French couple told us where we could cash our cheques. We crossed a wide dirt street past a long wall behind which a tower rose up like a tall sandcastle studded with ice-lolly sticks. The Agadez Grand Mosquée dates back to 1515 and was rebuilt in 1844, the tallest building for a thousand miles. Its strength against fierce Saharan winds owes itself to the timber shafts jutting out from each face, looking as if it wants to be climbed. The wooden protrusions are for supporting planks so that fresh mud can be applied to the walls from time to time.

We arrived at a kiosk to be offered fifteen per cent less than the official bank exchange rate. The patron of the second hotel we tried offered a better deal. The catch was that everything we bought had to go on the hotel bill. We signed the register, entered a basic airy room and took turns in the decadence of a shower. The precious water worked its therapy to free us of sand, sweat and grime. Feeling cleansed and pampered we ventured into town to explore and remind ourselves what legs were for. A man calling himself Hamid approached us as if we were long-lost friends.

'Welcome to Agadez, where have you travelled from?'

'Tamanrasset,' I replied.

'I will show you around, I have four Land Rovers for us to travel in, and then I will buy you beer.'

The black man spoke good English, an unusual skill in this old French colony. Being suspicious of such magnanimity we agreed but with reservations and at his insistence arranged to see him later.

'Hi how ya doing?' called the American Peace Corps workers.

Matt, Jim and Brad crossed the road to greet us. They had met up with Dale, Bernard and David, French-Canadians who also hitched rides. Without their own vehicle this was the only way to see more of the country where they had volunteered their services. They had opted for the Peace Corps rather than being drafted to Vietnam.

We chatted to this friendly bunch for a while exchanging stories. Such instant friendships had become the norm for us since we arrived in the desert. An unwritten code made all travellers we met seek and give mutual support. The overwhelming vastness of the Sahara demanded both locals and foreigners to stop on any road outside the towns for these exchanges. No one would ever pass another vehicle without a friendly greeting and offer of help if needed.

Here in Agadez the rule was a little different where westerners recognised each other as outsiders and always stopped to chat. Inwardly they marvelled at finding themselves in such a far flung barren land which was two-thirds desert.

The market sprawled across the dust and busy traders bought and bartered. Men wore head-covering for protection against flying sand and pulled the cloth down from their mouths when they wanted to shout conversations to each other. Noisy and productive spits punctuated their interchanges while piercing eyes shone out from sun-wrinkled faces to expertly judge the form of livestock. Hopeful sellers herded groups of donkeys, goats, sheep, and foul-breathed camels into pens for inspection by would-be buyers. Panicked livestock brayed, bleated, and grunted, suspecting their fate. A few barefoot children played in the dust. A little boy stopped to look at us strangers and flies crawled around his eyes, nose, and mouth the second he stood still.

We saw no hardware stalls for a shovel or sand-ladders.

Chergui's brother lived here, but we couldn't find him, instead Hamid found us. We accompanied him with four of the hitch-hikers to a mud-brick bar. On benches in the shade of a gnarled tree we all sat at a rough wooden table and he ordered seven bottles of Niger beer. We recognised it as lager and savoured the cool liquid trickling down our parched throats in the dusty afternoon heat. His generosity flowed with the drink.

'Have another beer!' he pressed.

'No thank you that was fine,' answered Ross

'I am very rich and I like to give visitors a good time. You have travelled a long way to Agadez and I like to make you welcome.'

This wonderful sentiment may or may not have been the truth, but ungratefully we wondered about ulterior motives. In one of the world's poorest countries we didn't know what to make of someone who was behaving like a lottery winner.

'You must come to my house for a meal this evening!'

The invitation was for all of us and the others accepted, but hardened by our experiences of the meal in Tamanrasset we made our excuses and returned to the hotel to eat.

As we got ready for bed the sight of pale reptiles darting up the walls and over the ceiling made me squeamish, wondering what their movements would be when the light went off.

'What are those lizards doing in here?' I demanded to know.

'I think they're called geckoes, and they will eat any mosquitoes,' Ross tried to reassure me.

'Yes, but shouldn't they be outside? I don't like the thought of them running over my face in the dark when I'm sleeping!' I protested.

Once I was convinced they had no interest in me and would stick to the walls for their hunting, I settled down. We celebrated a closeness that wasn't possible in the car and then sank back into a deep sleep. For one night our backs could lie flat and our limbs freely change position under the crisp, white, soap-smelling sheet.


29th October


At last a traveller's cheque could be changed in the morning. We paid our bill and left for Zinder, leaving the creaking fans of the hotel for another day of oven-blasting heat. Refuelled, revived and rested we entered the next phase hoping for an easier time. Zinder, the next town, was due south and Ross estimated a journey of over 300 miles.

We had been warned by the Americans that this road would be difficult in a car with little ground clearance and we soon hit drifts of soft beachy sand. These forced us into leaving the road and thus avoid being sucked down into the soft grains. About midday with the sun at its highest, hottest and cruellest Ross stopped to secure the bonnet which had shaken loose again. Apart from tufts of scrubby grass nothing provided shade and not a breath of wind cooled us or the hot engine. Two little boys in holey tee shirts and tatty shorts came to watch us as we sat on the ground eating. Offers to share our picnic lunch were as unfruitful as the terrain and they would not come close. We soon finished our old standby of sardine sandwiches and shaking off the crumbs we stood up from the ground. As we drove away I saw them run to pick up the empty tin we had left behind. My heart lurched at their poverty, and I wished I'd left something for them.

I'm ashamed to admit we disposed of rubbish like this as we went along. In the desert I'd had as little conscience about it as I would on the moon. Mostly our detritus amounted to banana skins, fruit stones and the odd cigarette packet. Bread came unwrapped and we filled a container for water, so empty fish or meat cans were our worst offences. If we saw other rubbish lying about we added to it, but otherwise we sometimes tried to bury it, an easy option in much of the desert.

Ross was looking at the scenery with uncharacteristic interest and urgency. I soon found out why. He stopped the car, threw open his door and shot off towards a straggly bush at the roadside.

'Be back in a minute…' his voice trailed from his hurrying bent form.

He'd been complaining of stomach cramps on and off since we left Tamanrasset and things had evidently gone beyond his control. Giving him privacy I kept my eyes forward with the intention of warning him in the unlikely event of another vehicle's approach. Our car was blocking the road and I could at least spare him the indignity of being caught with his trousers down. I opened my door to encourage a draught and released an immediate build–up of heat. The minutes ticked by. His return was more dignified than his departure.

'Feeling better?' I asked.

'A bit,' he replied without assurance, 'I had to leave my underpants behind under that bush.'

Ross wasn't in the mood for talking. Ten minutes later we stopped again. I wondered what he'd do this time if he was caught short like before. He hadn't replaced the underpants and only possessed two pairs of shorts so couldn't afford to leave either of them behind. Water for washing wasn't exactly in plentiful supply. I thrust our last few tissues into his hand. Poor Ross. If he felt anything like I had in Tamanrasset, he needed a cool room where he could rest and recover. Being forced to coax our wheels over hot stony sand under an unforgiving solar onslaught was not the prescription he needed. I felt powerless to help and he put on a brave face when he returned, but I knew he was struggling to cope. Twenty minutes later we stopped again.

'Try to sip water,' I suggested on his next return.

His skin had taken on a worrying grey tinge and he became very quiet. With the engine running again he grimly gripped the steering wheel. I sat attentively holding a plastic beaker in an attempt to keep him hydrated. Imodium wasn't working on this exotic bug waging war in his intestines, and I wondered what Sister Marie-Louise had given me in Tamanrasset. If we could make it to Zinder I resolved to find a chemist for another remedy. His normal verbosity turned to taciturnity and I watched as he used all his strength and resolve to maintain our quest for forward motion. The imperative to get to the next town weighed heavy and I could only watch and wait. Silent prayers were the best I could offer.

The going became difficult especially since tracks off the road kept disappearing into nothingness. When we had been in absolute desert with no scrub at all there were no obstacles, other than the odd small boulder, and we'd been used to driving where it suited us. Here the thorny tough bushes severely limited our options forcing us to stick to an impossible sand-drenched track. Heavy vehicles had preceded us on this main highway through Niger, leaving two deep ruts and a central strip of sandy earth a foot deep that defied the car's ground clearance. Concentrating intensely Ross coaxed, swerved, rushed, and then crept along the road which was to torture us all the way to Zinder for 465 miles. It was impossible to drive in the lorry tracks in an ordinary car, so with two wheels on the central ridge and the other two in one or other side of the lorry tracks we made wobbly progress.

The car kept stopping, wheels hopelessly turning without effect, but every time willing locals came selflessly to our aid. Full of smiles and sinewy arms they would drop their bundles to push our heavy vehicle and wave like new-found family when we resumed motion. Our only communication was sign language, and we always went on our way humbled by their generosity. When the sky darkened the car stopped unable to make headway against a heap of sand. We felt exhausted and demoralised at less than half-way from Agadez to Zinder. Our food, water and petrol were running low and the bonnet had shaken loose yet again. All except one of the rivets fixing its hinges were sheared and no amount of epoxy resin would survive the relentless poundings and vibrations. Ross decided that it would be safer to remove it completely in case it sprung open unexpectedly blocking his view at some crucial moment. Our last shreds of energy let us secure it to the roof-rack under the spare tyres, and then we both sank back into our seats with an unsettling view of the engine through the windscreen. At least the engine would cool faster.

We had expected to arrive sooner at the next opportunity for supplies. No signs of civilisation had appeared all day apart from the people emerging from hidden villages who helped us. Our desert quotas of spare water and fuel became vital and our vulnerability that night felt a world away from the comfort and security of the night before.

## 30ᵗʰ October

Waking at dawn we found ourselves still in the rut we'd become stuck in the night before, being too discouraged to do anything about it. A man passing on his donkey helped us to push the car back on to the road and within five minutes we were stuck again. There simply wasn't enough firm ground for the wheels to grip, and again we bemoaned our woefully inadequate ground clearance. We sat helplessly waiting for renewed energy and inspiration, or a Good Samaritan to help after our own efforts had failed.

As if on cue four Australians in a Dormobile trundled along from the opposite direction. Trevor, Susan, Andy and Jane helped us on to firmer ground with the use of their sand-ladders, cheering our mood with their collective enthusiasm and bonhomie. Sharing stories again animated our flagging enthusiasm. They had driven through East Africa and the Congo on a route that we planned to follow, and they in turn were following the route we had just done. Their report did nothing to hearten us since they had travelled up through Kisangani in the Congo with huge difficulty. Deep mud on the roads had been insufferable and they'd had the metal ladders made as a result.

We wondered if they had just been unlucky with wet weather, or if we would have to change our plan to avoid such bad conditions. They suggested cutting across the Northern Congo on higher ground into Uganda then circling round East Africa to enter Zambia from Tanzania instead. The ground clearance on a Dormobile far exceeded that of a Hillman Hunter, and even with four of them to dig and push they had experienced problems. The shorter distance of our original plan looked too risky even with time and money running low. We needed a rethink. Bad news can be welcome sometimes, and grateful for the warnings we bade them good luck on their travels and continued south.

Mostly we kept off the road from then on, but the bush became more and more overgrown and dense. A feeling of impending disaster hung over us. It was like an obstacle course requiring constant detours around impenetrable clumps of thorny shrubs, and sometimes dead ends necessitated going back as if in a maze to try a different route. If we landed in a patch of soft sand and couldn't get out other drivers wouldn't see us. Avoiding the road in this way cut us off from potential assistance so along with all the other considerations of land surface and avoiding bushes Ross tried not to stray too far from the official track.

Our foreboding became reality at the next sticking point and we knew we were on our own. The car wasn't in too deep this time because Ross had resisted spinning the wheels knowing it would only dig us in further. I climbed out to see if pushing would make it budge. I leaned my weight against the rear of the vehicle and out of nowhere a group of black Africans

appeared to help us. They were a merry lot defying us not to smile and laugh with them, and we gesticulated to each other for communication.

The loose-limbed bunch of men and women saw what needed to be done and without hesitation added their combined weight to propel the car twenty yards on to terra firma.

'One two three PUSH!' I shouted.

'Pooosh!' they sang and laughed.

We wanted to reward them somehow but we were at a loss. We had run out of cigarettes and spare food. The men took Ross's razor and the women my jar of Ponds face cream after I demonstrated a mini-facial. I cast a look at their faces, none of which enjoyed the flush of youth, and started to have second thoughts but they showed delight. These were not the anonymous *haik*-clad women of further north, in fact they were topless. Laughing and joking together one of them pointed meaningfully into the car. She had spotted my yellow floral Marks and Spencer's bra drying over the back seat, having been washed in our most recent laundering. I handed it over and immediately the eldest most wrinkled one put it on, parading around like a mannequin while the others laughed until they nearly fell over. This was the African way, to ask for things. In no way was it menacing or bribery, but a simple expression of what they would like in return for their assisting us. 'No' was an acceptable answer but some token of appreciation had to be shown.

In all we drove less than thirty miles that day with one tin of fish and some sugar lumps for rations to see us to Zinder. We had no heart for singing to raise our morale and barely dared talk to each other. The silence continued until the track covering hardened. Shortly before nightfall our progress quickened. Ross had not mentioned his digestive system for several hours, and I assumed he was feeling better. Not relishing the thought of dining on sardines again, we started fantasising about food.

'What would you give for a steak and chips right now?'

'Even macaroni cheese would be welcome.'

'Followed by apple crumble and custard.'

'How about sausage and mash.'

'Washed down with a pint of cold lager.'

'Strawberries and ice cream.'

'Or steak and chips with chocolate gateau for pudding.'

Our game continued for half an hour until we stopped to face our sad sardine tin. As a 'treat' I thought we might mix some evaporated milk with water but as soon as the water hit the thick milk it curdled. We drank it anyway to give ourselves sustenance. The game switched to comfortable beds with crisp linen sheets and ...

We woke in a sandy landscape under an immaculate sky. There would be no respite from the sun's grilling later in the day every time we left the shelter of the car. My shoulders and nose were crusty with sunburn and too late I put on a long-sleeved shirt. I'd given away my only face cream.

The land became sandier and blended with the road until we found ourselves in the middle of a brown ocean. Diminutive bushes dotted it like flotsam. Sandy waves made hills, valleys and stretches of flat nothingness reaching out to a hazy horizon. *Erg* looked beautiful, but driving across it was a nightmare in our vehicle. The sun too quickly rose directly above making reflections off the golden surface and shimmering around us.

'Is it this way?'

'Is that the track over there?' We both spoke at once and our words collided after a lengthy period of silence. The road had been covered by sand-dunes and clues to its whereabouts amounted to zilch. The solution lay with the compass, the last minute present from my father. It was simple; head south. How easy it would have been to go round in circles without it!

Soon we found a set of lorry tracks which we hailed as a blessing. For two hours we followed them until the realisation dawned that they were not heading in the right direction. This puzzle taunted us for a few more miles as we waited expectantly for the tracks to turn.

And then they petered out completely.

We had been following windrows of sand; two parallel ridges formed by the wind. Their span matching exactly the width of a lorry's wheels for such a distance was a fluke of nature that left us in real danger. Far removed from the correct route we were unlikely to meet a living soul in a country where population was less than three per square mile. Worse, we had used up precious fuel, a double waste if we made our way back along the windrows the way we'd come. A fresh wind blowing in a different direction could cover our tracks and we'd really be in trouble. Trying to suppress panic and think clearly we weighed up our options.

'I reckon that we've been travelling slightly west of due south,' announced Ross after thoughtful consideration.

So we decided to try to correct our position by heading slightly east of south and travel in a straight line. This was not ideal because it meant navigating over patches of soft sand where inevitably we ground to a frustrating halt. Without sand ladders and with no handy rocks that could be placed under the wheels we used the spare wheels as the only option for solid substance to drive over when there was nothing else we could do. The piece of wood we had salvaged back in Ghardaia came into use again and again as a base for the car jack. Like robots we systematically jacked up the car; dug away as much sand from under the wheels as we could; placed the spare wheels underneath then removed the jack. Ross then drove slowly over the wheel as far as possible, remembering to stop before the wheel spins dug the car in deeper. Sometimes only a couple of yards were gained before the procedure had to be repeated. It was slow tedious work. At other times he kept driving slowly if he could manage to keep the car moving. When that happened I had to gather up the wheels and run after him with one under each arm. The car in motion was less likely to be grounded, although it flashed through my mind that I shouldn't fall out with the driver!

Worse was to come. Driving up the face of a sand-dune we approached the top and realised too late it was a pointed summit. The front wheels sailed into thin air and the car came to rest with the chassis perched on a peak. The back wheels barely touched the ground. As we cautiously climbed out the car rocked like a see-saw. Back in robotic mode we started digging again, clearing the chassis and allowing its weight to fall back on to the wheels until there was enough traction to drive forward. Tired and hungry we worked in silence for an hour until darkness and exhaustion took over. Our hearts and backs felt broken. How carelessly we'd taken for granted the helpful young men on the date lorry who always leapt down ready to give us a push. Too tired to write anything in the log book, we fell into our seats and slept.

31st October

Halloween dawned and the witches were still out to get us. Repeatedly the car ground to a halt in the silky fine grains we had learned to hate. The wheels spun hopelessly unable to grip the surface. There was no one and nothing to fall back on. To make things worse Ross was still suffering from his stomach bug and had to keep stopping the car to disappear behind a thorny bush. He was digging deep to find the reserves to keep driving and I wished that I could do something to help. We'd tried a driving lesson back in the flat wilderness of the Sahara in case I had to take over in an emergency. It looked the ideal training ground with nothing and no one to bump into. Sadly we'd under-estimated the skills required to manoeuvre and navigate around problems. It soon became obvious that mastering those at the same time as learning to handle the controls would be impossible for me. The demands of driving lessons would have to be kept for later, so I stuck to my duties as driver's mate.

The relief on reaching Tanout lifted us out of despondency. Finding this tiny settlement was a miracle of navigation and luck, it would have been so easy to miss. Only a couple of hovels and a wind-blown sign indicated the village, but we'd been told this place marked the end of the sand drifts. Solid track soon turned into corrugations and in spite of the bumps we gratefully lurched along its hard and stony covering.

Ross had been doing some calculations.

'Do you remember I worked out that the distance from Agadez to Zinder would be about 310 miles? But according to the 'clock' we've actually done 600 which is practically double my estimate!'

'No wonder it's taken nearly three days then,' I replied.

'Across that terrain it's not bad!' He recovered fast from brushes with disaster. 'It works out at an average of twenty miles per gallon and that's because most of the journey was done in second and third gears. Back in the UK we were getting around 30 mpg. Keeping up the engine revs to carry the car over soft patches of sand is what did it. There's hardly any fuel left to get us to Zinder!'

All the jerry cans had been emptied and of the 35 gallons we'd had when we left Agadez only a quarter of a tank remained, the equivalent of two and a half gallons. It was a frightening margin of error with trouble lurking at every wheel-turn.

Without the constant challenge of avoiding obstacles our minds turned again to the suffering of our deprived stomachs.

'Oh for a big plate of fresh salad,' I started to play the food game again and we tortured ourselves with the thought of any food except sardines all the way to Zinder.

# CHAPTER SEVEN

## *Leaving the Desert*

In the relative cool of late afternoon we nearly cried with relief when we reached the town. We wanted to buy food and needed hard cash to let us shop. It was Saturday and all of the banks were shut. The customs post was open but its officers felt no need for speed, and our impatience to recover in civilisation again was hard to hide. At last we permitted ourselves to venture into a hotel. The young French proprietor changed our travellers' cheques and we sat in the breezy foyer sipping cool lemonade under a whirring ceiling fan. The joy of civilised comfort soaked into our souls.

As we sat there in a semi-daze of recovery, souvenir vendors arrived and one after the other set up their stalls in the hotel courtyard. It was all for our benefit since people who owned a car and could afford to frequent hotels obviously had ready funds. Not really wanting to buy anything Ross half-heartedly made a few low offers hoping to discourage them. The prices tumbled and we ended up with a pair of camel-leather sandals, two straw hats, a leather pouffé without the stuffing, and three ostrich feathers.

It was good retail therapy and the hats and sandals were necessary, but abandoning our budget on top of the extravagance of the hotel room left us full of remorse at giving in to their persistence. Our future mileage had stretched and fuel did not come cheap. We had second thoughts about the ostrich feathers too because they might be sensitive items to get through customs, so we wrapped them in newspaper and tucked them discreetly into a cranny in the boot. The hotel manager tactfully congratulated us on getting good bargains.

After all our troubles and privations we'd already decided a proper meal was a necessity rather than a luxury, so that evening we splashed out. As we sat down to eat, relatively clean, brushed and respectably dressed, we were about to realise our fantasy of food other than sardine sandwiches washed down with tepid chlorinated water. Our first mistake was to tuck into the freshly baked bread served with a salad for the first course, because it was all our shrunken stomachs had been led to expect from a meal for days. As a result the delicious steak and chips we'd fantasized about had to be forced down. After an ice-cream dessert we waddled uncomfortably back to our room to sleep it off. Our dreams had been made real, but the reality came with a bellyache!

## 1st November

On this 'All Saints Day' it was like entering the city of the damned. At the approach to Zinder market two parallel lines of lepers sat or stood begging for what little donation the locals could afford. In return they gave good luck to the market traders by laying their hands, or what was left of them, on the goods they were to sell including fruit, vegetables and meat. The lepers made a pitiful sight and made me want to turn and look away, but we ran the gauntlet and tried to be kind forcing ourselves to focus on the eyes of swollen but smiling deformed faces devoid of self-pity. We offered a few coins in return for heartfelt thanks.

The market measured the size of two football pitches, and the whole area was surrounded by several hundred Nubian vultures, the biggest in Africa, standing shoulder to shoulder on walls and rooftops. With a menacing force they stretched their huge wings from time to time to display up to three metres of untidy wing feathers. They watched and waited. When something was left unguarded for long enough they swooped, bounced forward and pecked with vicious hooked beaks, their pink wrinkled heads looking tender in the hot sun. Thin dogs competed ineffectively as scavengers. Fresh meat had to be guarded constantly and flicked with a switch of horsehair to deter swarms of flies.

In a separate section live camels, goats, sheep and chickens noisily waited for the day to end. Fruit, piles of dates, vegetables and dried pulses arranged in baskets sat on trestle tables or on cloths spread over the ground in a third area. Cooking pots, enamelled basins and household items piled up in another, but still no sign of a shovel.

A small child with dysentery squatted on the ground, holding up her dirty ragged dress. Her head was shaved showing signs of ringworm. Children like this seemed to belong to everyone and no one. She turned her dusty face to look at us strangers.

Everything was freely handled by all, and having to choose something to eat with our lunch we reluctantly purchased a little pile of tomatoes. Later we thoroughly washed them with chlorinated water.

As we wandered among the goods, two barefoot women approached us, each holding one end of the same broom handle. The girl at the front and leading was in her teens, the fragile old lady at the back was blind and begging for her livelihood. They both wore tattered shifts the colour of dust. Ross pressed a few coins into the old lady's hand and she immediately launched into what sounded like a tirade. We exchanged a questioning look.

'Elle vous remercie!' said the young girl with a beautiful smile, she is thanking you. Far from being ungrateful, she was chanting a lengthy song of blessing for us in return for the donation, a benediction to wish us a long and healthy life. Living didn't come easy in a country where life expectancy was only forty years, the lowest rate of all the countries we were to pass through and thirteen years less than its comparatively wealthy neighbour Algeria. I felt humbled and regretful about our overindulgence the night before after a relatively short period of deprivation on our part. This All Saints Day was showing us a few deserving of heaven.

## 2nd November

*'Allahu Akbar.'* The call to prayer woke us at dawn. We had hoped to get organised and away early in the morning, but no such luck. The puncture we'd taken for repair had still not been mended and they found two so it cost double. Our previous day's treats meant we had to change another cheque.

Back at the hotel we strengthened our resolve for the next lap with a cup of strong coffee. Matt, Jim and Brad, the Americans we had met in Agadez, came to join us. We discussed the road we had all just travelled, and related our experiences with local bacteria. Ross was still in a bad way. Dioralyte was not doing the trick and he had left three pairs of underpants behind bushes in the desert. They took us to the US Peace Corps pharmacy for medication. With instructions to 'take a slug' whenever he felt the need Ross hugged the pint of bluish liquid. If that didn't work they had given him a small phial with two tiny white pills inside and only one of these was to be taken if his condition became serious.

As we all walked away from the pharmacy, we somehow got on to the subject of veiled women and their place in society. To illustrate how the women depended completely on their men for support, and perhaps feeling that he knew us well enough after divulging intimate health details, Brad without warning said,

'Matt and I went to have a look at a brothel.'

'What did you do that for?' I asked stupidly, and instantly regretted speaking out in my effort to break the uncomfortable silence.

He ignored me.

'You've never seen anything like it,' he laughed nervously swatting a fly off his forehead, 'they were so old and ugly! They just sat on the floor waiting to be chosen, and the rooms were really dark and dingy.'

'I suppose that helped in the circumstances,' quipped Ross, trying to lighten the conversation.

'Well we didn't stay, no way. We were outta there believe me. Those women had hit rock-bottom and had no other way of supporting themselves. It was pretty tragic really. It was a hell-hole.'

Matt looked at his feet and kicked the dust as his friend made his revelation. We nodded not wanting to mock his candour but were a little taken aback by this salacious piece of unsolicited information. I struggled to block unwelcome images invading my thoughts and taking flight.

We left them with waves and good wishes and headed out of town.

To avoid taxation in each country, we carried a *Carnet de Passage en Douanes* for the car which we'd arranged in London. We arrived at the border with Nigeria and entered a building marked *Douanes* to get the *carnet* stamped. A

97

clerk told us the customs officer would be back at midday. There was nothing to do in the remote backwater and when we returned bored and frustrated at twelve we found we'd just missed him. Until he returned from his lunch break in a further hour and a half we'd have to wait again. Although we were getting better at dealing with this sort of thing it didn't come easily, especially at the height of the day's heat. To remain sane in Africa passive acceptance and an absence of hurry looked to be the only way. Nigeria beckoned and a new chapter was about to begin.

# CHAPTER EIGHT

## *Durbars and Guinness*

Most people would avoid a country recovering from civil war. This had been our original intention but plans change. Visas for the Congo could not be organised in London, and we'd hoped to get them in Madrid. Spain was enjoying a *Fiesta* due to run for several days when we arrived in the capital and the Congolese Embassy's doors remained shut. Too impatient to consider waiting for a few days on the off-chance of getting the visas we went on our way. Our budget covered living expenses for five weeks and a week hanging around Madrid would eat into our precious funds. Lagos had just made itself part of our itinerary being the only other town on our way south where we knew we could get a visa. We had studied our map of Africa to check the revised route and read ominously familiar place names. They were the stuff of news bulletins about the recent Biafran War. Getting to Lagos meant simply heading due south through the Sahara and onward on well-marked roads. But leaving the capital would take us through the South-Eastern part of Nigeria which is Biafra itself. Were we in the process of making a stupid mistake?

'It should be okay,' said Ross as I looked fearful, 'the war's been over for ten months, things will have settled down by now.'

I nodded, wanting him to be right. Any alternative on land would involve back-tracking for miles and using extra fuel which we couldn't afford. There was one other option. The port of Lagos would have ships bound for the southern shores of Africa and we might buy a sea passage. We could keep a plan B in reserve to avoid the Congo but still take us to Zambia. We might yet get the chance to travel up from Cape Town as originally intended all those weeks ago. The decision could be made when we arrived in Lagos and more information became available.

Before we'd started to plan our trip, friends destined for the neighbouring

Copperbelt town of Kitwe had set sail in July on the Union Castle mail ship with their two little girls. Dave and Sandra reported back on a fun-filled cruise followed by the drive of a lifetime up to Zambia in their new Ford Capri. They marvelled at the Garden Route along the southern coast of South Africa; raved about the hotels, wine and scenery; enthused over the game reserve Hwange, then called Wankie; and best of all Victoria Falls on the border between Rhodesia and Zambia had taken their breath away. We couldn't wait, and we didn't wait. Our impatience came at a high price and we'd missed a different trip of a lifetime.

In spite of the war a wave of anticipation swept over us as we entered Nigeria at Daura. This would be our first ex-British colony where we could drive on the left and speak English. Even the currency was still in pounds albeit the Nigerian pound or NGP, and I looked forward to feeling more connected and less alien.

Northern Nigeria, land of Emirs, the Fulani-Hausa tribe and dashing durbars crunched under our wheels. To get on to well-maintained roads again was sheer bliss. Being in the sub-Sahara now was what we considered the real Africa, and although we had imagined each country to become more exotic than the last, communication with the people seemed to be much easier and less alien, by virtue of speaking English.

The culture in the North has been Islamic since the late 15th century but women's faces did not hide behind veils. We passed through Kano the capital of the region. The thriving sub-saharan city had been built up from trade in salt, slaves and grain. Long after the Atlantic slave trade had been cut off Kano had one of the last major slave societies in the 1850s, with an estimated fifty per cent in the population living mostly in slave villages.

The Emir of Kano hosts Durbars to celebrate the two annual Muslim festivals: -Eid-el-Fitr at the end of Ramadan and Eid-el-Adha, to mark the Hadji or Holy Pilgrimage. The Durbar culminates in a procession of elaborately dressed horsemen who pass through the city to the Emir's palace. We were not lucky enough to coincide with either of these dates, but much later we enjoyed the experience.

## *Ashaka, Northern Nigeria Thirty Years Later*

*A long open-fronted marquee had been erected for the Durbar, and lines of every available chair in the staff accommodation had been mustered for this gathering of VIP's. The most important dignitaries, the chiefs, were already installed, the men sprawling their considerable weight over plush upholstered Dralon armchairs. Their women sat alongside looking self-contained and well-fed in heavily embroidered gowns of vivid purple, orange or green, their stiff head-ties artfully arranged at odd angles.*

*We were honoured with front-row armchairs, although a fair few down from the elite in the middle, but still a good position for what was to come.*

*The location of choice for the Durbar was the golf course, but to Western eyes this was not obvious. The day before we had been playing up this fairway, the ninth, accompanied by caddies who toted our clubs and the small square of Astro-turf from which our shots were played. Fairway was not an appropriate name for the long strip of dust.*

*The Durbar festivities began with a trumpet fanfare and parade of horsemen. Chiefs had travelled from all over the Northern region for their teams to take part in the display, and each section was announced with a fresh cacophony of sound before the assembled crowd. The bandsmen's tasselled instruments vied with a loudspeaker reminiscent of those in British railway stations which made barely comprehensible announcements throughout the event. We watched an exhibition of pageantry and pomp in all its glory with chiefs' sons playing major roles in the dozen or so teams of paladins. Video cameras and loudspeakers apart, the scene was medieval and uncannily reminiscent of the jousting ceremonies in Walter Scott's Ivanhoe.*

*The array of small Arabian mounts wore castellated cloths over their heads and backs, each bearing the distinguishing livery of their regional chief. The cloths were stitched into little tents around the horses' ears, whether to protect them from the sun's fierce rays or to muffle the alarming noises around them was unclear, and blinkers shielded their darting eyes from the terrifying proximity of other horses and riders as they charged at the crowd, with us at the forefront.*

*The horsemen were similarly attired in ancient battledress and threw themselves with enthusiasm into their warrior roles, waving guns and spears aloft as they spurred their mounts faster and faster. At the climax of the charge the warriors pulled sharply to rein in their mounts in front of us at the very last minute and the horses' heads jerked painfully back. Their eyes rolled and foam from tortured mouths flew through the mêlée. The smell of manure, human perspiration and horse sweat mingled in the heavy air. After a charge threw up the dust so close we could taste it, our cries of dismay brought undisguised looks of glee to the daring equestrians. This was far more exciting and colourful than a game of golf, but lasted just as long. Any emerging blades of grass on the fairway had been thoroughly downtrodden by nightfall that day,*

## 2nd November 1970

We drove on to Zaria, another major city like Kano on the A2, and on the outskirts of the town near a sharp bend a motorist waved us down. He stood in front of his written-off car, its front nearside corner mangled and steam wafting up to mingle with the damp jungly air. Trying to brake on the bend we'd just passed he had skidded off the road and found himself stranded but with only minor injuries. He didn't want to leave his ruined car unattended because it would be stripped of anything useful within hours.

We asked what we could do to help and he gave us a note to take to a friend in the university. We eventually found the address in town, delivered the gratefully received note, and mission accomplished returned to the centre of Zaria to find some food. The Harmattan winds blew particles of dust carried from the Sahara, stinging our eyes as we searched for somewhere open late on a Sunday. An hour into our quest we heard music coming from the 'Jamboree Club,' and ventured in to make enquiries

'It is too late for eating,' Joseph, the manager replied to our enquiries. 'The cook, he has gone home. We are only open for beer.'

Then he relented and organised some chicken with bread and butter for us. An errand boy was dispatched for provisions. He returned with two loaves of bread and two raw chickens. We had hoped to eat fairly soon and were relieved to see him sent straight back. Half an hour later he returned with a plate of cooked chicken pieces, bread and butter, and coffee.

It was already late when Joseph brought out his six-year old son to dance for us. Henry was blessed with a proud father and a wonderfully natural sense of rhythm so after twenty minutes of his show we applauded enthusiastically and still grinning broadly he went off to bed.

Our bill paid we sat with Joseph until one o'clock in the morning and long after everyone else had left. We listened to the jangle of Nigerian music which he proudly played on his record player.

'Come with me to a night club now,' said Joseph 'then you can stay at my house for the night.'

We felt dead on our feet and refused, promising to send him a card from Zambia. He gave us a bottle of beer 'for the road' and we left to find our usual out-of-town parking spot.

## 3rd November

Excellent roads took us down to Kaduna, but new hazards in the form of reckless truck drivers emerged. The road in this area was pot-holed, sinuous and narrow, forcing us to go off track every time we met another vehicle. Some lorry drivers used the size of their truck to bully other drivers into pulling aside, and played 'chicken' when it came to crossing narrow bridges which could only accommodate one vehicle. Numerous wrecks at the roadside and in the ravines beneath bridges served as a warning and made us take our time preferring to be live chickens than dead winners. Giving way every time we met another vehicle was a small price to pay for our safety rather than challenging crazed truck drivers.

The heat and humidity made us crave a cool drink but none of the roadside stalls which had cropped up had anything to offer but beer or Guinness. These were a sign of our leaving the Moslem North. We gave in eventually, still optimistic about a hidden stash of cool lemonade, and stopped in a village at an open-fronted wooden shack with a hand-written sign proclaiming 'Hotel'.

'What drinks do you have?' asked Ross of the cheery barman.

'We have Guinness,' came the reply

'What else do you have?'

'Just Guinness that is all we have.'

'Is it cold?'

'No, it is warm. Ha, ha, ha! We have no fridge or ice.'

'Okay we'll have one Guinness please.'

'Buy me one too,' he demanded grinning from ear to ear.

We laughed not really appreciating the joke while he still chuckled away to himself and took our money for one beer. Four onlookers emerged from behind the hut to witness this exchange with unusual customers, and we handed round cigarettes as a friendly gesture. Everyone took one. We soon discovered that only one of them smoked and he openly collected everyone else's cigarettes to keep for himself later!

The label on the dusty bottle handed over the counter to Ross looked as though it had been through the bottling plant several times without renewal. He gave the rim a rub against his tee shirt then offered it to me. I sipped tentatively. Nigerian Guinness tastes of liquorice and being treacly doesn't quench the thirst at all, its heavy strength making it more suitable for Northern climes. We had our suspicions about the authenticity of the product. Ross drank the lion's share which he soon regretted as it heralded the return of his 'runs'. Later I found myself sitting patiently looking the other way each time he stopped the car to rush off behind a bush.

Years later we discovered that Guinness didn't travel well, which explained the vile taste of our experience. Production was subsequently set up in Nigeria, and allegedly the country soon boasted the second highest sales in the world after Ireland.

We found a restaurant among 'safari bungalows' at Kontagora and bought lemonade, sandwiches and coffee. Although we ached with tiredness, the food and cool evening air revived us enough to turn on to the A1 southwards and cover another hundred miles before stopping.

# CHAPTER NINE

## *A Chief's Garage*

### 3rd November

Huge dark trees towered over us blocking the sun. Such lush shade was the stuff of dreams on a desert crossing, but here it came with the price of humidity and pestilence. Close, sweaty, stultifying clamminess slowed our brains and reflexes, making every movement an effort. During the night we had left the windows open an inch to let in cool air for more comfortable sleep. I'd folded up the blanket and stowed it in the boot, and we'd enjoyed one comfortable sleep in Nigeria the night before. Last night brought a new experience. We'd given an open invitation to mosquitoes and the menu was a buffet of our exposed flesh. The most popular pickings were lower legs and ankles.

The 9th October when we left London was less than a month away. En route to Dover we'd made a diversion to shop early at the all-night Piccadilly branch of Boots, the only one in London to supply malaria prophylactics over-the-counter. Without guide books we discovered things for ourselves, and we'd come up with this consideration the day before.

'*Prevention has to start four weeks before entering the malarial zone,*' I had read out from the instruction sheet and without delay we swallowed our first dose. That was 25 days ago.

A car full of bloated mosquitoes was our day's awakening call. They splatted blood blots when we squashed them on the windscreen, our blood. Frantic to soothe the itching we dabbed after-shave on each bite and got respite for a little while. We had just entered dangerous territory as far as our health was concerned and hoped we'd started our preventive medicine in time.

The heavy weather sapped energy and put everyone including ourselves into slow-motion. The torment of bites would follow us for the rest of our trip and eventually threaten my health. While we slept in the car the exposure was unavoidable because even with the car windows closed they could smell our blood and find a way in through the ventilation system.

As we drew nearer to Lagos it became easier to buy fruit and drinks, and we shopped at a roadside stall grateful to find lemonade, bananas and oranges. The few English speakers in the villages we passed had only an incomprehensible smattering, but big smiles always greeted us and the one clear word, 'welcome'. We were beginning to fall in love with the welcoming warmth of sub-Saharan Africa. Unfortunately this feeling did not mitigate the endemic frustration of third-world life and our first impression of Lagos, which in 1970 still held the title of capital, was the atrocious traffic.

Portuguese explorers became the first Europeans to begin trade in Nigeria, and called the port Lagos after its namesake in the Algarve. The principal commerce made its mark not only on the coast but also on the inland tribes, because it soon became evident that the most valuable cargoes would be slaves. In 1901 Great Britain claimed the country for Queen Victoria's Empire and Nigeria began a six decade term as a British protectorate until its independence in 1960. We can't have been such bad colonial masters judging by the way most people greeted us.

Thanks to directions from passers-by, we found the Congo Embassy where we could get visas, but predictably closed at eight in the evening. Then we located the general post office which was also shut. Thirdly we looked for a Rootes garage. We asked a man for directions, and in African fashion he offered to take us there, squeezing into the car to share my seat before we had the chance to stop him. This Ibo had fought in the recent Biafran war on the losing side, and had a tale of woe. He had lost most of his relatives, his business in Lagos, and his hard-earned savings intended for studies in Britain. His dreams were in shreds. The three of us arrived at a closed garage.

'It will open in the morning at eight,' said the security guard.

The Ibo man gave us a wave and went on his way, happy to have saved himself a walk. We parked outside the garage under the watchful eye of the guard and went for a stroll. Uniformed watchmen lurked near anything worth guarding. The huge population of refugees in the city was not to be trusted and Lagos businessmen didn't want to tempt destitute, desperate people. Plenty of job-seekers were willing to stay awake all night for low pay. Their uniforms hung loosely over thin frames and I wondered at their effectiveness. The offer of a square meal looked like a possibility for many to surrender their truncheon or look the other way.

We turned our attention to eating. A light, cheap supper would suit us and we were directed to the Soho restaurant which looked a squalid hole but the prices conformed to our budget standard. The menu of the day offered spiced rice which we didn't think would suit our delicate stomachs so the accommodating proprietress said she would prepare us an omelette with bread, apologising for not having any butter or margarine. We ordered beers and sat at the pavement table listening to city noises.

A post-prandial walk around the area displayed a squalid post-war city, and we soon returned to the car to write letters and the day's entry in the log book under the courtesy light.

A large gentleman knocked at the window to catch our attention. Ross wound down his window.

'Good evening,' the man boomed in a deep rich voice, 'are you having some trouble?'

We were still parked outside the garage and must have looked a sight. Ross made a mental list of the car's ills.

- The bonnet was still tied to the roof.
- The battery rested between my feet by the passenger seat.
- There was no paint on the lower eighteen inches of the car body as it had been stripped off by sand.
- The black plastic of the dash-board had turned grey for the same reason.
- The bump stops glued back into place in the Sahara had subsequently fallen off completely.
- Two holes large enough to put an arm through were now in the body of the car above the rear axle. They had been made by incessant

hammering across the *piste* corrugations and pelting by stones.
- There was a dent in the steering linkage about the size of a tennis ball which had been caused by a stone hidden in the sand.
- The rear registration plate had been ripped off.
- The rear shock-absorbers were shot.
- The gear-box was still leaking oil as it had done since Morocco.

'No, we're fine thank you,' said Ross.

'Fine' meant that the car could still go which to our minds meant we were not in trouble.

Our new acquaintance introduced himself as the managing director of the garage He called himself Chief E.O. Adeniyi, and certainly looked imposing enough for a 'Chief'. Dressed in an expensive suit, he had emerged from an enormous Humber Super Snipe driven by a uniformed chauffeur.

'Would you like to go for a drink somewhere?' asked Ross after a brief explanation of our trip.

He was interested in our travels and we needed help with the car. We assumed he would know a suitable location. He declined but instead invited us to return with him to his home. We followed the swish Humber along grey streets and wondered what was in store. A night watchman opened heavy metal gates and both cars drew in to a small courtyard. The gates were locked behind us.

He ushered us into a spacious air-conditioned, mosquito-free house, and we sank into comfortable armchairs to pass the rest of the evening sipping beer and smoking cigarettes which he kept in a wooden box on the coffee table. We hadn't experienced air-conditioning in anyone's home before. He had met his English wife Susan when he attended university in UK. Her girth showed that she thrived on Nigerian cooking, making her the shape Africans prefer in a wife. He was a cheerful man and although complaining of a headache, carried on a lively conversation. Susan disappeared into the kitchen to prepare his evening meal and at nearly eleven o'clock they both insisted we join them.

We moved to a table to eat. The Chief had a bowl of beef stew and maize porridge which he rolled into a ball before dipping it into the gravy. This was considered too spicy for us so Susan served us with chops, frozen vegetables and potatoes. He explained that he preferred the traditional Nigerian way of eating and excused himself for using his fingers.

After eating we got up to thank them and leave, when they further insisted that we stay the night. We offered pathetic resistance, and accepted.

'I'll just go up and spray the spare bedroom in case of mosquitoes,' said Susan.

Twenty minutes later we climbed the stairs to a cool mosquito-free bedroom smelling of insect spray.

Our bites didn't bother us that night as we fell into untroubled sleep.

## 4<sup>th</sup> November

In the morning we met their two coffee-coloured daughters in school uniform finishing off bowls of cereal. The chauffeur whisked them off to their studies and we sat down to a cooked breakfast of bacon and fried eggs prepared by a housekeeper while the rest of the family got ready for their day. Leaving Susan to a blazing row with a servant behind the closed kitchen door, I wondered what had caused the drama. None the wiser we returned to the garage, following the chief in his Humber.

Our car rose up on the hydraulic ramp and the mechanic stood underneath it looking at the devastation.

'How old is the car?' He asked.

'Four months,' said Ross with a wry smile.

He laughed loud and long thinking Ross had made a joke. Ever polite in the African way he didn't want to dispute the truth of what Ross had just said but it was obvious he didn't believe him.

A complete ten thousand mile service was arranged, the punctures would be repaired, the bonnet fixed back into position, new shock-absorbers fitted, the holes in the underside of the bodywork plated and welded, the battery would be remounted and welded back into position, the wheels tracked and realigned, the leak in the gear box mended, bump stops fitted, and the car washed.

Chief Adeniyi disappeared on business and we hung around the garage waiting room watching the work on our car which was keeping a crew of mechanics busy. We looked at the date on the wall.

'Can you remember when the car insurance runs out?' I asked.

'We paid for five weeks' worth because that's how long I thought the journey would take.' Ross made some mental calculations. 'It's not going to last us until we get to Chingola, we're going to have to top it up somehow.'

'That's going to be quite expensive isn't it?'

'Yes it is, but we don't have a choice. If we're really stuck we might have to get some funds wired out to us.'

'I wonder if Chief Adeniyi knows where we can get more insurance cover.'

Our optimistic predictions had caught up with us. The car was still not ours to risk and we needed to arrange cover as soon as possible. The dangerous undertaking of our journey needed at least this safety net. We started to plan how to cross the new hurdle when another waiting customer interrupted us.

'I hope you don't mind me breaking into your conversation, but can you tell me who your insurer is?'

A little taken aback, Ross replied 'Lloyds'.

'I myself am a Lloyd's insurance agent! Can I be of assistance?'

The God of travellers was watching over us. Ross related the well-worn explanation of our travels and he assured us he could arrange insurance to cover us for the rest of our journey. We then explained our lack of funds, to which he replied

'Don't worry. Listen to what I am saying. I shall arrange insurance for you and send the invoice to your workplace in Zambia. When you arrive you can send me a cheque. I can see that you look honest so I can arrange it for you.'

A problem solved and we hadn't even left our seats! The agent told us where to find his office and we made an appointment later to finalise the arrangements. We imagined we had one thing less to worry about.

Meanwhile Chief Adeniyi had arranged for a journalist from a Nigerian

Motoring magazine to come to the garage and interview us. He planned to write an article about our journey, and brought a photographer to record our arrival.

On the surface our car looked good by this time, with all the underlying damage invisible. Two photographs showed us standing proudly beside an apparently pristine car. It was unrecognisable from the one we'd arrived in. The bonnet had been laid neatly in place for the picture, but still required fixing, and the roof-rack also sat unattached. A garage hand had put all his 'elbow grease' into achieving the polished finish, and we had an afterglow from our hearty breakfast. A hand-written notice stood at the side announcing:-

*WELCOME TO*
*NIGERIA*
*FROM LONDON*
*BY ROAD*
*IN A HILLMAN HUNTER*
*4TH NOV <-> 1970*

The Chief hoped to use it as advertising to attract customers to his garage, and made us feel very important. To honour the occasion we had shampooed our hair in the garage wash-hand basin using tepid water. The Chief explained that travellers crossing Africa rarely came through Lagos and none since the start of the war. He saw our arrival as a good advertisement opportunity. Surviving the Sahara was a positive endorsement of the car's capabilities, and one to spark the imaginations of prospective buyers.

When he returned in the afternoon he put his car at our disposal. We couldn't believe our luck and asked the chauffeur to take us to the Congo Embassy, where we filled in forms, and were told to provide an 'attestation of fitness' from a doctor. Next he drove us to the British High Commission to get advice for our onward journey. We sank into deep leather seats out of the permanent dust cloud thrown up by vehicles and breathed in air-conditioned coolness. Too soon the chauffeur drew up outside the little part of Britain.

Thrown back into British orderliness on top of the luxury of the car was as unreal as the devastation in the streets outside. Mr Samuel showed us into his office. Once he recovered from disbelief at what we were doing he gave us a grim view of the road ahead. The general advice from himself and his colleagues was simple.

'Don't attempt to go through Biafra. It was devastated during the war and there are armed bandits on the roads at night. They wouldn't hesitate to kill you if they thought it necessary. There have been reports about it in the press and none of us here in the office would attempt it! It's bad enough here in Lagos.'

We asked about the possibility of a ship, our plan B. The answer was complicated and sounded like a lot of trouble requiring significant funds, paperwork, and time. We weighed up our options. Officially the border with Cameroon was not closed as it had been a year earlier and we decided to go ahead by road. From Cameroon we'd travel through the Central African Republic then on to the Congo. The decision was made in the blink of an eye, and we rejected our plan B.

He gave us directions for the best route to take for both safety and driving conditions, and wished us good luck.

From there we went to the insurance broker's office, and caught Mr Awolukun just as he was turning his key in the door to go for his lunch break. With a cheerful smile he re-opened his office. Extending our existing insurances would not be a problem, and without having to pay until we got to Zambia we were 'quids in'. The paperwork done we had some well-deserved lunch back at the garage pleased to think of our safety net back in place.

Some weeks later when Ross arrived at work in Zambia there was indeed a letter from Mr Awolukun waiting for him, but no invoice. He apologised for not being able to renew our insurance because the underwriters considered our journey too dangerous! We had travelled in ignorant bliss from Lagos to Chingola unaware of the consequences that a serious accident would bring! Most of the two weeks after leaving Lagos would explain all too well the underwriters' reluctance to give us cover. How Ross had managed to get insurance from Lloyds in the first place remained a mystery.

'Give me money. Give me a cigarette. Give me a job,' we were constantly being asked, but rarely was it a request for food. We imagined that the aid agencies had at least taken over that requirement and it could explain the convergence on the city.

In need of a good haircut and wearing well-worn clothes we certainly didn't match the smart Humber in which we travelled but they could not believe we weren't wealthy, because we were Europeans. Compared to them we were. Our temporary homelessness was self-imposed and we had the prospect of a house and job to go to, albeit thousands of miles away.

Prices were high, even for the fruit which we found so cheap north of the city. Consequently we went hungry rather than pay four shillings for a sandwich, and instead bought some bread and a small tin of poor-quality corned beef from a street trader. While waiting for the repairs and however long our visa application would take, we were given the use of a room next to the garage office. Basic and clean, the only thing lacking was a curtain so we rigged up our blue blanket at night-time for privacy; it wasn't needed for warmth. Our usual bedroom was up on ramps. Fidelis who lived in another room in the building showed us around the immediate area of the garage on foot that evening.

Stepping over the recumbent bodies of drowsing refugees we wondered how they survived, where they got their food and water, and how they managed washing and the basic needs of life. These were not beggars, although a few had lowered themselves to that to survive, and we never felt threatened. Mostly they hung on to the shred of dignity left to them, and appeared to be waiting for something or someone to help them get their lives back. Fidelis took us back to our room and made sure we were comfortable. Unlike the poor souls who slept on the streets not a hundred yards away, we had access to a toilet and wash-hand basin. I couldn't banish the plight of the refugees from my head. What terrible experiences had they endured? What were their lives like before the war? What would this city be like when the country had recovered from civil war?

A restless dream-filled sleep claimed us that night.

### Thirty years later on a busy highway through Lagos

*He looks a big strong young man, far too robust for what happened to him.*

*We are in a chauffeur-driven locked Mercedes, the other company wives and I. Our husbands are elsewhere in the city making important decisions on this short visit. Anne and Hilary chat about other places they have visited as I gaze out of the window absorbing the sights and sounds of modern Lagos now sprawling even further along the coast than it did on our first visit. There are more cars, bigger roads, more people, taller buildings, and the refugees are gone, but the poverty, the grime and the hopelessness still linger on from that post-war city that our younger eyes saw in 1970. We ladies have every comfort, reminding me of how Ross and I relished Chief Adeniyi's air-conditioned vehicle. Outside there is nothing but concrete and sky in view as we coast along one of six lanes of traffic on a flyover.*

*He must have been trying to sell something. Joseph, the marketing manager, said you could buy practically anything from your car window on the main roads in Lagos because shops were inconveniently positioned far apart. Few shopping centres made life easy for shoppers the way street traders could. They position themselves strategically beside slow-moving traffic, and wave their wares at you as they trot along beside the crawling car shouting their sales pitch. But a flyover is an unlikely place for trade, so perhaps he was running away from something, too intent on escape to notice the speeding vehicle that hit him. He has been there for a while because rigor mortis has set in, the last throes of agony set on his large frame for all drivers and passengers along the highway to witness.*

*Although horizontal, he looks as if he's still running in black leather shoes and khaki shorts, his open shirt torn. The full horror shows in his face. With head arched back his mouth is open wide in a final silent cry of alarm. A huge protruding purple tongue is his last gesture to the harsh city.*

*I gasp and look around. I have never seen a dead body before. The others are still chatting, unaware and I have no intention of upsetting their morning as well as mine. Not one driver slows down. No one else looks shocked like I do, or even shows surprise. We drive for another two hours before we reach our destination. I say nothing.*

That afternoon there is a gathering of wives in a homely suburban bungalow. I try to do the social bit joining in with their friendliness, discussing expatriate life, but cannot escape my thoughts, and seek refuge in another room. The solicitous hostess comes to see if I am alright and I can't contain it any longer. I sob uncontrollably in her arms, a woman I have never met before. I thought I was tougher than this.

'If you report a dead body to the police in this part of the world you become the person responsible for it,' said Geraldine. 'So no-one wants to get involved. The time, trouble and expense it would incur deter anyone from doing anything. So it's up to the police to deal with the problem and corpses can lie for weeks before anything is done.' She patted my hand. 'It's something we've learnt to live with out here, but the first time you see a body is a bit of a shock.'

Travelling again a day later, we see a woman lying face down by the roadside. Her basket has spilt its meagre contents of plantains and a bag of unripe tomatoes, and is lying beside her lifeless head which had been neatly swathed in a bright scarf before she set out for her errands. Shoppers, schoolchildren, mothers with babies on their backs, old and young, glance at the body and look the other way.

'She is sleeping' said Geraldine, fearing another emotional outburst, but I wasn't fooled. I had recovered my sang-froid and smiled at her solicitousness.

Five days after our arrival Ross and I are being driven back to the airport. The toll road ends and the cars fan out to pass through a dozen kiosks for payment. The car glides easily from the shadow of the booth and the chauffeur puts his foot on the accelerator to match the speed of other cars converging in a funnel to rejoin the road. At the centre of the convergence our driver swerves violently to avoid hitting a man in a pin-striped suit, white shirt and tie, who is lying on the tarmac. We move too fast to see if he is still alive.

'Shouldn't we stop?' I asked, knowing the answer but helplessly wanting to do something. Somehow it is all the more shocking that the victim this time is a smart businessman, bringing the true abomination closer to our understanding. It would be suicidal to stop and along with all the others who passed that morning we left his body to its fate. Thirty years of progress. Plus ça change, plus c'est la même chose.

## 5th November 1970

The Chief's generosity continued as he instructed his chauffeur to take us to the Congo Embassy. Slow unruly traffic would challenge the patience of a saint, road signs confused the issue, and we had not appreciated the extent of the city's sprawl. Ross enjoyed not being in the driving seat and we both looked out at the post-war city. Awnings in front of buildings sheltered families of refugees lying apathetically side by side. Sad-looking men and women surrounded by bundles of their worldly goods watched us with vacant stares as we passed them. Their children had no room for play in their lives and scavenged what little they could in the dust. Our hearts ached and the difference in our circumstances made us feel humble.

Regular traffic jams allowed an impression of the city to sink in. Air-conditioning units dripped from walls streaked with slime and grime. There were no shops, only open workshops and markets. The combination of humidity and dust claimed pristine new buildings within months absorbing them into the dirty huddle of structures sprawled across the city. Stray threads from a mess of wires strung between telegraph poles betrayed unreliable power and communications, and hung like unfinished cobwebs over the squalor below, ready to catch unwary bodies in their snare. A swathe of the city would not have electricity. Normal conversation was shouted to rise above the noise of car horns and revving engines. Street hawkers carried snacks and drinks from car to crawling car hoping to earn a few shillings. When the traffic moved, the hawker ran alongside the cars first to make his sale and then to collect his money. Salesmen kept fit in Lagos. Rotating fans whirred from drab dashboards to cool overheated faces and only a patient attitude would get you through the average day on the road.

At the Congo Embassy they asked for medical reports of our fitness, and letters of 'no objection' from the British High Commission before visas could be issued to us at a cost of four Nigerian Pounds and fifteen shillings each. The chauffeur duly took us to the British High Commission for the letters. Without a working knowledge of the city this foray alone into chaotic daytime traffic would have challenged us hugely. Unwittingly arriving at a good time in the relatively quiet evening, we had been lucky to find our way around the city two days previously.

Like a magic genie the chauffeur then drove us to the General Post Office for our mail in *poste restante*. I held my hand over my nose as I stepped out of the car to block the stench of a blocked sewer. Half-hearted beggars sat by the doorway. We wove around disorderly queues in the main part of the building, Ross pulling me through by the hand and trying to avoid collisions with babies tied firmly onto backs. The acrid smell of sweat brought my other hand back up to my nose. We found what we were looking for in a less frequented section of the building beside the post office boxes. With a letter each, we greedily devoured their contents and felt connected to hear from home, that safe place so far away. We sank back into the car's plush back seats to reread bland morsels of news and enjoy a small escape to familiarity. The joy of breathing air-conditioned air again was sweet.

Our problems were being solved for us. Someone in the garage was making sand-ladders; they told us where to buy a shovel; and Chief Adeniyi had a cousin who could give us the medical reports needed for our visas.

Back on the road after lunch, we headed for our doctor's appointment. An hour out of the city we never broke free of roadside dwellings and people. The chauffeur turned off the main highway and five miles on we came to a bush road. He found a shady parking spot near the remote clinic, and we climbed steps cut into the bank up to a painted concrete building with a corrugated iron roof covering two rooms. Someone had written a sign on the door saying 'Reception'. A polite assistant asked us to sit down and wait. A wooden table stood in the centre of the small room. Papers, a full filing tray, and a framed photograph of three smiling children sitting with their mother, made an orderly arrangement on its surface. I looked through a cracked window pane past burglar bars to a crowded compound where the sick huddled in groups patiently waiting their turn.

A tall tired-looking man in a white coat came in twenty minutes later and shook our hands warmly. He wanted to know all about our experiences on our journey, enjoying every detail when we related them. He reciprocated our story with his own. He had trained recently in London and compared his work in Nigeria to what would have been expected of him in a British job. His responsibilities were at least tenfold, the pay a pittance, the area one hundredfold and the complaints he dealt with were not coughs and sniffles but often the life-or-death variety. All of this responsibility came with low funding and shortages.

'Why didn't you get a job in England?' asked Ross.

'Because this is my country,' he shrugged with a wide smile. 'These are my people and they need me. Yes it is hard and I could be a rich man in America, but this is important work I do here. Maybe one day I'll go somewhere else for better pay but for now this is where I belong.'

We nodded.

'So what can I do for you?' he asked smiling.

Ross explained about the visas and the medical certificates.

'Do you want to examine us now?' I asked.

He laughed. 'If you have survived that journey you don't need an examination. Tell me what to write.'

He wrote the necessary letter which would enable us to get our visas for the Congo. We gave a donation and grateful handshakes, and then left him to get back to his workload. He thanked us for an interesting and welcome break in his routine.

Leaving the vegetable plots, goats and washing lines of the suburb we returned to the city grime. Endless miles of Lagos passed the car window. That year Lagos had the highest urban population in the world, albeit temporary. The mainland was squalid, dusty and home to hundreds of beggars and dispossessed people from the Biafran war. Further south on Lagos Island and Victoria Island cleaner air and more space gave a fresher feel but deprivation still spilled over into this more privileged quarter.

At the garage we discovered the sand-ladders would not be ready for another day and would cost us five NGP, our first and only bill from them. To kill time we went to the market and bought a clay pot as a souvenir. The foul smell coming from meat and entrails crawling with flies speeded our exit and brought our sight-seeing to a swift stop. We sheltered in the haven of the cool garage office for the rest of the afternoon. Echoes of the young man in the Nigerian Embassy in London sprang to mind.

'You want to travel through Africa for pleasure? For pleasure?!' He had asked.

It had taken three afternoons of queuing before we could admire the three-week entry permit to Nigeria stamped in our passports. Pleasure had been in short supply in both the Embassy and the country.

We passed the time studying the map and comparing routes through the Congo.

Stretching our legs in the cooler evening air we met two more Ibos from Biafra. One of them, a garage attendant, had his wages cut after the war by eight NGP a month

'It was just because I'm an Ibo. The others got the same as before,' he said without self-pity and resigned to the new order.

This left him with fifteen NGP a month to live on, so we hoped that he had a cheaper source of food than the ones we had come across. We returned for our last night in the room next to the office.

'They'll be letting off fireworks and lighting bonfires back home tonight.' I reminded Ross.

We had other things to occupy our minds.


## 6th November


We expected the ladders to be ready in the morning but only the raw materials had arrived. The job had been given to a young man who had to saw all the pieces by hand. He looked grey with exhaustion when the finished ladders were ready late in the afternoon. Meanwhile we sat idle trying to keep cool. At last the time came to leave and they made us feel like celebrities with the send-off they gave. The mechanics and office staff all stood outside the garage and waved until we were out of sight.

We stopped outside the city sprawl when we realised we hadn't stocked up with drinking water. A wide tree-lined avenue offered a shady parking spot and we stepped out to look for somewhere to buy drinks. The character of English suburbia had unmistakably influenced the little hamlet with tidy bungalows sitting cosily in their square plots, a garden in front, a vegetable patch at the back, and fruit trees down each side. A gate stood in the centre of each low brick wall marking their boundaries. Leaving the car under a Tulip tree we stepped over some huge fallen petals, orange turning to brown. The shady trees gave some coolness to the stifling humid air. I imagined expatriate Brits trying to recreate some English calm here in West-Africa, an area known as 'The White Man's Grave'.

The market opened out on rough ground at the end of the avenue. Dirt, human poverty and decayed buildings matched that of Lagos and reminded us of the recent troubles. No white faces could be seen in the crowd, the war having chased the last of them away. Prices were still high so we bought a minimum, and turned to go when a young laughing couple in European dress approached us carrying a baby boy.

'Good morning, how are you?' said the young man with a friendly smile.

'We are well thank you,' we replied. 'How are you?'

'We are well. What have you bought?' He was laughing still.

'Some tomatoes, bananas and bread,' I said, wondering what he wanted.

'Those are not bananas, they are plantains,' he said pointing at what we'd thought were very big bananas. 'You must cook them. They taste good fried.'

'Oh,' I said, 'we didn't realise.'

They laughed.

'Would you like to buy this baby? Here take him!'

The woman thrust the little boy towards me, but gorgeous as he was I resisted even holding him, being worried they might run away and leave me literally holding the baby. They kept laughing and holding him out for me to hold until we took our leave thinking the joke was on us but, apart from confusing plantains for bananas, we weren't sure why. New experiences continued to assail us.

Wide-eyed, I entered the classroom on my first day at school. Bombarded by new experiences on that day too, I looked at the 'Black Baby Box'. It sat on a reachable shelf, but we were forbidden to touch. A smiling black mission boy with red lips and white teeth held out his hand. If a coin was placed on it, a lever behind his head could be pushed to raise the hand to his mouth making the coin drop into the box. It implied that giving money would put food into hungry mouths. As a five-year old I came to the conclusion that all African children must be hungry. The real baby we were being offered looked well-fed, so that could not be the reason.

Still wondering whose baby it was and why they would joke about selling him, we travelled on and stopped for the night before Benin City, on the edge of the danger zone.

'Don't attempt to go through Biafra …there are armed bandits on the roads at night. They wouldn't hesitate to kill you if they thought it necessary.' The words Mr Samuel spoke in the British High Commission repeated in my head, and I fell into restless asleep.

# CHAPTER TEN

## *Road through Biafra*

7th November

Back to reasonable food prices again we invested a shilling in our first paw-paw. Its name alone was the stuff of foreign tales and mystery, and we'd never seen one before. We chose one the size of a rugby ball and the fruit instantly seduced us with its soft sweetness, the beginning of a love affair with all tropical fruit. Food was not only cheaper but easier to source, so on the surface things appeared normal in the Eastern provinces.

Although we had left the squalor of a city teeming with refugees, this part of the country had seen the real horror. We were getting closer to the worst part of the war zone, Biafra itself. It had metamorphosed into a crushed and ravaged place with horrible stories lurking in the shadows which the lush greenery of the forest could not disguise. An outbreak of bullet holes pockmarked the houses in Onitsha and some had been boarded up. The people who had stayed wore masked faces and were in the process of healing their scars by immersion in ordinary life, a life made harder by the destruction of conflict. The survivors held on silently to their tragic memories and a palpable heaviness burdened everyone. The children with kwashiorkor, the horror of television news reports, had disappeared. But by the end of the war five and a half million children and their mothers had become totally dependent on medical relief and food supplements from the charity UNICEF. Graphic News footage had shown swollen-bellied children before help reached them and dedicated charity workers braved the dangers of hostilities to provide a thousand tons of supplies daily. Benevolent organisations had been able to increase their activities since the ceasefire in January. Post-war relief and reconstruction was well underway by the time we arrived ten months later and all of the children we saw looked well-nourished.

At a small-town where at last we'd found an open-fronted store to buy a shovel, junior school children stood in regimented lines in front of a flagpole bearing the Nigerian flag. Standing to attention in their spotless royal blue and white uniforms, shrill voices sang the National Anthem.

*Nigeria we hail thee,*
*Our own dear native land,*
*Though tribe and tongue may differ,*
*In brotherhood we stand,*
*Nigerians all, and proud to serve*
*Our sovereign Motherland.*

The civil war had not started because of differing tribes and tongues, but because of different concepts of government. Independent kingdoms had been self-governing for centuries before Great Britain carved out an area from the coast inland in which more than three hundred different ethnic groups managed their own affairs. Disparate groups found themselves clumped together as Nigerians whether they liked it or not.

The Ibo kingdom around Biafra was one of the oldest and differed radically from those of the Yoruba further west, and those in the Muslim north. After independence in 1960 they all had to share the new country's government for the first time. Being as diverse as Spaniards and Russians, Italians and Scandinavians, Scots and Albanians, after seven years their incompatibility resulted in war.

Outside the town another puncture hindered forward motion and as we dealt with it Ross noticed a distortion in the frame of our roof-rack. The newly-made ladders added in Lagos combined with the spare wheels amounted to overload which would have to be alleviated. The weight was considerably over the recommended maximum of 100 pounds, and that was without the 'shock loading' caused by bad roads.

Somehow we shoehorned two of the wheels between the top of the pile already on the back seat and the fabric of the roof. One wheel and the ladders remained up on the rack and relied on the remaining strength of the bent metal. Life would be even more uncomfortable from then on because retrieving any of our stores from underneath two heavy wheels would involve first heaving them out of the way. Contortions from the passenger seat would prove practically impossible from this time on and we had to stop the car to find whatever we wanted or manage without. Limited comfort had become even more restricted, and tested our tolerance to its extreme.

Women are the vegetable farmers in Africa. In and around every town small patches of land reclaimed from the ever-encroaching bush sprout without boundaries. The women, often with a baby strapped to their backs, plant their plots with rows of maize underpinned with twists of pumpkin vines and clumps of spinach to feed their families. After a day's work they could be seen ambling home with bundles of firewood balanced on their heads. We saw brilliant green leafy banana trees marching intermittently into the dense bush and star-shaped leaves of cassava studding the fringes of smallholdings. The latter had been introduced by the Portuguese five centuries earlier. Chickens and goats pecked and nibbled close to the houses, but were free to roam. Boys responsible for goat-herding sometimes stood restlessly watching their herd, stick in hand at the ready. Yet mostly the creatures seemed to roam free as we discovered with countless near-misses on the roads. Everyone knew their own livestock from their neighbours' even if they had dozens to account for and we were wary of damaging anything belonging to people who had lost so much already.

'Is there a bridge at Abakaliki?' Ross asked a lorry driver at Enugu who looked as though he'd come from that direction.

We'd heard it had been destroyed in the war and washed away but wanted to verify the rumour before embarking on a lengthy diversion. Going to Ogoja through Gboko instead would add two hundred miles to the journey.

'We understand that the bridge over the river has gone,' said Ross pointing at the map. 'Surely there is some way of getting across the river rather than following such a long diversion?'

The man studied our faces and then our map.

'But you can still go that way,' he said, 'there's a pontoon operating now, you can drive your car on to it and it will take you across the river. A man will charge you some money, but it will not be much and it will save you from going on the diversion.'

So with an absence of further information and preferring to travel only one hundred miles on the shorter road we took a risk and headed for Abakaliki. We knew it was a gamble and at the end of the long day discovered there was no such pontoon and our only option, unpalatable though it may be, was to turn back and take the detour. It took us years to realise the importance of phrasing a question to Africans correctly. Politeness and respect prevent them from suggesting the slightest disagreement with what you say. This could have explained his answer, but we shall never know. Our irritation at unnecessary mileage and waste of time soon paled into insignificance when we spoke to local people before turning back to take the tedious diversion. The Ibos who had seen their land and lives ruined shook their heads and looked at the ground as they remembered the recent horrors. Our recovery from a bad choice of road would take at most a day. Theirs would take a lifetime.

We stayed outside Abakaliki for the night and bought two overpriced bowls of soup for our supper.

8th November

Heading back towards Enugu we covered the same long road as before and hoped for the best when we finally embarked on the bumpy surface of the detour. Our fears were realised as we slowed to a stop again in sand. We thought we had seen the end of this hazard, but it didn't compare to our struggles in the Sahara and we soon freed ourselves with the newly acquired shovel. A push from a dozen chattering schoolchildren who'd enjoyed watching our efforts helped us on our way again. Then we made good progress on a stretch of tarmac road but sadly this patch was over almost as soon as it began; a tantalising reminder of how things could be.

We stopped at a village to buy food, and a barefoot boy approached us to offer a selection of flimsy baskets. The young trader looked so crestfallen at our refusal we relented and asked the price. His beaming smile was worth every one of the few pennies we paid, and I crammed the straw creation on top of an already full back seat.

Several times we had to stop and rest. The combination of heat, humidity and strenuous driving took its toll, and each time giggling locals swarmed round to watch our every move. A dense population settled on fertile land meant short distances between villages. One group of women we suspected had much to do with servicing the large military presence nearby. The oldest one who was no spring chicken kept telling me to take off my dress if I was hot. She had found the answer by wearing nothing but a rag tied around her waist! Then they all doubled up with hysterical laughter, it was one way to survive.

We were entering the forested region of Biafra, the centre of the war-zone that still had a curfew. The long road to Gboko had not been repaired for years, steadily accumulating pot-holes and water damage, but we managed to get there by late afternoon. A particularly deep rut caught on the back number plate ripping it off again. Luckily Ross noticed it when he looked in the rear mirror, and I climbed out to reclaim the sad rectangle of metal which inevitably joined the other paraphernalia on the back seat. The repair in Lagos hadn't lasted long. From Gboko we made better time to Ogoja but we were still nettled by the extra three hundred miles we'd had to travel.

During the 1950s Biafra had been one of the worst affected areas in the world for endemic leprosy. Ross remembered a talk given to him at a Boys' Brigade meeting by a missionary who worked with the lepers.

'There are three very big leper colonies in Nigeria,' he had said to his morbidly fascinated audience, 'and each one is bigger than the size of Scotland, can you imagine that?'

'There has been a cure since 1930,' he went on, 'but there aren't enough workers in our missions to go round treating everyone. It doesn't take much to train the helpers, but insufficient numbers are coming forward. So sadly people are still catching this terrible disease.'

The unforgettable talk and slide-show still resonated,

'I always wanted to come here and help to treat them,' said Ross wistfully, 'I wonder if those colonies still exist.'

But thankfully the only lepers we saw on the journey were those back in Niger at the entrance to Zinder market.

The mark of missionaries could be found in unlikely places including the road. Nearly all trucks and buses had been elaborately painted with colourful patterns and cryptic biblical quotations written in large letters at front and rear. The size of the script limited the length of the message leaving us puzzled as to its meaning. 'Let them say,' rumbled towards us with at least a dozen hitchhikers hanging to its rails. This would be a profitable journey for the driver because he charged each one. 'What is written is written' had been inscribed mysteriously on the back.

We bumped over war-torn roads wondering what trouble might lie ahead. At least five signs predicted a twisting road and just as we rounded the first hairpin bend a hand-written notice said, 'You have been warned!' The distracting sign alone could have been the cause of the two car wrecks we passed soon afterwards. On a particularly bad bend we saw another notice, 'We told you!' as Ross swerved to avoid a truck in the middle of the road bearing a picture of Christ and the words, 'And he sayeth'.

A sound surface let us drive after dark and, afraid to stop because of bandits, we hunted for somewhere safe to spend the night. Eight miles from Ogoja Ross drew up at an army road block. The night curfew had been in operation for over three hours allowing no passage through after six in the evening. We chatted with the friendly guards for five minutes and they invited Ross into the Officers Mess. Shiny black boots clattered through the doorway and the door closed. I felt abandoned.

He stayed for half an hour talking and drinking the local palm wine, leaving me alone in the car, probably the only female on the road. I had locked myself in and waited under the watchful eyes of the young armed guard. Gazing out at the dark green shadows of the forest I wondered what my grandmother would think of this situation. There were certainly plenty of trees nearby for men with sinister motives to hide behind.

Ross must have convinced the military that we were not a threat so they excused us from the curfew and let us through to look for lodgings in the town.

By ten o'clock Ogoja crouched dormant and only soldiers immune to the curfew dared to be out of doors. Still hunting for the rest-house we crawled along dark streets to the outskirts of the town when a guard stepped into the road and pointed a rifle at us shouting,

'Halt who goes there?'

Ross wound down his window and started to explain. The soldier showed no comprehension and Ross might have been shouting abuse to get the nervous gun-waving response. This youth didn't speak or understand English, the official national language, other than his prescribed question.

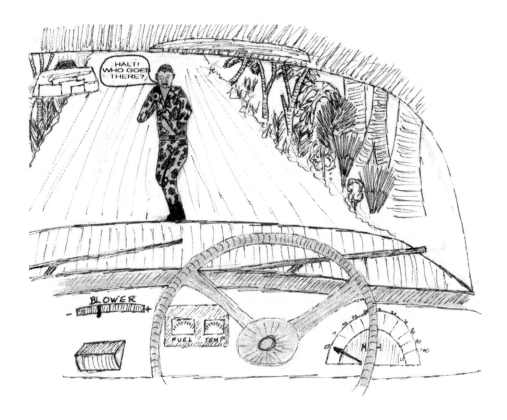

Our lives depended on the right answer and getting it wrong made things worse as we soon discovered. Any attempts on our part to communicate met with the same 'Halt who goes there?'

The elusive reply would probably be simple if we could only think of it. Adrenaline flowed but not to our brains and I gripped my seat with damp palms. Ross tried again to explain in simple language. It was not the prescribed answer the soldier wanted, and he became more agitated, shaking his rifle angrily while still pointing it directly at us screaming,

'HALT WHO GOES THERE'.

We both froze. Every muscle in my body tensed and my heart raced. His watchful eyes searched to see us through the glare of our headlights on full beam and trying to make him less jumpy and more comfortable Ross dipped them. He brought the rifle up against his face to take aim, his hands shaking. We steeled ourselves and hardly dared to draw breath, sitting motionless in the dark road. A loud frog chorus shrieked in the silence to orchestrate our discomfort. The guard kept us in his sights and our tortured tableau waited.

Our minds did not match our motionless bodies. They were turning somersaults as adrenaline kept pumping around our immobile limbs. I imagined my grandmothers words '*I told you this would happen!*' And wondered how it would feel to be shot at close range. How long would it take for the British press to get hold of the news? I started to stray into the morbid realms of our assailant being a bad shot when a noisy Army Jeep brought an English speaking officer to our rescue. He accepted our explanation and took charge of the situation.

'Friend,' he said to the guard.

It was as simple as that. The soldier lowered his rifle and returned to his post, all aggression gone like a switch being flipped. He looked almost as relieved as we were.

The officer ordered us to accompany him and demanded to sit in the car with us. Seeing the crammed back seat he shoved his way in beside me but found himself in danger of falling out so he stood his large frame beside me on the sill hanging on to our fragile roof-rack with the passenger door flapping open.

'Drive forward this way to the camp!'

He waved his left arm vaguely forward and we crawled along the dirt road in case he fell off. We didn't need more trouble. Several times along the two mile route guards with rifles stopped us and the officer used the magic word 'friend' each time for us to proceed without a murmur. The officer slapped the roof twice each time he wanted Ross to start or stop and his final two slaps brought us to their headquarters.

A circle of painted concrete houses with corrugated iron roofs represented the army camp and we parked in the middle of a swept clearing near the flagpole. Ross was taken into an office to complete some formalities and again I locked myself in, all confidence gone and unable to stop my imagination from conjuring up possible scenarios for what could happen next. He soon emerged looking untroubled and calm, and they allowed us to continue our search for the rest house. I felt safer with Ross in the car beside me but still kept the doors locked. Unfortunately he wasn't given any pass or signed declaration to see us through the rest of the night.

I opened my eyes and jolted awake. An inch away from the window next to my sleeping husband was an angry black face, shouting belligerently at us. Yellowed and bloodshot eyes gawped in at us, a recent scar ran down his left cheek, stained teeth lined his furious mouth and the pock-marked face set on a short neck gleamed with sweat. Although he wore a uniform and a soldier's Webber belt he did not look like other soldiers we had seen that night. This uniform and woolly head had not passed any recent military inspection.

The car clock told me it was midnight and with panic rising I scrutinised all the doors checking we had remembered to push the locks down. Sleeping rough in the car was not for the faint-hearted in this recent war-zone where shocking atrocities had been everyday occurrences. The rest house still eluded us and we thought we'd secured a safe spot away from the road and close to the barracks for protection. We vowed to be more careful next time.

Our dreams of sleep had mutated into a nightmare of wakefulness. Ross was struggling to rouse himself from the depths of slumber and trying to

make sense of the situation. He inched down his window and croaked
'Can I help you?'

This communication seemed to take the edge off the man's fury and an ugly grin touched the edges of his thick lips. The stench of stale sweat and beery breath wafted through the gap in the window and he staggered as he motioned Ross to get out of the car. Ignoring his plea Ross opened the window a little further. He tried 'friend' but alcohol had undone its spell for this man. Our aggressor was barely comprehensible from a combination of drunkenness and poor English.

We picked up the words 'police', 'lies', 'I have seen you before', and 'kill' as he waved his arms about wildly raving. With the unpredictability of drunks he then lost all control rising to a new peak of fury and hitting the car with the metal buckle of his belt. Preventing things from getting worse became paramount for the second time that night.

The newly made mud-ladders took up all our roof-rack space and the spare wheels now had to be carried on top of everything else on the back seat. We had taken to putting these wheels outside the car at night chained to the rear bumper to allow us enough room inside the car to stretch out a little and recline the seats. The wheels were valuable and not just in financial terms hence the chain. This precaution prevented us from simply starting the engine and fleeing.

When our assailant's limited concentration made him forget his mission, whatever it might be, he turned away ranting to himself. Ross grabbed his chance and slipped out of the car, quietly unchained the wheels and threw them in the back. As we shot away I looked back at the enraged inebriate waving his fist and demanding we come back.

Still shaken we returned to the relative safety of the army camp to find refuge. By this time it was one o'clock in the morning and we craved sleep. Again the guard confronted us yelling
'Halt who goes there?' and pointing his rifle.
'Friend,' called Ross now confident in the light of experience.

Two smart and sober soldiers approached and Ross explained our predicament. Drunkenness had no logic and they sympathetically took us to the army barracks where we could spend the night in peace. We parked as instructed near the flagpole in the centre of the compound and in spite of the exposure of our new location, looked forward to a restful sleep.

No such luck. At two o'clock we were woken with another face at the window, not angry this time but with a far more alarming prospect. I had left my window open an inch for air, and the end of a rifle barrel was pointing at my drowsy head. The vision was a variation of the previous nightmare.

'Halt who goes there?'

'Bugger off!' murmured Ross, his eyes still closed.

He opened them and sat up.

'Friend,' we chorused.

'Oh' he said 'You are friends?'

'Yes' we replied trying to hide our sleep-deprived irritation with respect for his weapon that was no doubt loaded.

Ross gave the bored soldier the detailed explanation he wanted and we returned to sleep. The guard had changed and no one had explained to the new watch why two Northern Europeans were asleep in their car in the middle of camp. Nor did it occur to that guard to relay this information to the next one and at four o'clock the whole performance repeated itself. However ridiculous the situation, an armed soldier must be respected. Daylight came too soon two hours later.

Distracted by a small monkey tied to a tree at the side of the compound we watched in a stupor as it performed acrobatics. Ten long months had passed since the ceasefire and an entertaining monkey would be a welcome diversion for bored soldiers who had been used to action. We must also have been a diversion that night. Still desperate for sleep there was no question of grabbing any more shut-eye so we forced ourselves awake and rolled out of the camp.

After this we always tried to drape something over the front windscreen and clamp tee shirts with the side windows for makeshift curtains. The claustrophobic coverings would be preferable to another rude awakening.

## 9<sup>th</sup> November

Before we left Edinburgh a popular song had often been played on the radio, called 'A *Wandering Star*' made famous by the gruff voice of Lee Marvin. The grumpy message it gave stopped us from singing the miserable lyrics very often, but today the words rang true. So to stay awake for the next stretch we sang what we could remember of the song, albeit without much energy, until the words '*I never seen a sight that didn't look better looking back.*'

Outside Ogoja we came to another army roadblock. Stern-faced soldiers searched the car, questioned us about our journey, and then allowed us through. No longer on the diversion we found the road bearable compared to what had gone before. At least it appeared to have had some maintenance. We passed through cocoa plantations and the vegetation grew taller, greener, and thicker. At a village we bought some food from a roadside stall and being pleasantly surprised at the prices stocked up on a dozen bananas; four tomatoes; and a huge paw-paw. This last item had been freshly picked by a boy who'd been dispatched with a machete to cut it down. We wondered how tall the tree had been when he ran back with the prize, panting and grinning. We'd seen some paw-paw trees as tall as fully grown Palm trees and imagined him struggling with a machete to limber up its heights and then bring the fruit safely back down without dropping it.

The customs should have appeared at Ikom and instead we came to our last army security road check in Nigeria. They looked at our papers and had difficulty accepting that Ross's passport photo was genuine. He had lost weight which showed on his face, his hair had grown long and wild and he hadn't shaved or had a proper shower since Lagos four days previously. Having convinced them they subjected us to another search. We exchanged exasperated looks but didn't dare complain. Twice in one day was a trial. Ross started to empty the back seat and I got going on the boot. At least they didn't insist on everything coming out, just enough to check we weren't gun-running. Then it all had to go back and fit in the same space. They let us through.

The frontier with Cameroon had not officially been opened since the civil war and we would have no proof of the car leaving Nigeria without a customs officer to stamp the *carnet*. The army officers refused to stamp or sign it.

'We don't want to be charged for leaving our vehicle in the country,' Ross explained.

'You can just write a letter to the authorities,' suggested one of them, 'Me myself, I will sign the letter for you if you like.'

'Thank you that would be a big help.'

I found some writing paper and an envelope, and we composed a letter which the soldier duly signed and promised to post to Lagos for us.

'They all said we couldn't get through,' said Ross triumphantly as we drove out of the country. We thought about the AA officers in Edinburgh and London, and the Embassy staff in Lagos.

I smiled at him and he held out his hand to squeeze mine.

'We're a good team,' he said and smiled back.

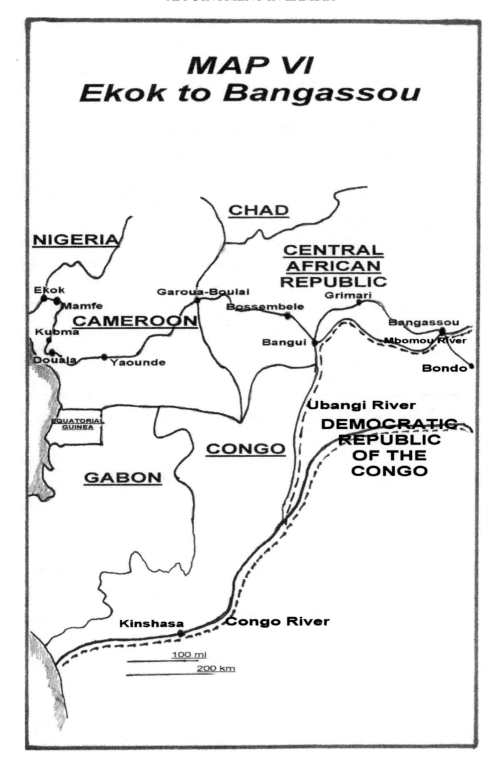

MAP VI
Ekok to Bangassou

# CHAPTER ELEVEN

## *Potholes, Mud and Manic Hens*

Escaping from the ghosts of war we left Nigeria behind to its constant road checks and army officials. Relief settled over us and we headed for Ekok, Cameroon, arriving at midday.

Two rubber-stampers were there but not the crucial passport officer who was not expected to return from Mamfe before evening so all travellers had to wait.

This part of the country had been a British colony from 1919 until the early sixties when it joined the neighbouring French Cameroon in gaining independence for the whole country.

A young man had already waited for a day and sat listless in the shadows fiddling with a blade of grass. Since no one else had the authority to stamp our passports, we had to wait too. We looked around for a profitable use of time and decided to walk to the river for a picnic lunch.

Women had left some laundry to dry on the rocks and hundreds of blue and yellow butterflies waltzed low over the riverbank. Cattle had been there to drink and the butterflies settled and basked on the cow pats which we carefully stepped around. An army of large toe-biting ants filed past across the footpath adding to the obstacle course as we stepped through clouds of butterfly wings. Being aware of bilharzia we resisted the temptation to paddle although we saw no telltale reeds growing nearby. The tiny organisms use snails as their hosts and they in turn live in reeds. We didn't fancy any unwelcome guests burrowing into our skin and making their way to our internal organs. Untreated bilharzia can cause life-threatening urinary system or liver damage, as countless victims in developing countries discover every year.

A fish eagle shrieked over the chorus of cicadas. Moments later the span of its fingered wings stretched between us and a torn scrap of white cloud, and my eye met his cold stare as he expertly scanned the muddied watery reflections. The river murmured on over the rocks and into the slouching jungle

Back at the customs we whiled away the rest of the afternoon chatting to the staff. Being in the smaller English-speaking part of Cameroon, Ross could still communicate easily and of the two of us he was the chatty one. The remaining four fifths of the country to the north and the east where we would be travelling next had been a French colony, and I would soon have to return to my attempts at simultaneous translation. The customs men were killing time too and wanted to hear about our journey.

More men and women, one with a tiny baby, had arrived to wait with us, and everyone sat passive to the tedium under the trees in the dwindling afternoon heat. As a cooling diversion we did a little laundry in the river, the washerwomen having collected their clean clothes. But we hadn't thought it through and couldn't dry it. The heat of the day when the sun would dry washing in no time, had passed. Unlike our experience in the Sahara the wetness of our clothes lost nothing at night to the humid air. Another hidden danger lurked. Leaving our laundry to dry outside would be an invitation to Putsi flies to lay their eggs in the damp clothes, and without an iron to destroy them, the larvae would hatch and burrow into our skin. If that happened a boil would develop with the grubs feeding off flesh until they were ready to hatch out. Newly arrived expatriates in Africa occasionally forgot the warning and neglected to iron everything. The worst cases involved babies in the nappy area. We spread our wet things out on the back shelf and dashboard.

As the darkness grew, frogs provided sound effects while fireflies silently performed pyrotechnic shimmies. But our accumulated mosquito bites soon distracted us from the show. Irritating fresh red mounds on arms and legs demanded to be scratched as always in the evenings and threatened another good night's sleep. So we retreated to the less exposed but oppressive and now damp shelter of the car. Since central Nigeria I often woke in the night with the torment of my bites, and tried to cool the burning itchiness by dabbing them with a flannel dipped in water. Ross gently snored oblivious of my dabbing and sometimes I gave in to crazed scratching which always made me regretful but gave some sense of satisfaction at the time. He admitted doing the same as I slept.

By nine we had settled down for the night and an hour later insistent knocks on the windscreen woke us up. The customs officer had just returned and a woman was offering us an invitation to his house where the rest of the family sat on the floor indoors propped against the mud walls watching us. Still drowsy from sleep we shook hands and he motioned for us to sit down. At first he presented an officious veneer, asking searching questions about why we chose to travel in this part of Africa. No European customers had passed this way for months and he wanted to know what we were about. Discovering we had borrowed money didn't help and he assumed we weren't married since we had separate passports. Ross patiently explained our marital status and about the job in Zambia which cleared up the misunderstandings. Afterwards he became much friendlier; in fact he invited us for a meal.

He called it 'relish' which consisted of rice and chunks of roughly butchered meat in a mouth-numbing hot sauce which burned the roof of my mouth. He ate with his fingers and the woman provided us with spoons, but didn't join us, just watched from the sidelines. The meat gave plenty of opportunity for chewing, and we soldiered on politely acknowledging the honour of the invitation. Afterwards he produced some whisky which didn't help our recently challenged constitutions or the burning sensation in my mouth from the chilli sauce but we sipped away politely. I left the conversation to Ross since no translation was required and listened quietly with the others. All I wanted was to get back to my interrupted sleep. The clock said midnight when we settled down for the second time.

### 10th November

Feeling better at last from a proper sleep we completed the customs formalities, got a positive forecast for the road ahead and left with high expectations for Mamfe. Roads disfigured with dried mud forced us to advance with caution. Pot holes large and small dotted the surface and to make reasonable progress Ross could only attempt to avoid the biggest ones so the car had a good shaking yet again and our bodies went uncomfortably with it as they had done in the Sahara.

'Watch out for that one!' I warned.

At that moment the front wheel sank into a small but deep hole making the car jolt and I bit through my tongue. Tasting blood I decided silence would be safer from then on and only pointed to indicate hazards, saving conversation for later.

Ten miles from the border we had crossed the day before we came to an uphill stretch which could only claim to be called a road by its connection to what had gone before. Scarred by torrential rain which had left deep ravines in its surface it looked more like a steep river bed torn apart by a torrent. The car could lose wheels in the impassable crevices and with dense jungle pressing in on both sides of the road no alternative route presented itself. We sat pondering what to do, unbelieving and despondent after the customs officer's positive forecast. The road would have to be rebuilt to make it passable and we would be the ones doing it.

Collecting stones and lumps of wood to fill in the holes, and using the ladders to bridge the worst gaps, we set about making a serviceable track. With fifteen yards repaired and passable Ross drove as far as he could and then we started on the next section, using the infill materials from the previous section to repair the one ahead. Three hours later we had travelled fifty metres. A puncture then added to our woes. After that a semblance of reasonable road surface returned allowing us get to Mamfe and we considered our first day's initiation into Cameroon complete. The road we had found so bad in the Rif Mountains in Morocco now looked quite acceptable.

'How could he call that road 'good,' it didn't even look like a road?' Asked Ross.

He was now ready to make conversation after our gruelling day.

'Big trucks must be the only traffic using it and their weight makes things worse, churning existing holes into bigger ones with their huge wheels. Even they must have problems with a road like that!'

'Can you imagine what it must be like after heavy rain?' I asked. 'The road must look more like a waterfall!'

'I think we'll have to be careful how we word our questions in future, before we rely on information like that again.' Then he added 'At least we've done it, and it's not as if there was an alternative! Let's just hope the worst is over!'

Arriving in Mamfe, the first town in a new country, we had to sort out money and food. We also managed to swap some leftover Nigerian money. The rate of exchange was pitiful, but we considered ourselves lucky to get anything at all because of the war. Inflation was burgeoning in post-war Nigeria.

While waiting for a puncture to be repaired we enquired about the road to Kumba which we planned to travel the next day. Our nerves cried out for a rest from driving and we planned an overnight stop in the town to allow ourselves some recovery time before the following day's exigencies. But the next bit of road between Mamfe and Kumba only opened for one-way traffic on alternate days, so with sinking hearts we realised that we had to cover it that day or wait and lose a day. Disregarding our waning enthusiasm we doggedly continued and found it not much better than the one we'd just travelled. Lake-sized puddles stopped us in our tracks and we climbed out to poke them with sticks, checking the safety of the road surface under the water and the depths of holes.

'Be careful of the puddles on the road to Kumba,' the mechanic in Mamfe had told us. 'A lorry on that road nearly disappeared recently. There was a huge hole hidden under the water and he thought he could just drive through it!'

We still laboured on after dark but at least found that night-driving was a little easier than during the daytime because the lights showed up the worst pot-holes and ruts. During daylight hours friendly villagers waved as we passed their settlements. At night policemen at road-checks were not so friendly, and these sprang up nearly as often as in Biafra. By this time we had left the English-speaking part of the country behind, and just before Kumba, a policeman waved us in to stop beside him.

'Vos passeports s'il vous plaît,' he demanded.

We handed over our dark blue documents embossed with the royal crest in gold and the words BRITISH PASSPORT on the cover. Our names had been hand-printed in capital letters in a recessed lozenge at the top. He had a good look through the pages.

'Vous êtes Français ou Américains?' he wanted to know.

'Britanniques,' I replied trying to muster patience. He didn't smell of drink but something slowed his mind. We wondered about the qualifications for becoming a policeman in Cameroon.

Next he demanded to know which one was which. Considering my hair was long and blonde and Ross had dark curly locks we were dumbstruck and I had a compelling urge to giggle. He clung to our precious documents as he continued this line of enquiry, enjoying his power, and I soon found myself translating between his inanities and Ross's fury. We had to explain ourselves to this dimwit more than to the customs officer back at Ekok.

'Nous allons a Zambie pour travailler là,' 'we are on our way to Zambia to work there,' I said

'Pourquoi?'

'Parce que mon mari a un emploi là,' 'because my husband has a job there,' I ventured.

This exchange went on for some minutes until the trials of the day finally made Ross lose patience. Between clenched teeth he growled,

'Tell that fucking bastard to give us back our passports!'

I took a deep breath to find strength knowing that Ross had reached the end of his tether. The heat of the road burned through my flip-flops. Ross's tone was unmistakeable.

'Mon mari n'est pas content,' I translated. This assertion that my husband was not happy obviously understated the situation but my monstrous understatement went over the officer's head.

He insisted that forms needed to be completed.

'Attendez,' he clipped and handed us back our passports.

He walked off to fetch the paperwork from his wooden hut expecting us to wait. We looked at each other, nodded in a silent pact, slipped into the car and drove away, Ross gripping the steering wheel with white knuckles and me looking back over my shoulder for signs of trouble.

11th November

Huge mud patches presented themselves on the road from Kumba to Douala for the morning's first challenge. At their edges the sun had curled blisters the size of truck wheels. Tough driving had become the norm again as it had in the Sahara and Ross needed all his concentration for the road ahead. We stopped for another puncture. Welcome relief came on the well-maintained urban approach and the first town gardens of Douala blazed with Flame Trees and multicoloured bougainvillea rampaging over their walls.

'Look at those gorgeous colours,' I enthused, grateful for the prospect of civilisation and trying to lighten the mood.

I could safely talk again without the risk of biting my tongue.

At that moment a metallic screech tore from under the car. Our nerves jangled.

'Sounds like the exhaust has just fallen off,' groaned Ross with weary resignation. We both stepped out to face the truth. The front number plate hung from one corner scraping the ground, and we heaved a sigh of relief as Ross yanked it right off and chucked it on top of the jumble on the back seat. This we considered cosmetic damage!

Our early start had us arriving before noon in Cameroon's largest city. The Peugeot estate car ahead of us carried a full branch of ripening bananas on the roof rack and three French children turned their tanned faces to stare at us through open car windows. They recognised us as not belonging to the diplomatic service, nor did we look like contractors and they were trying to place us. We had become accustomed to being seen as oddities and we waved to them, but they didn't wave back.

A garage became the first port of call for our latest two punctures which we considered light punishment for what we'd just put the car through. Ross supervised the repair while I looked out at the busy street. On the opposite side of the road outside the garage sat a tailor complete with a treadle sewing machine. We had watched him arrive at the same time as us, carrying his machine on his head with the ornate iron frame and attached treadle knocking behind his legs. His eyes darted back and forth without any head movement to choose the best spot under the mango tree. Needing to rest after his exertions he sat on a tall log which he retrieved from a nearby ditch before setting up his shop to start late on a market day. A transaction took place between a man and a trader, and the customer reached down to retrieve some worn notes from inside his shoe for payment. A few feet away sat a cobbler on a matching stool and on the other side of the tree a hairdresser supervised her salon.

Two ladies broke lengths of black thread with their teeth and busied hard fingers over their clients' heads, dividing and plaiting and binding unruly froths of black hair. Wooden combs with three long teeth made tidy partings and soon intricate rows were taking shape over neatened scalps. Their manifestations looked far from gentle as heads were jerked this way and that to achieve the perfect tight braid. The heat of the day notched up a few more degrees and half moons of sweat waxed under the hairdressers' arms.

We went to explore the market. Returning two hours later the coiffures had risen into basketwork concoctions. Delicate and springy they stood up like crowns joined in the middle of each elegant head, two individual masterpieces defying gravity. Pieces of broken mirror appeared to show the results and two satisfied customers gathered their belongings to set off home. They helped each other load large bundles of market-wares on to their heads which instantly flattened the artistry. Unperturbed they gracefully swayed back to their families. I longed to ask them if it would bounce back.

A man walked past the garage carrying a book balanced atop his curls rather than using his hands. Universal good posture and perfect alignment would put to shame the hunched shoulders of Western civilians.

Back at the garage to claim our mended tyres we saw glass flagons of cloudy liquid lined up on a shelf.

'Would you like to taste some?' asked the English-speaking cashier seeing us looking, 'It is wine made from the palm tree.' Then she added proudly, 'I made it myself!'

'Yes please,' I said, looking forward to trying something new.

Ross looked hesitant muttering warnings of uncontrolled conditions and brain damage from ethyl alcohol. She ignored his hesitation and whipped out a dusty recycled beer bottle and two china cups with their handles missing. Hoping that the alcohol would destroy any germs we sipped tentatively. The wine appealed to my sweet tooth and we succumbed to buying a litre from the enterprising lady, promising ourselves to ration the strong liquor sensibly.

On red laterite road again we passed through villages and found a new hazard in avoiding the livestock. Manic hens panicked at the car's approach and ran straight into our path. Goats were nearly as bad while dogs either lay in the middle of the road defying our passage, or yapped at the wheels mindless of danger. Between villages one of the latter came too close and the animal's leg was crushed by the front wheel. Another dog barked at us incessantly as we slowed wanting to solve the upsetting problem. But fearing a rabid dog-bite or possible retribution from villagers, we hastened away from the howling animals, feeling dreadful about the unavoidable accident.

The red dusty road led us on. Several times we passed cyclists most of whom simply stopped to watch us pass. Others went into a panic and drove straight into the roadside ditch landing in a heap with arms and legs flailing in the damp hollow. The rarity of vehicles jerked their usual complacency into over-reaction. Their self-made predicament stirred up guilt again especially when there was a passenger sitting on the crossbar, but they really didn't need to go off the road and Ross always slowed down in case they swerved in front of us in their panic. Approaching a man who was barely visible under a huge bundle of sticks tied to his back, we were greatly relieved to see him stop his bicycle on the roadside and solemnly watch our passing before balancing himself back on the two wheels and wobbling his way home.

Mosquito bites continued to torment us and our next near-miss happened when Ross bent to give his ankles a good scratch. The momentary loss of concentration brought us close to trouble. He had to do an emergency stop when a surprise herd of goats trotted across our path. Killing livestock would be unforgivable and would have landed us in real trouble with their owners.

We stopped within reach of the capital where we planned to visit the British Consulate for advice on our route.


12th November


We drove into Yaoundé about midday, travelled up Avenue General de Gaulle and collected welcome *poste-restante* letters from the Post Office. Our first connection with home since leaving Lagos had a calming effect on our stretched nerves and we read and re-read the comforting little pieces of home news, hearing the voices of those who had written them.

Having found the British Consulate appropriately situated in Avenue Winston Churchill, we made an appointment to see the vice-consul in the afternoon. We walked out of the building and passed an old man lighting up a cigarette. He put the packet into his pocket, but the box of matches he balanced on his head as he strolled off along the pavement puffing away with his head held high.

Our usual town activities of food-shopping and arranging puncture repairs followed. The mechanic quoted nine shillings, an exhorbitant fee, but when he couldn't find the hole he offered to fit a tube for the same price and Ross looked happier.

I was watching a man walking past the French Embassy with a rolled black umbrella on his head when I noticed the *Tricolore* hung at half mast. Back at the British Consulate we wrote answering letters to our parents as we waited for our appointment, taking advantage of the spotless air-conditioned waiting room. The letter finished I picked up a copy of the Observer from a coffee table. General de Gaulle had just died, explaining the French flag.

The vice-consul in a tie and linen jacket ushered us into his office and showed genuine interest in our journey. We felt a change in attitude from past experience. Successful transit across the Sahara and Nigeria brought respect and we no longer felt defensive as we had in past institutions. He couldn't offer much help regarding our proposed route ahead through the

Congo, but he helpfully phoned the Congolese Embassy and found that a train definitely ran from Kisangani (formerly Stanleyville) to Lubumbashi in the south of the country. This was just to the north of the Copperbelt in Zambia but we were not keen on the plan. Remembering the description of the roads in that area from the Australians we'd met in Niger we preferred to head for East Africa. We'd come through so much we also wanted to drive the whole way and it would be like giving in to take a train. The hope for a passable route by road persisted in our minds and we needed reassurance and information on road conditions. In truth we were virtual pioneers to venture in these parts of the continent in a two-wheel drive vehicle and no one could predict our success or failure with any certainty. We had to try for ourselves and our youth and ignorance let us take that risk.

Rain had fallen refreshing the air and we inhaled a warm, earthy, damp straw kind of smell that comes up from the newly-wet ground and which would always remind me of Africa. It was the first rainfall we'd seen since Algiers. Ready to move on we studied the map, found the road to Garoua-Boulai and headed north-east out of the capital.

After nightfall fork and sheet lightning flashed over distant trees for hours lighting angry black clouds above, but little rain came down around us. We sat cosy in the car watching the show, praying for it not to turn in our direction. Luckily the storm raged to the north of us and not to the east or south where we were heading. Rain on dirt roads would mean flooding, mud, and water damage and we'd had enough of that experience three days earlier on our first day in Cameroon. Lightning flashes through the dry night were like someone switching the bedroom light on and off. They illuminated our recumbent forms and the bushes around us. Exposed and vulnerable I struggled to sleep. Thunder rumbles and Ross's snores punctuated my restlessness, but no unwelcome visitors knocked on the window.

13th November

We were getting closer to the border with La République Centrale Africaine,

CAR in English and formerly French Equatorial Africa. The narrow snake of ochre track blinkered by elephant grass on either side was certainly equatorial. Just as we congratulated ourselves for making good time, visibility became impossible from thick dust stirred up by another vehicle ahead. We could barely see further than the car bonnet. Any attempt at overtaking would be suicidal, so for an hour we crawled along afraid to overtake and hoping that whatever travelled ahead of us might turn onto another road. We swigged heavily chlorinated water to wash away the taste of dust, not knowing which was worse. Our smarting eyes forced us to close the windows, but then we lost the current of air and started to sweat, while the fan on full blast prevented conversation and only served to swirl warm air.

We stopped for half an hour to allow the dust to settle. Peace descended, a dove cooed and crickets rustled in the dry grass. Not a breath of wind whispered to disturb the hot air. Ross started up the engine again and a welcome draught flowed through the sweltering car. Half a mile further up the track we came to a wooden store standing in a clearing. As we approached two heavily-laden trucks pulled away from the store and out in front of us. They had stopped at exactly the same time as us on the otherwise deserted road. Because the drivers couldn't see us for their own dust, or hear us for their noisy engine, we'd missed our chance. We were sentenced to hours more of travelling at fifteen miles an hour just far enough back for the dust to be bearable.

The roof-rack didn't look as if it would last much longer. The middle section had sunk low under too heavy a load and one of the feet had sheared so that it rubbed on the car roof like squeaky chalk on a blackboard. Apart from these annoyances we were pleased to travel a good distance on better roads than those we'd first experienced in Cameroon.

An evening stroll around Garoua-Boulai prepared us for the next customs experience in the morning. The daily remission from heat at the end of every day had to be grasped and enjoyed before mosquitoes woke up for their vampire feasting.

Over the border a country we'd hardly heard of waited to give us a memory we'd never forget.

# CHAPTER TWELVE

## *Back of Beyond*

14<sup>th</sup> November

'Avez-vous un fusil?' Asked one of the customs officers.

'He's asking if we have a gun,' I translated.

Before we left London Ross came back from the city alone one day with a package.

'I want to show you something,' he said in a low voice. 'Come upstairs.'

Intrigued I looked around to see if any parental ears were pricked, and followed him up. He unfastened the wrappings of a parcel with great care. A gun tumbled into his hand and I gasped.

'What did you get that for?'

'Keep your voice down! It's only for an absolute emergency. I've been worrying about trouble in the Congo and wondering how we'd defend ourselves if we got into real trouble, so I decided to buy this. We'll keep it well hidden and only use it as a last resort.'

I looked at the resting weapon. As a replica of a German Luger it looked ferocious. The mechanics sounded less scary since it worked off a compressed air cartridge, the same as that used in soda fountains. Around forty aluminium pellets could be fired without reloading.

'So it's an air-gun,'

'Yes.'

I was relieved but unsure about this turn of events, and took little interest in how it worked. To me guns spelt trouble and I wanted no part of it, but understood why he had bought it. We hadn't discussed it since, and it lay mischievously at the bottom of the glove compartment. I put it out of my thoughts.

'Tell him we have an air-gun for shooting snakes,'

'Nous avons un pistolet d'aire pour tuer les serpents,' I guessed the translation.

The customs officer looked puzzled and asked to see it. Ross went back to the car and some minutes later came back with the air-gun held carefully dormant in his hand. They backed off with their hands up in the air. Alarmed by their reaction we assured them we meant no harm. Ross offered to demonstrate how it worked and when they realised that it only fired aluminium pellets they laughed in an over-exaggerated fashion, we suspect to hide their embarrassment. I wondered what my translation had said.

The head of state Bokassa looked down with a smug smile at this exchange from his framed picture on the wall. He'd gained power in a coup d'état a few years earlier.

'This will be an era of equality,' he announced on the radio to the surprised nation.

Seven years after our passing through the country he had himself crowned as Emperor, styling himself on Napoleon complete with gold epaulets, gold-embroidered jacket and fancy hat. The coronation cost more than the annual budget of the country and included a throne made of solid gold. Allegations of cannibalism were never proved.

'I thought that things were going to get nasty back there,' said Ross as we drove into our eighth country. 'They had guns of their own, only theirs were rifles and not air pistols. We would have been pretty helpless if they'd decided to turn against us.'

We pondered this as we rolled along until at ten o'clock we reached Bossembélé. The petrol situation took over as our latest anxiety. I wrote in the log book:-

'Petrol here is 9/- to 9/6d a gallon which for 88 octane fuel is hell of expensive.'

This was priced according to the prevailing exchange rate, but we had no local currency so couldn't buy petrol regardless of what they were charging. We might just have made it to Bangui without filling up, but decided against the risk. The AA book had two hotels marked where we hoped to change a traveller's cheque, but they had long gone and after numerous enquiries we tracked down the police station to seek advice. This proved to be the right decision and the charming constable grasped our situation immediately, giving us a coupon for twenty litres of petrol in exchange for a traveller's cheque.

Having local currency was always a problem when we arrived in another country. It had happened for the first time in Spain on a Sunday. Up on the Meseta of the central plateau we arrived at a smooth new three-lane highway freshly demarcated with bright white lines. We'd settled into enjoying the empty straight road when a barrier and toll booth blocked our way ahead. The toll-keeper put down his copy of *El País* as we drew up alongside him. We'd not yet bought Spanish currency.

'Diez pesetas por favor,' he requested.

'No tenemos pesetas,' I started to explain since I was nearest. We couldn't pay the ten pesetas and I was trying to think what the Spanish for travellers' cheques could be. Between us we tried to offer sterling, tangling ourselves up in the unfamiliar language and causing more confusion. This was no good to the isolated toll-keeper, and after much explaining and sign language he told us to '*peess off*.' He uttered the order with fluency, apparently the only English words he knew, with an angry wave of his arm but also a raising of the barrier. Giggling we passed through gratis on to a motorway to let the miles fly past.

On the road to Bangui we ground to a halt in sand again, reminding us of the Sahara and marginally preferring it to mud. We were taking it in turns to dig ourselves out with our new shovel bought in Biafra when a large truck arrived from the opposite direction. The driver couldn't pass on the narrow track so he reluctantly had to stop, and a Ugandan hitch-hiker who was travelling with him came to talk to us. He had just come through the Congo and related horrifying tales of the local people, corrupt officials, and impossible roads which forced even large trucks to be stranded.

'It would be better for you to cross into the Congo at Bangassou,' he advised. 'You should avoid a lot of trouble that way.'

'But is there a bridge there?' asked Ross, knowing that none was marked on the map and that the river in question was the main tributary of the Congo River.

'No, but there is a ferry which can take you across the river,' he assured us.

The Ugandan was so sure of himself we decided to trust his advice. His stories of corruption and dreadful roads were exactly what we feared in the Congo and his suggested route would minimise the time and distance we'd have to spend there. Ever guileless and with an absence of any better information, we altered our plans to head for Bangassou before crossing the huge river and thus delayed our entry into the dreaded Congo. The road would still take us through Bangui, our original destination, and we could reassess the situation when we arrived there. We drove on another twenty miles before stopping for the night, bringing the day's total to over three hundred.

## 15th November

Based on calculations using a distance-measuring wheel over roads on the map Ross had estimated back in London we had to travel 4,000 miles to Chingola. His father suggested we add fifty per cent on to this amount, making the total 6,000, and with this in mind we planned to take five weeks for our journey. We had long passed the seven thousand mark and still had a third of our journey to go. London was exactly five weeks behind us. The realisation made us press on. Our original budget for five weeks would have to keep stretching. Petrol would be a fixed cost, so our only way to minimise the rest would be to hurry on and save on living costs.

The broad avenues of Bangui led us down to the wide River Ubangi which marked the border. Its waters would wind their way through dense forest for several hundred miles and flow into the great Congo River. This had been our planned crossing over to Zongo in the Congo until we'd changed our plan and we stood looking across the wide stretch of lazy muddy water. The barge that served as a ferry sat solidly against the quay. A faded notice stood alongside with a timetable. We'd just missed a crossing and the next ferry wouldn't be sailing for a few days, further endorsing our decision to continue to Bangassou.

The French colonial capital beckoned us to linger for a better look. Instead we followed a smell redolent of France to a local bakery for warm baguettes, changed some money and headed out of town. A hedge of hibiscus lined the central reservation of the wide highway, and a woman with a basket was collecting its scarlet flowers. We imagined it was for tea or medicine.

Lush colonial gardens restrained by high walls hinted at abundance. A fifty-foot tree dripped with dangling green avocadoes, banana fronds thrust untidily upwards, dusty mango trees branched out over the pavement casting welcome shade for passers-by, and between towering trees leggy Poinsettias were coming into flower in time for their festive Christmas splash. Glimpses of an old crumbly building evoked a past life of masters and servants, of pink champagne and canapés, but also of diseases, disasters and rebellion.

A police checkpoint stopped us and polite officers asked us the usual questions of where we were going, where we had been and why, and then let us pass with their good wishes. Could this smart efficiency be happening in darkest Africa? Would we have a different tale to tell after we crossed the Ubangi River?

We'd been dreading the Congo and if we were honest shouldn't have been going there.

'I will let you have the loan if Mr McCarry gives this journey his blessing,' smiled Mr Johnson the bank manager, back in Edinburgh. He was talking about my father, his predecessor

We sat in the Leith office with a mid-September sun shining through the window. Ross had presented our scheme admirably and we were full of hope. Mr Johnson had taken over the Bernard Street branch from my father when he retired and we were appealing to him for a loan of £350 to cover our living and travelling costs for the journey. We had estimated this to be enough to cover modest living accommodation and one hot meal a day for five weeks, our estimated time for the trip. The company N.C.C.M. offered nothing towards our costs. Normally they paid in advance for the ship's passage and motoring expenses up from South Africa, or direct flights to Zambia. But they would not risk any funds up front for our unprecedented scheme. No encouragement came from that quarter. We didn't qualify for the 'induction' or hotel accommodation in London either and had little idea of the life waiting for us when we arrived.

Back in Colinton Road at my parents' house I suspected that Mr Johnson had just cleverly thwarted our plans. I lifted the heavy black telephone receiver with an equally heavy heart about to appeal to my father who was visiting London with my mother. He had already coughed up a loan for the new car out of the lump sum he received on retirement. It wasn't only a question of capital. Was this going to be stretching his generosity of spirit? My request would put the burden of sanctioning our enterprise onto his shoulders.

I tried to sound confident and sensible, and then passed the phone to Ross to have his say. We must have presented our case well or caught him at a weak moment because rather taken by surprise he reluctantly but unmistakably agreed to our scheme. He made one condition. We must not travel through the Congo. We had secured our bank loan!

A stretch of tarmac road led us out eastwards on the RN2 out of the city for over 100 miles, a luxurious surprise after the rutted roads in the rest of the country. It allowed us to reach Grimari by the end of the day having plenty of miles under our belt and another satisfying mileage for the day.

### 16th November

Encouraged by the good progress we'd made up to Grimari our hopes were high for crossing into the Congo from Bangassou later in the day, but we were too optimistic. In the late morning our roof rack finally broke, which wasn't really surprising considering the load it had been supporting since

Lagos. It happened just beside a village so we soon had an audience of ten. We removed the offending roof-rack and left it in a ditch. Before long someone had made their claim, scurrying away with it carried aloft before Ross could change his mind. The remaining wheel and ladders now had to go into the car and after a lot of thought Ross decided to cut the ladders shorter so that they would fit inside with the windows closed. I helped to find the hacksaw in the boot which involved unpacking half of its contents and creating a turmoil which kept me busy rearranging for the next twenty minutes. Sweating away under the watchful gaze of the villagers Ross managed to reduce the length of the sturdily-built ladders while still leaving them useful for an emergency. We tried from every angle to squeeze them into the car but they solidly refused to fit, so he had to cut off another tiny section which took just as long. The young men were amused by all this activity and one took the saw off Ross to lend him a hand, grinning broadly. Finally we arranged everything for a reasonable fit, including the three spare wheels, but our personal space had been reduced to a minimum with my knees pressed against the dashboard, and Ross with barely enough room to manage the car controls. It also meant we both had to use the driver's door, and the prospect of driving thousands of more miles didn't look appealing. It did however get rid of the disconcerting noises from the roof every time we hit a bump. The show over, our audience gave us a cheery wave and dispersed back into the bush.

In the early afternoon we had to stop again for our tenth puncture since leaving Lagos. This meant changing not just the punctured tyre, but two in order to keep the wheels balanced, as well as the tiresome need for both of us using the same door as we climbed awkwardly in and out.

'We're not going to get across the river today after all this,' said Ross.

I agreed and produced a flannel with some soap and water for a wash after handling the dirty wheels. As we sat on the green verge of the red national road rubbing the oily stains from our fingers, we watched an old man approaching. He carried a large knife, a spear for fishing, and a branch of bananas. Using sign language we persuaded him to sell us some of his fruit. They were still green but would quickly ripen in the warmth of the car.

Dusk was approaching when we arrived in Bangassou. Anxious about the ferry we headed straight for the river. Slightly narrower than the stretch we'd seen in Bangui, it flowed faster. A swathe of solid green bush covered the Congolese side in dark mystery.

Blank faces answered our enquiries. If there had ever been a ferry it had long ceased to operate. Perhaps taking advice from unknown hitch-hikers had not been a good idea and we would have to backtrack. We asked several more locals about a river crossing and our fragile hopes took an upturn as each one assured us there was still a means of getting across.

'Yes, you can get across the river with your car. There is a raft,' said one.

'Maybe three, maybe four years ago the men of Bangassou, they made a raft to carry a car. But it was smaller than this one that you yourselves are driving,' said another.

Each time we phrased it differently just in case of misunderstanding, and after half a dozen positive answers decided they must be right. As the daylight seeped away and the hated mosquitoes began to whine we stood and looked at the fast-flowing barrier where crocodiles and hippos lurked. They call the river Mbomou here before it merges with the Uele River to form the Ubangi River that we'd seen in Bangui. Although this was not as wide as the lazy stretch we'd seen before, it would need a sturdy carrier to transport us across its swirling depths.

Using the last hour of the day to make a start with arrangements we set off, and tried to out-pace the mosquitoes as we strode from place to place.

'You know we have to find a way to cross this river, don't you?' said Ross

'Well we could always go back if it looks too dangerous,' I replied.

'But we can't.' He looked at me helplessly. 'We don't have enough petrol, and there hasn't been anywhere to buy it. It's really remote here. We're in the back of beyond!'

'What about that little petrol pump we passed in town?' I asked.

'That was diesel, it seems to be all they have on offer out of the main towns.'

Ubiquitous trucks ran on diesel, and anyone wealthy enough to have a car made sure their vehicle did too.

There wasn't much demand for rafts since most transport used the ferry at Bangui. It would cost ten pounds, a price which came down to about six pounds but still we weren't very happy although unclear of what was actually involved. Being British we decided to consult the police to find out if these prices were correct, ever trusting of the constabulary. But the policeman wasn't helpful at all and asked for all our papers. He couldn't understand our passport and visa arrangements. The remains of the day faded as we offered lengthy and patient explanations to convince him all was in order. Satisfied at last he slipped our papers into the drawer of his wooden desk.

'I will keep them here until tomorrow.' He announced.

We couldn't understand why, and suspected he was simply wielding his power. It meant we couldn't change a cheque at the hotel to pay for the boat crossing. His obstreperous attitude got us riled, although I tried not to show it, but it was tricky trying to keep the lid on Ross's frustration. Finally we persuaded him to hand back our passports, promising to return them when we'd changed the money. His was the worst face of officialdom. Bored by a lack of action, a little alcohol made the day pass more pleasantly. It fogged his brain and made him belligerent, which was not at all pleasant for us. Exhausted and demoralised by all the argument, we treated ourselves to a meal and a glass of beer at the hotel.

We found ourselves the only diners although others were expected judging by the tables laid out with bread baskets. French custom is to eat late, and they had set the standard in the country's restaurants. Communication with the waiter left us unclear of what was on offer and conscious of our tight budget we opted for the bargain set menu which had not been written down. Thinking about food had our juices flowing and ravenous we started on the bread. The waiter appeared with a salad as a first course, and then an omelette, which he cut in half. Fearing this was the main course, we helped ourselves to bread on the next table. Ross had just popped a sugar cube in his mouth when a puzzled waiter returned to ask if we'd like more bread. We accepted and soon regretted our request when the main course of steak and chips appeared, and then a choice of crème brûlée or cheese board. It turned out to be another taxing evening for our previously under-used digestive systems, reminiscent of Zinder.

The 'patron' of the hotel offered to exchange some Congolese money as well as the local currency. There was no petrol to be bought in this backwater before we made the crossing so it would be essential to fill up the tank as soon as possible across the river. We'd learned this lesson when we first entered the country from Cameroon, and we jumped at the chance to get Congolese currency in advance. We returned the passports to the unpleasant policeman as promised and drove out of town for a quiet spot to spend our last night in the country.

### 17<sup>th</sup> November

Our passports reclaimed, we set off for the garage to arrange puncture repairs. We'd been led to believe the owner might also help with the promised river crossing, but we spoke to five people before reaching the man in question. He promised to solve our problem, saying the punctures would be repaired free-of-charge, and suggesting local prisoners could assemble a raft for crossing the river. Reassured, we left the tyres with him, went to the market for fresh food and posted letters home.

A small boy called Emanuel who claimed to be twelve but looked the size of an eight-year old, became our shadow. He longed to run errands for us and was never far from our sides until we left town.

We reclaimed our mended tyres and ready to leave, went to see what was happening about the raft… nothing. It had all been a misunderstanding and another failure of communication. The garage owner agreed to hire some workmen to do the work but we would have to pay them.

We went to the customs, a mud hut with resident official sitting at a small table and wielding a rubber stamp, left the *carnet* there ready for our departure from the country, and went down to the river to see how things were progressing. We would have to pay for the use of the local's dug-out canoes and also the workmen, who didn't look like prisoners, for constructing a raft and getting us across the water. This work would cost us the equivalent of ten pounds, the original sum quoted and one we could little afford. We realised after much discussion it was the only way and a better alternative than returning to Bangui, particularly with no fuel being available. Still groping our way through the fog of misunderstandings we then found it rested on us to obtain the planks for the car to stand on, and rope to tie everything together. Emmanuel led us to the Catholic mission which had not been our first thought when looking for rope and planks.

We emerged from the cool peaceful building accompanied by a brown-robed Brother Paul who understood how things worked here. He greeted Emanuel, our shadow, and with long rosary beads clinking with every stride he led us to a locked storehouse. Its well-ordered interior revealed all manner of useful objects and he selected a large coil of rope. The planks had to be at least eighteen feet long and wide enough to support the car. Emmanuel was dispatched to the river for carriers from our new workforce. Four men appeared and were instructed by Brother Paul in their own language to return the wood at the end of the day. Ross and I carted the rope with Emanuel holding the tail-end, and our little procession made its way back to the river.

The call had gone out to the neighbouring village chiefs for the biggest pirogues or dugout canoes to be brought, of which the four longest and deepest were selected. The mission's planks would be laid at right angles over them and secured with rope to form a craft similar to a catamaran with two canoes on either side. Another two planks made a short bridge between dry land and the raft.

'Where will it land?' I asked, surveying an apparently impenetrable line of bush across the river.

The foreman pointed to the bank directly opposite us. I looked again more closely, and saw a narrow break in the greenery with a barely discernible clearing from the bank into the unknown.

The men busied themselves with ropes, canoes, and planks and we watched with apprehension, wondering about the wisdom of trusting our lives and our golden car to such a precarious craft. We thought again about returning to Bangui, and remembered the lack of petrol. Even the mission vehicles ran on diesel. Every time we looked at it the river looked wider and faster-flowing, so when the time came for the car to embark on the precarious raft our hearts raced with something akin to terror.

'If it capsizes Ross will have to swim to the nearer bank,' I thought to myself. A faint hope should disaster strike, given the speed of the current and the resident wildlife.

'The raft is ready now so you must pay us the money,' said the foreman with African directness.

'You can have a deposit now and I'll pay you the rest when you get us, and the car safely over to the other side.' Replied Ross firmly. I translated.

Some muttering ensued, but after a few minutes he nodded, took the cash offered and got down to business.

'Allez y!' he ordered, waving Ross on to the planks.

'That won't work,' protested Ross, 'the raft will just float away if I try to drive on without it being held.'

The boss man scratched his head.

'The men will have to get into the water on the other side to hold it still until the car is in place,' Ross explained gesturing to demonstrate what he meant.

An extensive discussion followed in the local tongue, and then they did as Ross asked. Mindless of lurking crocodiles, eight of them stood up to their chests in the murky water pushing the raft towards the bank while another eight held the dugouts to the shore.

I became the guardian of all our money, travellers' cheques and passports for safekeeping, and our heaviest luggage had already been stashed in a separate dug-out canoe where I would be travelling. I was considered the better risk.

Ross coaxed the wheels cautiously on to planks nine inches wide to board the bobbing raft and it plunged instantly and alarmingly under the weight. Sixteen men strained to their limits trying to hold the lashed canoes close to the bank. Struggling to regain his *sang-froid* Ross inched the back wheels onboard amidst shouts and waving hands about how far he should take it. Too far would topple both car and driver straight into the river, and not far enough would upset the balance. Sweat streamed down faces still trying to hold the raft to the bank. Ross pulled hard on the hand-brake. No rope had been left to secure the wheels in place.

The young men took up their positions with two in the front and two in the back of each dug-out. Another man to orchestrate the chanting and rowing amounted to seventeen in all. Ross sat in the car with his arms folded, a 1970 version of a nineteenth century explorer.

Two men jumped into the water to push the raft from the bank, and the chanting started.

'Aye oomh. Aye oomh,' they sang plunging their paddles into the swift current.

Sweat glinted on their straining torsos. My heart lurched and I felt as if I'd strayed onto a film set.

Two boats let in water and soon one man gave up paddling to bale them out. The car slid a fraction with each rhythmic pull of the paddles and Ross opened his door frightened by the wheel movement, gesturing to the conducting foreman in dismay. Already the wheels strayed a few millimetres over the edge of the planks.

'Aye oomh. Aye oomh.'

The foreman did not flinch and on they laboured upriver, keeping close to the shore where the current was weakest up the hurrying river, chanting their refrain with deep rich voices.

'Aye oomh. Aye oomh.'

They looked unaware of a possible slide into the murky water, and it

seemed they were taking the car and my husband away from me, the distance became so great between us. Then they started to turn into the full strength of the current to make a wide arc downriver towards the opposite bank.

I set off in the single dug-out with two boatmen but without the need for chanting or to travel so far upstream. Our documents had been stored in a bag around my neck and I clutched them while I studied the murky riverbanks for signs of crocodiles.

'People always see them too late,' Brother Paul had remarked unhelpfully earlier.

I'd read somewhere that it was a slow and painful way to die, starting with a death-roll before being dragged semi-conscious into their lair to slowly rot. Ross looked at me across the liquid divide and I forced a smile, hardly believing what we were doing and not sure of my emotions. He grinned back putting on a brave face and showing me he couldn't believe it either.

'Aye oomh. Aye oomh.'

The lack of film for our camera was a tragedy.

Our smaller craft arrived first and the paddlers helped me to offload the luggage. I stood on Congo soil and watched the raft approach with the chanting getting louder at every stroke.

'Aye oomh. Aye oomh.'

They had safely reached the weaker currents on the Congolese side of the river and could let the raft glide through thick reeds and down to the bank beside us. The temperature rose as the hot oarsmen pulled the raft close in a sweaty haze.

'There will be no problem with landing at the other side,' the foreman had assured us before they set off.

But he had not allowed for the water level being low at the start of the rains and thick mud stretched between the water and the bank. It was too thick to take the boats and not solid enough to drive over. The men who had transported my dugout stood up to their knees in water wanting their work to be over and waiting expectantly for the car to roll off the raft across glutinous mud. 'Don't pay the ferry man until you get to the other side' had been a good motto to follow.

'We have to make a ramp across that mud or it'll be disastrous!' Ross pleaded, refusing to move the car off the raft.

So the planks from the previous ramp were duly laid over the divide as a bridge for the car to drive over.

'It's still not good enough,' he insisted, 'We'll need to collect wood or stones to provide a firmer base. What is there?'

But there were no more planks or other hard material.

'We'll just have to go for it then, everyone cross your fingers!'

The men standing in the water pushed the raft as far as they could into the shore while others pulled from the muddy bank. The main concern was the front wheels being plugged in mud while the rear wheels were still on the raft. So with the engine running and everyone in place holding the raft, Ross pushed down his right foot on the accelerator and made a run for dry land. Half way across the planks slowly disappeared into the mud with a crack. We all looked on helplessly as the car slid uncontrollably sideways. Men pushed to stop its downward motion but within seconds the wheels also sank out of sight into the brown muck. The slurping river looked as if it would be claiming our golden dream after all. I hardly dared watch.

Sunk too deep, the car doors would not open. To get out Ross had to climb through the window and the mud sucked at everyone's feet. The oarsmen tried to lift it out and the body of the car rose up but the wheels and axle stuck firm refusing to budge. Ross produced our shovel. They started digging, digging and digging, and finally ramming the wooden planks downwards in an effort to slide them at an angle under the wheels.

Sinewy arms and shoulders got stuck in, and tried once more to lift the car back into place, chanting 'drrrr-ya,drrr-ya' with an upward lift on the 'ya'. Pushing and heaving they tried again and again, and just as it slipped into place the malevolent slime claimed another wheel.

'Drrrr-ya,drrr-ya.'

This sequence kept repeating itself but each time a few more inches were claimed. The mud ladders were indispensable.

'Drrrr-ya,drrr-ya.'

Including Ross there were twenty strong men labouring for an hour to secure the car on to solid ground and we certainly got our money's worth.

In the process of freeing the car, one of the planks split without warning and stabbed two men in their legs with deep dirty cuts. Torn red flesh gleamed out through four inch openings in mud-encrusted skin, one in the calf and the other on the outer thigh. Stifling my abhorrence I rushed to retrieve our first-aid box. Their stoicism shamed me into denying any squeamishness and I did my best to patch them up. They revelled in the attention from this pale European girl and soon a queue had formed, each man displaying his wounds. Our stores of antiseptic and Elastoplast quickly depleted as I felt obliged to treat even the tiniest cuts which I'm certain under normal circumstances would have been ignored. I sat on an anthill to administer sticking plaster and sympathy until each one of them wore his badge of honour.

We paid our dues, and in true African fashion they all decided what they would like us to give them: – cigarettes; sweets; money; shirts; hats; blankets, medicine. We parted with a few sweets, aspirin, and cigarettes, shook many hands and everyone smiling and the job accomplished we left them to row back home. We had just shared one of the most unforgettable experiences of our lives with these men, and were heavyhearted to think we would never see them again. We owed them our survival.

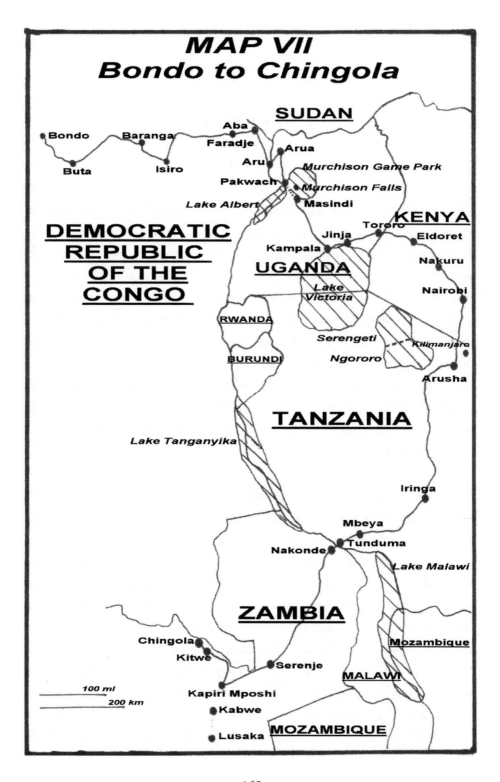

MAP VII
Bondo to Chingola

SUDAN

Bondo  Baranga  Aba
Faradje
Aru  Arua
Buta  Isiro  Pakwach  Murchison Game Park
Murchison Falls
Lake Albert  Masindi

DEMOCRATIC
REPUBLIC
OF THE
CONGO

KENYA
Tororo  Eldoret
Jinja
Kampala  Nakuru
UGANDA  Nairobi
Lake
Victoria
RWANDA
Serengeti  Kilimanjaro
BURUNDI  Ngororo
Arusha

TANZANIA

Lake Tanganyika

Iringa

Mbeya
Tunduma
Nakonde  Lake Malawi

ZAMBIA

Chingola  Mozambique
Kitwe
Serenje
100 ml  MALAWI
200 km
Kapiri Mposhi
Kabwe
Lusaka  MOZAMBIQUE

# CHAPTER THIRTEEN

## *The Congo*

### 1960

It is an ordinary evening of a school day in Edinburgh, and I am spending the evening at a friend's house. Her mother sits in an armchair near us in the sitting room, knitting and watching the news. The worst place to be in the world is the Belgian Congo and images unfold of African bush and simple mud houses along dirt streets. The presenter speaks a warning and her mother sends us from the room since the news report is too shocking for our tender ears and eyes. This is a novel turn of events so immediately on full alert; we sit outside the door trying to glean information. We don't discover much, but our appetites have been whetted and we take to reading the papers about horrific tales of rape, murder, and cannibalism of priests, missionaries and nuns. The thought of the nuns at school being eaten is something to ponder.

That same year The Congo gained independence from Belgium's particularly harsh administration. On that first independence day in June, Lumumba the first president before Mobutu's coup, proclaimed:-

'Our lot was eighty years of colonial rule ... We have known tiring labour exacted in exchange for salary which did not allow us to satisfy our hunger ... We have known ironies, insults, blows which we had to endure morning, noon, and night because we were 'Negroes' ... We have known that the law was never the same depending on whether it concerned a White or a Negro ... We have known the atrocious sufferings of those banished for political opinions or religious beliefs ... We have seen that in the towns there were magnificent houses for the Whites and crumbling shanties for the Blacks, that a Black was not admitted in the motion-picture houses, in the restaurants, in the stores of the Europeans; that a Black travelled in the holds, at the feet of the Whites in their luxury cabins.'

17<sup>th</sup> November 1970

The country we had tried so hard to avoid and then struggled so hard to enter was the source of our greatest fears in the whole trip. Crazed cannibalistic rebels apart, one of the cruellest colonial regimes in Africa had existed here and the Congolese owed Europeans no favours.

Relief at arriving relatively unscathed after our recent ordeal, mixed with apprehension at how we'd be received. Tall grasses brushed both sides of the car and we cautiously proceeded. A muddy red track unused by any vehicle bigger than a bicycle for years, twisted between lush green vegetation leading us to our fate. Ross stopped the car.

'I don't think we should risk it. I'm going to get rid of it and throw it away.'

With that he took the gun out of the glove compartment, walked to the edge of the forest and performing a wide overhand throw dispensed of our weapon far into the greenery.

'After the reaction of the customs officers when we entered CAR I think we'd just be inviting trouble if we kept it, especially if we didn't declare it and then they discovered it.'

He climbed back into the driver's seat and I felt a weight lift from my shoulders. We continued another hundred yards to the junction with a better-frequented road and approached a tiny hut marked '*Douanes*' with a clear conscience ready to meet our first villainous Congolese customs officer.

The simple customs house stood alone in a clearing behind a flagpole with chickens pecking around outside its mud walls. We parked in a shady spot, gathered up our papers and stepped inside trying to look inoffensive. Under a framed picture of President Mobutu with signature heavy glasses and toque perched on his head, the officer shook our hands and welcomed us to his country. His clientele would normally be local travellers on foot or bicycle. We couldn't imagine many other vehicles venturing up that dust track to keep him busy and his spruce appearance and efficient manner took us by surprise. He spotted that the *carnet* had been wrongly dated, something that customs officers in eight other countries had failed to notice. We expected a bad reaction and watched nervously waiting for him to grasp the opportunity to bribe or fine us. He shook his head at the careless blunder made in London showing a start date after the termination date, altered it with black pen and then requested some aspirin.

'It's hard to get hold of medicine in our small village,'

I translated his words to Ross, and like some fawning peon went to fetch some pills, grateful and relieved at such a small request. We suspected that our first aid kit's reputation had run ahead of us, and gladly handing over a handful of aspirin we were free to go.

Sixty miles further up the road at Monga we knew that the immigration officer would have closed his office for the day so we stopped to rest. We watched Congolese walking or cycling along the roadside and going about their daily business. They were just like other Africans but as many as a third of them had enlarged thyroids. Deep in the forest a thousand miles from the sea there must be a lack of iodine.

18th November

Ours was the only vehicle travelling over the red mud. We climbed a gentle incline while the forest dripped around us and hid rustling secrets. Something moved on the road ahead and I peered through our insect-stained windscreen to see. A small troop of man-sized gingery monkeys looking like orang-utans but much hairier, heard our approach and within three seconds had disappeared into the tangle of greenery to either side, scooping up their babies as they scrambled to safety. The sight we hoped to catch at the spot where they vanished eluded us, while they probably had a good look at us from the leafy shadows. Our hopeful eyes strained for other wildlife sightings without reward until the immigration office distracted us with practicalities.

Again anticipating trouble at immigration we approached the office with friendly diplomatic smiles pasted onto our faces and again all went smoothly.

We left with less trepidation than before. The people reacted to us the same as everywhere else and the trouble we had expected at every turn didn't manifest itself. At first they looked unfriendly and suspicious of two foreigners in their strange car, but it only took smiles and waves for their whole expression to change as they reciprocated our friendliness.

By nine o'clock we arrived at another river, but this time a pontoon was in operation. The floating platform would be hauled across the river by ropes, and looked a much safer vessel than the raft of our recent adventure. We didn't mind waiting in the least after our experiences over the last twelve days and felt like 'old hands'.

Two pale girls also waited. They stood out like beacons amongst the smiling black faces. We guessed they had something to do with a mission, probably the American Baptists. Silent and joyless in their teenage years their mousy hair hung lank under straw hats to frame faces deprived of sun, a commodity not in short supply. Shapeless pastel cotton shifts covered thin shapeless bodies revealing nothing of arms and legs. Off-white socks hid ankles above cheap canvas shoes. I tried to catch an eye to say hello, perhaps enjoy a customary exchange of experiences. Not a flicker betrayed any willingness for social contact. This was a strange meeting of young white women in the heart of darkness.

A large wheel was fixed to a sturdy tree at each side of the crossing, with thick rope attached to each end of the boat. The rope went around each wheel and hung like a taut washing line above our heads. A shout from the man in charge prompted three others to heave on the forward rope and pull us closer to the other side. Ours was the only vehicle on board, and timings of crossings corresponded to the number of passengers and the workers inclination. We looked forward to a free passage across the swirling water which was only fifty yards wide but half-way across the ferrymen asked for presents. We parted with a few cigarettes and aspirin, a gift proportionate to effort and goodwill. They thought us mean but returned to their heave-ho, not in the mood for mutiny.

Bad roads followed but not as drastic as before until about five miles from Bondo when we met two young American men whose Jeep had skidded off the road into a sea of mud. We did our best to tow them out but even with the help of our ladders the task needed the power of a truck not our townie saloon car, and we risked pulling ourselves in with them.

'We've come from Malawi and are heading for Mali,' said Gary, 'how about you guys?'

They had journeyed up from the south of the country through Kisangani. This was not their first problem with mud, and they were not the first people to advise us to stay on higher drier ground.

'You wouldn't believe the state of the roads back there,' he said. 'It's the trucks that make it worse, and there doesn't seem to be any maintenance programme, at least not during the rainy season. It was tough enough for us in the Jeep; you wouldn't have a hope in that car!'

They planned to cross the border at Bangui as we had originally planned, and were interested in our alternative route. We didn't fancy their chances of arranging a raft- crossing from this side of the river with a much heavier vehicle, and left them to make their decision.

'Is there anything else we can do to help before we go?' asked Ross after we'd failed to pull them out.

'Well you could send someone out for us. We stayed at the Catholic mission in Bondo last night, it's easy to find. Ask for Father Aloysius, he should remember us. If you tell him our situation he'll know what to do. Just say Gary and John sent you.'

'You stayed at the mission?'

'Yeah, you should do the same. It's not safe in this country after dark, and the police and army are not to be trusted, never mind the bandits. There are plenty of missions to choose from but we find the Catholic ones are the best. They make a small charge to cover their costs, oh and sometimes they'll give you breakfast and dinner as well!'

No rain for two weeks made for reasonable driving conditions and we hadn't realised how lucky we'd been until the heavens opened. We hit a wet patch as slippery as an oil slick carrying us careering sideways into a ditch. Luckily the car fared better than our nerves. Still shaken Ross stepped out and skidded as badly as the car, ending up on his back. Trying not to laugh at his slapstick performance, I helped him up. We clung on to branches to prevent another fall, manoeuvred the ladders, and got the car back on to the road. Cleaning up effectively was impossible and the reddish-brown slime carried back into the car with us on clothes, sandals and worst of all the ladders did nothing to enhance our living conditions. Since I still had to exit and enter through the driver's door the mess spread badly, but it dried out in time and the worst could be scraped off.

At Bondo we tracked down Father Aloysius to report the message from the two stranded Americans. He set out immediately with a small truck and a length of sturdy rope. We felt part of the 'bush telegraph'.

The ferry for crossing the next river was not in operation and it looked as if we might have to cross on dug-out canoes again.

'When does the ferry leave?' I asked a passing African.

'Ne sais pas.' The African shrugged. He didn't know.

As in Bangassou every reply to our enquiries gave no, or at best vague information. This time unfazed by the prospect, we accepted the possibility of raft-building with resignation and decided to leave it until morning. It was pointless to fret about something over which we had no control, and our main worry would be the cost. Within two days we had accepted this mode of river crossing for our nearly-new car to be normal practice.

Meanwhile the petrol gauge had dipped dangerously low so we explored the town for supplies. Purchasing fuel didn't involve anything as modern as a petrol station. Instead we had to visit 'Comaco,' a contracting company which had fuel supplies for their own trucks. Few cars existed or survived in the small town and most people relied on bicycles. We arrived at a fenced store and parked outside.

'Nous cherchons l'essence,' I explained to a man in oily overalls.

He nodded and led us over to a small stack of forty-five gallon oil drums. One of them was fitted with a hand pump. He quoted a price and we returned to the car for jerry cans. We filled them with his help and in turn lugged them back to the car parked outside the gates, pouring the fuel into the tank. An extra two cans were filled as spares as supplies could be scarce in this country, paid and headed back to what passed as a town.

To fill ourselves up we found bananas and mangoes in the market, but for the first time since leaving home we couldn't track down any bread.

'I think we deserve a beer,' said Ross.

'That's a good idea,' I replied, 'I don't think I can face any more chlorinated water today,'

'I wonder if you can buy it here.'

In the town's only small shop we had found the usual tinned sardines, corned beef, and basic bags of flour, sugar and maize meal but no cold drinks of any description, so we stopped a man in western dress to ask. He directed us to a nearby house. Thinking there had been a mistake we asked someone else and got the same reply with the added information that it was the doctor's house.

Puzzled, we climbed side steps up to the first floor of the house, feeling like trespassers. A balding bespectacled man inched open the door.

'Excusez moi, on nous a dit que vous avez de la bière,' I ventured.

The smiling and somewhat bemused Belgian doctor insisted on inviting us in. He produced three bottles out of an ancient fridge and we sat down with him in his bachelor-status sitting-room diverting him from work. A desk in the corner was piled high with papers abandoned with our arrival. 'Santé,' said the doctor looking glad of an excuse for a break. Our payment would be to regale him with our experiences since leaving UK.

We returned to the mission to see if we could spend the night and take a badly needed shower. For a voluntary donation we were offered an evening meal and a room for the night. There was no shower but a monk brought us a fresh jug of hot water in our 'cell' for washing in Victorian style, placing it on the small wooden table next to an enamel bowl. We could use the visitors' lavatory down the corridor.

Alongside silent monks we sat at a long refectory table watching the others for clues on the form. After Ross tried to make conversation with his neighbour, a senior monk intervened and told him that Brother John would not reply because like most of them he had made a vow of silence. The senior monks were exempt allowing them to manage the place. After grace the abbot talked to us while the others sat mute, passing dishes of small potatoes and stringy spinach along the line with a nod or half a smile. The small chunks of meat were wild boar and so tough they had to be swallowed in their entirety, but leaving any was unthinkable. I wanted to know who had caught the animal, and how; what other bush meat was available to them; did they raise chickens; and how much they grew themselves. But answers were not available in this conversation-free zone for such trivial exchanges so I kept my questions to myself.

Ten of their missionaries had been murdered six years ago, and the few survivors had all returned along with compassionate new recruits eager to restore some sort of order. Local people had suffered far worse at the hands of the rebels from beatings, rape, torture and ritual murder. Their homes, families and lives had been devastated and the monks offered humanitarian, medical, and spiritual support. Now things were slowly returning to what they called 'normal'.

At half past eight a key turned in our door and we felt like prisoners. Sleeping indoors rather than in the car had been a luxury every other time we'd done it and I was looking forward to the same in spite of it being called a 'cell'. We had half an hour before the noisy generator would be switched off, and all the lights with it.

The Abbot had given us the choice of one or two rooms and we'd opted for one. Our single bed was a concrete slab covered by a thin mattress and we soon discovered that comfort was impossible, let alone intimacy. It wasn't long before Ross opted for the floor as a more comfortable option for us both as it was only a little harder than the bed but without the risk of falling off. Neither of us slept well because of the cold, which was the price of keeping to a route at higher altitude. We'd been given one thin blanket, and being locked in couldn't go to the car for more clothes or our own lovely blanket. My mosquito bites kept me awake and by now my feet and ankles had swollen up badly with bites scratched too often during my sleep and becoming infected. I got up to dip a cloth into the water-bowl for dabbing at the hot red mounds. It helped for a while before I succumbed to scratching again, which would be to my cost later in the trip. A cockerel with a bad sense of the hour started to crow at three in the morning and with uncanny timing crowed again just as I had nodded off. He kept this up until dawn.

19th November

It was a relief to get up at six, and then we found that the time zone had changed shrinking the day by an hour. We drank black coffee and ate thin slices of homemade bread and pineapple jam for breakfast as silently as the monks but without their company. They'd been up since before daybreak, courtesy perhaps of the cockerel.

Neither of us could summon up much energy to arrange a river crossing, but we went through the motions. The same lack of reliable information surrounded us again like fog. At Comaco where we were looking to organise another raft, we met a Greek called Andreas who took us back to his shop to change a traveller's cheque. He offered us a good exchange rate and a beer. Perhaps he'd spoken to the doctor, but beer and mornings don't go together in my experience. It was good to talk, albeit in French, after the stilted conversations of the night before and this man had useful information. The road between Buta and Kisangani was virtually impassable and he wouldn't even attempt to take his trucks through. Looking for a detour we brought out our map to make a plan.

Meanwhile it transpired that a new Monsignor was arriving on the opposite riverbank at midday bound for the Catholic mission. Consequently all efforts had been made for the VIP and the old ferry would be repaired by 11.30am when we could cross. Relieved of the task of organizing another river crossing we spent the rest of the morning chatting to Andreas and he produced more cold drinks and salami sandwiches. We got on to the subject of bushmeat and wild animals.

'There are many wild animals here,' his eyes sparked at the thought. 'I would like to show you something, but you must tell no one. Do you promise?'

We nodded, intrigued. We finished our drinks and followed him outside.

Plenty of game could be found nearby, and sworn to secrecy, he led us through tall grass on a narrow path for half a mile. We didn't see any animals and assumed they were hiding in the dense bush, but arrived at a large wooden shed the size of a single garage. A heavy padlock and chain secured the double doors which he unlocked, looking over his shoulder and scanning the bushes for inquisitive eyes.

'Et voila!' he announced proudly. Packed from floor to ceiling were piles of elephant tusks. The biggest ones arched up to nearly touch the ceiling, and dozens of smaller ones wedged them in. It was a miserable sight. He boasted about the biggest ones and how big and old the animals had been. His shed load of ivory was worth a fortune on the black market and in a land devoid of proper controls he would probably get away with it. It was a struggle not to show disapproval to our kind host

'Here, you can have this one as a souvenir,' he offered generously.

Ross held up the small tusk to admire, and then passed it to me. A hollow centre ran halfway down the curved length where it must have been attached to the soft tissues of its victim. I visualised its bloody removal from the beast and shivered.

'We would have trouble at the customs I'm afraid,' said Ross.

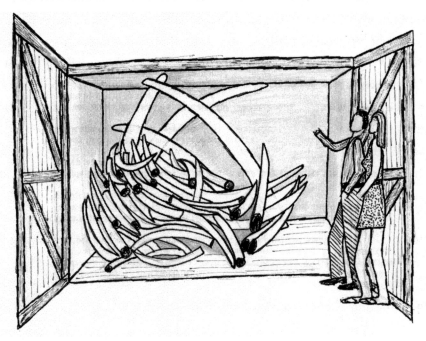

'Yes that's true, but you can easily hide it in a corner of your car,' insisted Andreas.

'Thanks, it's very kind of you,' replied Ross, 'but we'd rather not take the risk.'

At 11.30am we boarded the ferry which was another pontoon. Although the jetties at either side of the river had railings, the platform itself had none. It was nothing more than a bobbing raft, but too big to be held still as the paddlers in Bangassou had done. Ross boarded with supreme caution, and I stood on deck to attempt guidance.

The crossing was a miracle of precise timing we had learned not to expect and we arrived safely on the opposite bank before midday. To welcome the Monsignor a large crowd had assembled by the river, singing hymns in rich African harmony. Glorious arrangements of brightly-coloured flowers adorned the jetty and I wondered where they came from since all I'd seen for weeks was leafy growth. What a lovely impression the Monsignor would get of life here!

We'd been warned to expect the worst on the road to Buta and it lived up to its reputation. We were forced to stop several times in the full range of mud, deep pot-holes, rickety bridges, and sand that had become part of every journey. We thanked our lucky stars that the ladders always helped us out.

The travellers' code we'd discovered in the Sahara also operated here for Europeans. A Belgian who stopped to chat told us we could get entry permits for Uganda at the frontier with the Congo so there was no need to go to Kisangani on the dreaded road. This was the one that the Australians in their Dormobile and the Americans in their Jeep had told us was virtually impassable.

It wasn't only us who gained from these impromptu exchanges; we brought a taste of Europe to far-flung outposts and found ourselves eagerly invited into discussions.

'That's the best news we could get,' I said to Ross as we drove on. 'I didn't fancy our chances on that road, or even a detour!'

'No, neither did I. It sounds suicidal to use that road, so I'm glad we've been let off the hook. The only problem is the increase in mileage by going round East Africa. I'm not sure we can fund the petrol so we'll have to do some calculations and maybe get some more money sent out if necessary.'

This last possibility was one we'd move mountains to avoid, as it would involve pleas to our parents and admission of failure, if only of our budgeting.

Repeatedly freeing the car from muddy situations had us covered in grime, slime and sweat by the time we got to Buta. We made a roadside stop and tried to make ourselves respectable with flannels, cold water, combs, and a change of tee shirt, but the mud still clung to our sandals and under our fingernails. To cheer ourselves up we succumbed to another glass of beer.

At eight o'clock we headed for the mission but everyone had already gone to bed and the main gate had been padlocked, so we parked just outside the grounds. After the previous night I can't say I was disappointed!

### 20th November

Looking for bread again we had no luck. Everyone seemed to bake their own and no one had any to sell. There was another Comaco depot in town, so we stocked up with petrol and then set off on the detour to Isiro. It was a higher road deemed to be better than the main one since it had suffered less in the recent heavy rainfall. We found the alternative route slow and tiring, so realised that our chances would have been slim on the other road. The car took many bumps because we couldn't judge the depth of pot holes under the puddles, and we soon had another puncture.

The forest spread dark and tall around us with shafts of sunshine struggling to dapple the leafy floor. While we changed the wheel the usual crowd gathered. Amongst them were pygmies, mainly men but also two women standing chest-high beside the other Africans watching. They giggled at us as Ross heaved a spare wheel from the back seat and I helped to loosen the flat one with a wheel wrench. Ross lifted the bonnet to inspect something and instantly shadows fell over the engine from numerous woolly heads bent over to see inside. Not wanting to spoil their entertainment I found Ross a torch. As we all looked into the engine, I felt a slight tug at my hair and turned to see one of the women looking guilty. She'd been feeling my hair to compare with her own, and might not have seen hair my colour before. I held out a lock and invited them to have a better feel, and grinning they all reached fingers forward. We had their full attention, and as we finally drove away on the fresh wheel, they all waved enthusiastically and laughed behind their hands. We could have been a travelling circus put on for their amusement.

Further along the road a snake slithered across the damp red track disturbed by our engine's rumble and later a badger lumbered bear-like away from our noisy approach into the shelter of dripping vegetation.

Ten miles short of Baranga we'd exhausted the energy needed to reach the town. The drudgery of constantly freeing the car from difficulties, and with constant shaking and bumping when we were in motion had taken its toll. We stopped unable to go on. Somehow we felt safe enough to spend the night on this little-used road, and were too tired to care or even miss the comfort of a bed. Before dark a flock of birds descended on a nearby tree and I remembered the swallows in Algeciras five weeks earlier. They would be in South Africa by now. Their route took them over the Sahara too, but from Nigeria they could fly due south without our restricting need for dry roads and visas.

### 21st November

We had run short of food and tried again to buy bread. In a shop at Baranga the lady shopkeeper gave us some of her own, it was not for sale. We still had a tin of condensed milk to make a sickly but energy-giving sandwich.

The roads didn't get any better and loud creaking noises were emanating from one of the back shock absorbers. Perhaps it had absorbed one shock too many. An investigation found that one of the rubber stops which had been welded back in place in Lagos, had fallen off, and now the other one had loosened. Without their protection the back axle had punched holes in the chassis of the car through repeated hammering from dreadful roads. To prevent further damage Ross had to drive more carefully and on roads full of pot holes our progress felt like snail's pace.

Most of the bridges we came to looked perilously close to collapse. The first dilapidated crossing made us stop to stare at it in disbelief. Gaps, through which our wheels could easily fall, had to be bridged by the sand-ladders and this became the formula for the next few bridges too. Ross crossed over each one at a snail's pace.

The ladders came in handy again when we were stuck in mud. A man who'd stopped to help was thrilled when Ross gave him the ladder we'd just used. We only ever used one at a time and it gave us more room inside the car. They had made a horrible mess of the seats, scratching the upholstery and leaving ingrained stains.

At four o'clock we arrived at Isiro and went straight to the mission hoping for a badly needed shower. A cool reception, possibly due to our unkempt appearance, prevented us from returning at a more convenient time for further enquiries. Instead we stayed dirty and went into town for petrol and a mechanic.

We met some friendly young Greek men who told us where to go for car repairs, and instructed a small African boy to take us there. The manager of the garage, another Greek called George, spoke good English. He promised to help us the next morning. We chatted for a while and soon beer was on offer along with a room for the night which we gladly accepted. Living and travelling the way we had been made that cold beer taste like nectar.

Greeks had established communities in the Congo before Belgium claimed it for a colony. They held a strong presence all over the country, setting up businesses in coffee, trade, fishing, and transport but stayed out of politics and kept their religion to themselves. They were survivors and only concerned themselves with commerce.

We went into town to buy some bread, successfully at last from a Greek baker, and then ventured into a building calling itself a hotel. We started to feel human again as we sipped cold drinks and our taut nerves relaxed. We were still lingering on the sweat-stained armchairs after nightfall, listening to the chanting of the cicadas and marvelling at being in the depths of Africa. Wanting to hang on to our upbeat mood we stayed on in the shabby establishment for a proper meal, leaving the bread for later. George came to find us and took us back to spend a very peaceful night with the luxury of a bed each that wasn't made of concrete.

### 22nd November

Breakfast was coffee and a ham sandwich, another treat for us compared to chlorinated water and bananas squashed onto bread if we were lucky. Work started on the car an hour later.

They glued one rear-suspension bump stop back into position and replaced the other with a part salvaged from a wrecked Dodge. Thousands of miles of awful roads had given these protective blocks a machine-gun hammering, starting with the Saharan *piste*, and it was a miracle that the leaf springs hadn't broken. Another fist-sized hole in the chassis was welded. Oil, water, brake and clutch fluid levels were all topped-up and our long-suffering car was once again ready for its next onslaught. The wheel alignment could have done with some attention but would have to wait.

The next two days would bring local festivities to celebrate the anniversary of Independence. Like our New Year it would involve the consumption of copious quantities of drink. The Greeks advised us against passing through the Congo customs until three days hence by which time the effects of alcohol would have worn off. Having already suffered at the hands of drunken officials we welcomed the chance for a rest, and celebrated with a long overdue wash.

Late in the morning our hosts left to visit one of their coffee plantations, and we waited until early evening for their return. There was nothing for us to do or organise and the enforced rest was bliss. The cook would prepare dinner for us – roast beef, beans, salad and chips – a feast that brought reality to some of our hungry fantasies. Their kindness knew no bounds, and when we left they refused payment for the work done on the car.

We managed about thirty miles on bad but not impossible roads with the only distraction and diversion being around an enormous spider about the size of a child's hand sitting in the middle of the track. We poked the poor thing with the end of an umbrella and luckily for us it didn't retaliate.

## 23rd November

Sleeping in the car again came hard after the comfort of a proper bed, not least because of invading mosquitoes. We stretched limbs stiff from an uncomfortable night, washed out dry mouths with the hated chlorinated water and set off. Big trucks had not used the roads we were on, so driving wasn't too difficult in the absence of deep ruts. When we felt hungry we looked for a market but all trade had stopped because of the holiday. An old man carrying a branch of bananas was making his way up the road so we stopped the car and walked back to him offering to buy some. He looked threatened and backed away. We tried to gesture friendship but he kept hurrying away, and finally cried out something which sounded pretty desperate so we gave up and left him in peace.

Later we had more success in a village where an eager young man disappeared for a few minutes then emerged with an enormous branch of very ripe fruit. The bananas were falling off as he walked towards us. Because of language difficulties it seemed easier to buy the whole lot, but we doubted if we'd get through them all before they rotted. We could manage on banana sandwiches for at least one day after the good food in Isiro.

Ten miles from Faradje we had to slow down for a tribe of Vervet monkeys sitting in the road. They had strayed from nearby Garamba National Park. Continuing into the town we met up with the young Greeks from Isiro again. They had been visiting the game park and enjoying a break from work. We drove on to Aba.

As usual our first thought on arrival was a cold drink, so we asked for directions to the hotel. We parked outside and I was preparing to clamber out of the driver's door in my customary undignified fashion. A van drew up beside us and the European inside told us there were no cold drinks at the hotel, but to follow him.

No longer surprised by this welcome, we arrived at Costas' house, missives were relayed to the kitchen, and a small but mature Congolese cook wearing an apron appeared with a tray of strong Greek coffee, some creamed rice and cinnamon, and apples. Japhet padded barefoot across the red polished concrete floor on broad dusty feet. He bowed as he laid the food down, and backed away from the table respectfully. A few minutes later a stream of invective drifted out from the direction of the kitchen. In his own territory the humble servant was loudly wielding his power over his own underlings.

Conversation became easier with everyone speaking English, and we were delighted to accept a room for the night. We sat around a huge sitting room sparsely furnished but with worn upholstered armchairs for everyone. An enormous snakeskin stretched nearly the height of the room at its middle. It continued the length of the wall and tapered to a point at the end of the adjacent one.

'I shot that python five years ago,' said Costas, 'It measured a full ten metres.' He added proudly. 'It was only about six steps from our front door, and when we cut it open there was a whole goat inside its belly.'

Later George's nephew, who we'd met in Isiro, appeared and we talked away the afternoon about travelling and living in Africa. The repair to the bump stop that had been done in Isiro had loosened again, so Ross also discussed with him the options for a temporary fix until we got to Kampala in Uganda. 'Temporary fixes' were seeing us through equatorial Africa as they had done when we crossed the Sahara.

The busy noise of saucepans drifted through from the kitchen followed by a harsh volley of shouts in the local dialect. Costas disappeared for ten minutes and shortly afterwards dinner was announced. Three barefoot Congolese silently laid out salad, potatoes, tomatoes, bread and feta cheese. Japheth cast a critical eye over the proceedings, and rearranged some of the dishes.

We made up a party of seven. This being our first Greek meze we didn't understand the need to pace ourselves through the meal, so our stomachs groaned when the first course was cleared away and we were faced with steak and chips, herring, and chicken in tomato sauce.

'And here is the Queen Mary,' announced Costas, as an enormous platter of spaghetti was carried to the table by two of the kitchen staff and put alongside the rest of the food.

Dessert of creamed rice and cinnamon finished off both the meal and us. To top it all we toasted each other with a glass of the liqueur Marie Brizard.

The organisation and sourcing of ingredients for what we'd just eaten must have been monumental. It was likely that all the fresh vegetables were home-grown, but the rest must have been brought in by special deliveries or by the Greeks themselves. The country's infrastructure was practically non-existent, the roads unreliable, and only good managers could enjoy a reasonable quality of living.

Between seven of us we ate about half of this feast, and we'd hardly dented the mound of spaghetti. Blatant over-catering gave Costas the reputation of a generous host and wise old Japheth knew that the remainder would be left for him to share out between the staff and their families. It was a game that was played out all over the colonies, even after independence, in a silent agreement to let both sides win. Costas disappeared again into another room.

Sitting back replete after the marathon food fest the subject of war atrocities came up again. We sat out on the veranda to a shrill chorus of crickets, and moths throwing themselves against the yellow lights above our heads. During the uprising in 1964 the whites were attacked at night without warning in their homes. The rebels would burst out of the bushes with guns and dance around them. Their faces daubed with mud, and their bodies covered in leaves and feathers, to complete the picture they wore saucepans on their heads in an attempt to mimic military helmets. Their resulting comical appearance was a reality of horror. All the servants and factory workers ran into the bush when these trouble-makers arrived in town. Brutal men took what they wanted, helping themselves to food and women and generally throwing their weight around. The least show of resistance met with blows from fists and rifle butts. Dimitri showed us his deformed arm which had been repeatedly beaten with the butt of a rifle when he found himself in the way of an angry rebel. Driven out of their homes they watched helplessly from a distance for eight days as the order they had coaxed out of wilderness was trashed and vandalized. Treasured furniture shipped from Europe and painstakingly transported over miles of bush roads broke easily under hammer blows and burned with a strong flame under black cooking pots. The smell of roasting human flesh pervaded those eight gruesome evenings. Mostly it would be hapless villagers dragged out from their hiding places. Atrocities fuelled by the stash of Ouzo they had found in the Greeks' houses were the stuff of pre-dinner entertainment and gave the perpetrators an appetite for the meat of their victims. In Aba all of the nuns and missionaries had been killed and eaten. Raw fear forced many village boys to join the rag-tag army and most were never seen again.

A loud banging of saucepans made us jump and two Congolese men with their faces painted white and their bodies covered in leaves, leapt out of the shadows at Ross and me, grabbing my arms. They had tin cans on their heads and carried bows and arrows as they danced around us.

'What's going on?' I gasped, completely taken by surprise and adrenaline already pumping around my system, the pictures of torture, rape and murder fresh in my mind. Ross looked equally confused and had jumped to his feet. We both looked to our host for an explanation and saw Costas' shoulders shaking and a hand covered his mouth. The men then all started laughing aloud at their staged joke. Costas had dressed up the staff to re-enact the rebel intrusion. We were grateful they hadn't left us to face the scene alone and at least there were no guns involved.

Costas talked again about the violent chaos they had survived. Greek traders and businessmen kept out of politics, and they all managed to escape into the bush with minor injuries. From there some managed to flee the country, but our stalwart hosts had stayed. Not knowing how long their ordeal would last, they lay low until the rebel forces moved on to their next target. Most of their businesses and properties were ransacked or destroyed and they lost everything, as did all the European settlers. Men had started returning to get things up and running again, and it would be a while before they had any female company. Those few women and children who had come from Greece to be with them had mercifully been sent back to Europe at the first sign of trouble.

At the end of the evening Costas presented us with an ivory snail as a souvenir of the Congo. We didn't enquire about its provenance but his generosity touched us and the next day he also pressed a kilo of coffee beans from his plantation into my hands. Another night in a comfortable bed made us feel properly pampered.

24<sup>th</sup> November

We enjoyed a light breakfast, and then I stayed in the house while Ross went to see about more car repairs. I heard raucous singing and went to the window in time to see a lorry crammed full of Congolese men and women going past, celebrating the anniversary of Mobutu's coming to power with everyone already the worse for drink at ten o'clock in the morning.

'We would have been sailing from Southampton to Cape Town today if we'd stuck to our original plan.' I said to Ross when he returned.

'Yes, but think what we would have missed!' he replied.

In the afternoon Stavros took us to see his parents' soap factory, ransacked by the rebels in 1964. We stepped warily over weeds which had taken over the path, looking for snakes, and followed him into a bare echoing concrete building. All of the machinery and vehicles had been taken away or destroyed. He took some photos then we headed for his old house, now inhabited by a Congolese family. At the entrance the pungent perfume of Frangipani hit us, and we spotted the surviving plant reaching up from a tangle of weeds defiantly producing fragrant waxy flowers in the chaos. A turbulent bougainvillea clambered high and wild over an adjacent Mopane tree, and the remnants of a stone wall guarded thin leggy geraniums with tiny red blooms that hinted at once carefully tended flower beds. Not a stick of furniture remained and the cold ashes of a cooking fire lay in the middle of the 'sitting room'. A malodorous heap of accumulated rubbish and what smelt like sewage was piled up in a corner and a listless young woman sat on the floor with a rag-clad baby clinging to her breast. Stavros greeted her and she nodded and looked away. His lovely house had gone to ruin, and acknowledging his painful memories we returned in silence to Costa's house to wait for dinner.

Still waiting for the festivities to finish we enjoyed another lazy afternoon, decadently taking showers and chatting away the hours. Stavros appeared later on and presented us with a finely carved ivory antelope as yet another souvenir of the Congo. We protested at such generosity, but he was determined to spoil us. At dusk Japhet had disappeared for the celebrations, so Andreas commissioned his own cook to prepare the next feast for us all.

Another evening of good food worked wonders on our deprived systems with dolmas, (spiced meat and rice rolled up in cabbage leaves and served with yoghurt), steak, vegetables and chips.

### 25th November

Having been thoroughly fed, watered and rested by our wonderful hosts, we said farewell and made an early start. They had made our memories of the Congo a good experience instead of the horror we'd expected and we couldn't thank them enough. Fearing evil in this country we had found nothing but kindness.

The longer but less risky road took us north onto higher ground then east to Faradje. By this time midday was approaching but our bellies were still full and we didn't waste much time looking for bread. We did manage to buy cigarettes to keep us going, and used up the last of our local currency on a badly needed pair of shorts for Ross. The roads had already improved and promised to continue to do so. With the prospect of better roads ahead in East Africa Ross decided to off-load the second sand-ladder and we deposited it in a ditch at the roadside. It wouldn't be long before someone would claim it and put it to good use. I got back into the car by my own door at last. At Aba close to the border with Sudan we turned south once more.

Again apprehensive, we approached the customs at Aru, but as before they were efficient and very friendly with no hint of trouble at all.

# CHAPTER FOURTEEN

## *Big Blue Skies*

As a country which used to be part of the British Commonwealth with the Queen's head printed on the corner of its stamps, we relaxed for the Ugandan customs and expected a smooth entry. The stamps represented 'Kenya, Uganda and Tanganyika' and two of those countries had kept the same name. Feeling on home ground we expected no real threats to lurk in the string of countries which had been the stuff of geography lessons, and we looked forward to a psychological turning point.

Before the horrors of Amin's administration and long enough after the Mau-Mau uprising we regarded East Africa as safe. This might have been true, but didn't exclude irritation

The customs officer acknowledged us and promptly disappeared to make us wait for over an hour while he enjoyed a late lunch. As in the Embassies and Consulates around Grosvenor Square in London prior to our departure, we felt small and powerless in the face of officialdom.

Swallows which had departed Europe at the same time as us would not have to suffer the indignity of enforced waiting. They would be soaring through skies further south by now, diving and swooping for South African insects.

The minutes moved sluggishly, and away from the protection of thick Congo forests hot sunshine increased our irritation. A lizard darted across the dusty compound outside the customs house and stopped dead, motionless. He caught a fly in one swift movement and jumped on to a rock digesting his mouthful with sudden head jerks. The freshly fed official reappeared and gave us a look to make us feel like his next victims.

'Entry Permits, please!' He demanded. We flustered through our papers, brain-numbed in the heat. With evident satisfaction he found we had none.

Unaware of this requirement, we had been advised that our British passports would be sufficient for an ex-Commonwealth country. After eight years of independence the Ugandan officer relished the power he had over us children of his former masters. He soon admitted we didn't need an entry permit but 'sorry' was not part of his vocabulary.

President Obote looked down from his picture on the white-washed office wall. Sir Frederick Watesa, King of the Baganda tribe had enjoyed the first presidency for four years before Milton Obote deposed him in a struggle typical of emerging African nations. Another four years had passed and Obote still held on to his precarious position as an African Head of State, but it would only be for a few more weeks. We didn't realise at the time how close we'd come to being caught up in the chaos of a military coup.

Form-filling followed a thorough car search. This man was determined to find something wrong. We were unusual customers and he was suspicious.

Knowing we wouldn't be seeing another Scottish winter for three years we had taken our warmer clothes to donate to a Salvation Army store before we left home. Oxfam shops had yet to arrive in Edinburgh. We lugged two holdalls down past the Greyfriars' Bobby statue into a cold stone building and down a dark passageway where clothes hung ready for distribution to the homeless of the Grassmarket and other unfortunates of the city. The Salvationist rooted through our bundles. She took out three items from about forty, and pushed the rest back across the rough wooden counter.

'These are the only ones we can pass on,' she announced coldly.

There was no other tactful way to put it and, mortified, we took our rejected garments away. Afterwards we realised some smartening up was in order and had gone shopping for new summer clothes.

'Have you anything to declare?' asked the Ugandan officer.

'No,' said Ross.

'What about new clothes?'

'Yes we do have a few,' I admitted foolishly.

I rummaged in bags and soon realised our purchases back home had been used and abused for the last six weeks and now looked far from new.

His look was as haughty as the Salvationist's. We got away two hours later, and lost another hour in the new time zone.

In Arua town centre we soon had local money for the tenth country of our journey. Petrol and food were easy to find, but with a poor exchange rate we would have to shop wisely.

The luxury of rolling over tarmac roads again felt heavenly and open country a treat after more than three weeks of dark, damp vegetation. Shortly before the border we had gained altitude and the improved clarity of thought that came with cooler air energised and lifted us. The rest of our journey promised to be much the same at high altitude and we relaxed a little in that reassuring thought. We left the oppression of humid lowlands to memory and allowed our nerves to slacken a little.

On through Pakwach and Masindi in the twilight hour we crossed the Albert Nile. We watched a beautiful sunset in dreamy silence having missed colourful farewells to the day since central Nigeria. Birds preparing for a night's rest flapped dazzling wings towards dark trees and broke the still air with shrill warnings into the forest. The rumble of a truck disturbed the peace and as it faded to nothing the humming dusk took over. We would have stayed longer to savour the moment but mosquitoes soon forced us to move on, twirling our wrists in unison over the window handles.

We ventured into a darkening Uganda and passed the edge of a game park where a herd of elephants grazed ten yards from the roadside. In the distance we could just make out a herd of buffalo in a dust cloud, standing with turned heads, cow-like and dangerous. Our first taste of big game viewing held us in awe. In fading light I saw a lion skulking through the bushes, but perhaps I imagined it. Later the headlights picked out herds of impala leaping away from us in elegant flight.

Soon pitch darkness let us pick up speed without the distraction of sights, but Ross proceeded with caution, wary of colliding into unannounced animals.

'Can you hear a noise?' I asked, trying to work out what it could be. 'It sounds like heavy traffic.'

A thunderous and consistent roar was getting louder as we drove.

'No, it's too constant,' Ross replied, 'Have a look at the map. Is there a waterfall nearby?'

I switched on the courtesy light and reached for the map. We had to be close to Lake Albert and heading for Kampala which sat at the north end of Lake Victoria. I located Murchison Falls where the entire volume of the Victoria Nile is forced through a six-metre rock cleft before plunging one hundred and thirty feet and rushing on to Lake Albert. But our road crossed the Albert Nile much further north. Could the roar of tumbling water travel over fifteen miles? None the wiser we saw nothing and pressed on, missing the chance to see another sight. Funds and time were running out, we had to keep rolling on and couldn't afford the luxury of gathering moss.

## 26th November

*Coo coo, coo coo.* A dove was my gently insistent wake-up call. I opened my eyes. My legs hurt, and I gingerly felt over the bumps of mosquito bites wondering if they'd become infected. I could feel the scars where Id scratched them during my sleep. *Chakera chakera chakera* sounded through the bushes from a brigade of partridge. They jerked into view pecking at plants and insects in a foray over sparse ground, smart in striped uniforms. The cool stillness of morning transfixed me with its peacefulness. No leaves stirred and no clouds stained the sky. *Chakera chakera chakera.* The brigade moved methodically around every bush, ever pecking, ever wary. Ross stirred, a car sped past, and the partridge ran launching themselves into heavy flight with a loud feather flutter. It was time to raise our seats to the upright position. I forgot about my legs and reached for the map.

It was still morning when we arrived in Kampala, and we found a clean, modern city with flowering trees lining every street. Our heads which had been fogged by heat and humidity for so long cleared in the freshness that came with twelve hundred metres altitude. In spite of being close to the equator the feel of constant English summers made the capital a magnet for Europeans.

A young couple on a scooter spun around a large city roundabout laughing. The girl's long blonde hair streamed behind her lightly tanned shoulders and she clung to the driver as he turned off and away from the city on a joy ride. We had seen very few northern Europeans in Africa until now and nothing approaching this breed. Chingola would be on a similar altitude and our enthusiasm to get there was revived. To our naïve eyes Kampala looked like Utopia.

The city had been built on hills, all bearing witness to history. On one the kings of the Baganda people had established their court long before colonial times; Captain Lugard, the representative of the British colonial company had his fort built on the one opposite; and various missionaries established themselves on other hilltops. Kampala grew alongside the development of cash-crop agriculture from the beginning of the century. It soon became a trading centre benefiting from increasingly good harvests of coffee, tea and cotton. By 1931, when the costly Uganda Railway finally reached Kampala from Mombasa, it was on track to rival Nairobi. Called the Iron Snake by Africans the railway revolutionised and opened up East Africa.

The peaceful exterior of the capital apparent to our unsuspecting youth did not betray the unhappy rumblings under the surface. Uganda was about to spew out Africa's latest despot. Forty-five year old Idi Amin had found himself out of favour with Obote at the time of our arrival. The president had enjoyed Amin's support over the years but a power struggle was underway and feeling threatened he had recently removed Amin from his powerful command positions. Unfazed by his loss of power, Amin, in preparation for such a fallout had already been recruiting from his own Kakwa tribe   He was born in Arua of a mother who became a camp follower of the British colonial King's African Rifles. Amin joined the same regiment as a cook. Having plenty of brawn as a boxing light heavyweight champion he rose up the ranks despite a lack of education, showing great leadership qualities. At thirty-four he gained the rank of *effendi*, a position specially created by the colonial army for capable noncommissioned Africans, and this led to further promotion. Three years later troops under Amin's command committed the Turkana Massacre. They had been sent to suppress cattle stealing by Kenyan tribesmen over the border and the Turkanas were tortured, beaten to death and, in some cases, buried alive. Amin should have been court-martialled, but with Uganda's independence imminent, it was overlooked.

A few weeks after we crossed the country, Amin discovered Obote intended to arrest him on charges of misappropriating millions of dollars of military funds. So while Obote was out of the country attending the Commonwealth Conference in Singapore, Amin staged a successful coup that was later reported to have been backed by Israel and welcomed by the British. We had unwittingly avoided disaster by a fine margin and later watched in horror with the rest of the world as events and atrocities unfolded over the following eight years.

In a road lined with stately jacaranda we found the Chrysler garage and discovered that our warranty had run out at six thousand miles. Our faint hopes of having work done on the shock absorbers or gear box under the guarantee evaporated. Our dejection at this bit of unwelcome news must have been obvious to the garage owner. On top of this disappointment, my legs ached again and I could feel them swelling up. I felt miserable.

As we discussed the problematic car parts Ross offered him a cigarette

'No thank you,' he replied, 'I had to give up. My doctor said I would be dead in six months if I kept on smoking. Until a month ago I used to get through two packets a day.'

'That must have been hard,' I sympathised.

'I had no choice,' he said matter-of factly, 'It was difficult for four days,' he explained, 'but I only ate fruit during that time, and afterwards it has been okay. I feel much better already.'

This sounded like an effective cure that I should try one day soon. It could also help our budget, but our nerves weren't ready for such a challenge yet. We lit up our cigarettes and inhaled the calming smoke.

Enchanted by our adventurous journey, and no doubt out of pity, the Indian manager offered to replace the bump stop free of charge. He refilled the gear box oil, changed the engine oil and fixed the wheel alignment too, smiling graciously as we delivered our thanks. One of the garage mechanics, also an Indian, had spent two years in Paisley.

'You'll be missing the Scotch mist then?' he asked with unexpected Glaswegian undulations in his voice.

Scotch mist was one thing we certainly didn't miss, and his cheeriness lightened our mood.

Our funds had dropped dangerously low, but we felt a shift in attitude to our journey here from which we could possibly benefit. Instead of shaking heads of disapproval, our story was bringing a favourable reaction. In fact we had to be a good bet for sponsorship having proved ourselves capable of covering the riskiest areas of our route. That afternoon Ross decided to approach some petrol companies. Our prayers were answered and a representative from Mobil duly obliged. Thirty five gallons of petrol were pumped into the tank and all five jerry cans in return for three advertising stickers being attached to the car.

'Well that has just paid for a few hundred more miles,' said Ross. 'Perhaps we should try the local newspaper for sponsorship?'

'I think I saw some Dunlop offices in town somewhere. Perhaps they would be interested too?' I added.

But losing our focus and finding the energy to persuade sponsors soon lost its appeal. We left the Mobil garage after closing time feeling at ease with the pressure off our budget. In fact we felt comfortable enough not to pursue further funding preferring the chance to put another day's mileage behind us rather than risk the uncertainty of more success. We headed east out of the city glad to be back on track.

Our journey took us through Jinja, the home town of an old friend of Ross's family so we decided to look him up. The fertile land around the town and close to Lake Victoria, Africa's largest lake, made for rich pickings by its owners, and he was one of them. Huge plantations of cash crops, including sugar cane, coffee, cotton, and tobacco fruitfully gave big payback and further benefited from intensive cheap labour.

'There's a train running between those fields,' I said, surprised.

Uganda's railway ran alongside the plantations and the planters had installed their own tracks next to the crops to connect with the main line.

For the last forty years it had been compensating the land-locked country by efficiently whisking harvests to coastal towns on the Indian Ocean and onwards to rich markets of the east and west. Labelled the 'Lunatic Express' by the British press when huge government investment was made at the end of the 19th century and many lives were lost during its construction, the railway opened up East Africa for future settlers and trade. Until that time pioneers and prospectors were restricted to following the old slave routes.

In 1970 most of the plantations in Jinja were owned and managed by Indians, some staying on after building the railway. Africans call them *muhindi*, while white people are known as *mzungu*.

'We'd better smarten ourselves up if we're to meet Raj,' said Ross. 'We can't turn up on his doorstep looking all clarty!'

He examined dirty fingernails and looked in the driver's mirror rubbing his stubbly chin.

We drew up at the roadside under a glorious Tulip tree for a scrub up, then a discreet change into clean clothes, a brush of unruly hair and our best efforts to look respectable. We had very little water left in our container, so only our faces, hands and lower arms, the visible bits, got washed and Ross managed a cursory shave.

We found the company offices in the early evening but failed to get in touch with Raj in spite of the staff making numerous phone calls. Ross accompanied Ashish to Raj's grand house. A uniformed maid answered the doorbell.

'He is not here,' she informed him.

'Will he be back tomorrow?' asked Ross.

She shrugged and held out her hands before closing the heavy ornate door.

The office boys cheerfully offered to show us around the estate instead, but touring had ceased to be a pleasurable pursuit for us. They chatted with us for a couple of hours and treated us to sweet potato chips sprinkled with chilli powder.

Leaving Jinja and looking forward to approaching the next country we remembered the problems we had at the Ugandan border. We had forgotten to check about entry permits for Kenya and Tanzania while we were in Kampala. British citizenship did not necessarily grant us immunity from local red tape, so we retraced our journey. Annoyed with ourselves for our forgetfulness, it was not the evening we had planned heading straight for the next country. Having the stickers on the car, we parked outside a Mobil garage for the night, feeling that they gave us this entitlement with the added benefit of using their facilities in the morning. We wouldn't normally have parked so indiscreetly in a city.

I rubbed my legs gently. The swelling was worse; both legs throbbed and hurt to touch. Bites were on top of bites, and my legs had hundreds. Perhaps sleep would help.

## 27th November

An arrow pointed to the Immigration Office at the entrance to the British High Commission. The appropriate officer wasn't there, a frustrating discovery after we had battled with their bureaucracy and wasted an hour on top of the journey back to Kampala. He finally turned up to confirm our original assumption that we didn't need additional papers when we had British passports anyway. Our application fee was refunded and we left, a bit heated. Thanks to a disagreeable customs officer two days earlier we had been running round in circles.

The low of the night before still dogged me, and sleep hadn't lessened the swelling.

At Jinja we tried again to get in touch with Raj but still without success, so continued to Tororo just before the frontier. When all Asians were exiled from the country by Amin we wondered if such an astute businessman had already felt the rumblings of trouble in the corridors of power. He might have been busy making appropriate arrangements at the time of our visit. Asian businesses formed the backbone of the Ugandan economy, and Amin seized all their property but allegedly Raj had left the country with less than £1 in his bank account.

Our funds looked healthier after getting free petrol, so a few Ugandan shillings remained in the kitty even after stocking up with food. We bought some airmail letters and stamps and caught up with correspondence to reassure our anxious parents.

I wrote:-

'...Hope to reach Kitwe on Saturday 4<sup>th</sup> December (still beat the ship)
Got some free car servicing in Kampala and hope to get more in Nairobi.
... You'll probably be relieved that we're out of the Congo, but we reckon we had less trouble there than in most of the previous African countries. The roads weren't too bad because the rains had stopped for 2 weeks – very lucky.
Still got £85 left to last us a week. Not bad going.
I hope that you'll get a telegram saying we've arrived, shortly after this letter. Feel that we're almost there now....'

I wrote this letter almost as a telegram, such was the need for haste, and I was obsessed with the cost of everything because we felt we had to justify everything to my father, our 'guarantor' as well as counting every penny to let us survive to reach our destination. The letter paints a prettier picture of the Congo than the reality, and perhaps they were wise enough to realise.

Using up our Ugandan money bought us the luxury of cold drinks and ice cream to give us a lift, and some chocolates to take to the Mistrys in Nairobi. One of their sons had lived with Ross's family in Edinburgh while he pursued his studies, and we had met the whole family before. They had introduced us to mangoes. Our traditionally British visiting gift was less than ideal, being expensive and likely to melt.

We put both sides of the frontier behind us without incident, on through Eldoret and an hour later we crossed the equator marked by a large painted sign.

'But it's really chilly!' I said, 'and not what I'd have expected at the equator.'

'Don't forget we've been climbing for ages,' said Ross, 'we must be at roughly seven thousand feet above sea level by now!'

I rooted around in the back of the car for jumpers which we'd discarded long ago. Later the blanket which had last seen service in the Sahara became a necessity again to let us sleep comfortably in the chill. My legs stubbornly remained swollen and sore.

## 28th November

Still on high ground our route took us through Nakuru to skirt around Lake Naivasha. We delighted in sightings of giraffe walking in apparent slow motion unafraid of the car at twenty yards distance. Ross slowed the engine to marvel at huge steaming dollops of animal droppings. They had to mean elephants nearby, but although we strained our eyes searching we couldn't see any. We stopped for a late breakfast but the real feast was for our eyes. Sitting at a high vantage point, miles of Kenya stretched out over the Great Rift Valley below our feet.

We soon arrived at Nairobi on good roads unaffected by recent rain. Wafts of flower scents drifted through our open windows. The young town approached its seventieth year and was emerging fresh and new, a larger version of the older Kampala. Following a long leafy avenue of flat-topped Flamboyant trees we made our first stop at the Chrysler garage to look for a Mr Turner, but his office was closed. Next we tried the General Post Office with the hope of tracing the Mistry's address since we only knew the box number. This proved difficult since the GPO didn't keep residential addresses, and the phone book offered no help either.

'Can I be of assistance?' Asked a smart elderly British expatriate lady. She had overheard some of our conversation, and we explained the problem to her.

'Do you know what Mr Mistry does?' She asked

'Yes he's in the building trade,' replied Ross, 'and his son is an architect.'

'Well if you'd like to wait here while I finish my shopping, I'll see what I can do.' We waited patiently as she went into the shop next to the post office and bought a few groceries which she placed carefully into her basket.

'All right then, now come with me,' she instructed, and we followed her like schoolchildren into another building. She approached a man at a desk and asked for the telephone number of a building contractor she knew.

'Try telephoning this man, he should be able to help you. Everyone knows everyone else here in Nairobi and I expect you'll soon find your friend through this contact.'

We thanked her and followed her directions for a bank to stock up on Kenyan currency, making sure we had change for a phone box.

We squeezed into a phone box outside a café. I held out the coins for Ross to feed into the unfamiliar machine. But Ross pushed the wrong button and the returned money shot out too quickly for us to catch before it slid under the metal grille of the floor. Once we'd retrieved the coins, it took only four telephone calls to contact Lakshman, the Mistry's eldest son, who happened to be working in a building next to the café! I struggled up the stairs on aching legs behind Ross into Lakshman's office. He started to arrange a hotel for us since his house was full up with visitors.

'You don't need to do that,' said Ross, wary of expensive accommodation. 'We'll sleep in the car as usual.'

'You have been sleeping in the car for seven weeks?' He was aghast.

'Don't worry we always find a quiet spot,' Ross tried to reassure him.

'But you mustn't risk that in Nairobi, it isn't safe! I'll pay for it, don't worry.'

Lakshman then insisted on taking us to a hotel set in well-tended gardens on the outskirts of the town, and we didn't put up much resistance. We wondered what he might have thought about some of the places where we camped for the night.

'Habari bwana. Habari Bibi. Karibu.' The doorman greeted us with a Swahili welcome as we entered the relaxed hotel.

This was luxury to us at any time, and after weeks of travelling a dream come true. Just to be there felt like therapy. As soon as our luggage had been installed we took it in turns to wallow in the ensuite shower. But cleanliness couldn't undo the pain in my legs and I slumped into a chair feeling unable to walk. Adrenaline had stopped flowing through me as soon as I relaxed. The accumulation of mosquito bites had taken its toll, and my legs were so swollen and sore that standing up was beyond my capability. Logic took flight along with my imagination and I convinced myself I'd contracted some debilitating disease like polio. Safe in the luxury of a hotel room in this English-speaking country self-pity overwhelmed me. I let my stiff upper lip slacken and burst into tears. Something would have to be done. When Ross contacted Lakshman later that afternoon he asked about seeing a doctor. It was arranged immediately and I soon had a prescription for a good rest along with penicillin tablets for infected bites. Since the doctor lived in the flat below the Mistry's we climbed the stairs to meet Lakshman's family. My legs felt fit to burst. Afterwards he took us to a chemist to collect my prescription.

Back at the hotel I swallowed the first antibiotic and collapsed on to the bed while Ross started to have a good sort out of our things, even tidying the car! Later we used the opportunity to relax, walk in the gardens amongst exotic birds and remember what civilisation felt like. In the evening I sipped lemonade and Ross enjoyed a Tusker beer before a proper dinner amongst smart diners.

## 29th November

By morning the antibiotics and a good night's sleep between crisp cotton sheets had started to work, convincing me that I would not lose the use of my legs. A delicious breakfast with napkins and plates, smiling waiters and flowers on the table helped too. We started with a choice of tropical fruits including my now favourite paw-paw, then a wide choice of cooked foods including a full English breakfast, but also fried plantains and Indian curries. Overcome by the unaccustomed variety we tried a little of everything new to us.

A souvenir stall set up close to the dining room displayed an extensive array of Africana, so we stepped out accompanied by birdsong to wander over and 'just have a look.' We spoke to one of the traders and discovered he would trade his carvings for second-hand clothes if we had no money to spare. Seeing we were still resistant to buying he gave us a carved antelope each. He perhaps knew that Ross would immediately go back to our room for one of his newly washed towelling shirts which was still in reasonable condition. Ross had done some washing the night before in an effort to present a smarter appearance for the hotel. We couldn't stretch our budget to the laundry service, and would have been ashamed to do so anyway.

Several American peace-corps recruits were staying at the hotel before moving to teaching posts in local schools. Their youthful enthusiasm spilled over and we enjoyed spending time with them. Another young couple from Switzerland had recently come from the Luanshya mine in Zambia and we jumped at the opportunity to talk to them.

'We were glad to leave Zambia, the local people are dishonest and lazy,' moaned the husband, 'and we didn't like the Mine accommodation,' added his wife.

Since we had pinned our hopes on the next few years being good ones, we didn't like the way the conversation was going so we avoided the disgruntled couple afterwards. A positive approach would be instrumental in seeing us through the last lap of our journey and we couldn't afford to put it in jeopardy.

Lakshman arrived and treated us to a tour of Nairobi in his car. He worked as an architect, so showed us new constructions, a 'rich-man's' housing development, and the buildings his father had constructed. We stopped at a very grand hotel for a drink then returned to his house for lunch. The women were creating dishes from exotic foods and spices in the kitchen. Never had I seen so many ingredients going into one dish. They chatted and laughed as they stirred and tasted, but when the meal was served to us in the dining room, they didn't eat with us. I sat with Ross, Lakshman and his father at the table thinking that the women were probably having more fun in the kitchen. They had made a specially-mild curry for our western palates and we enjoyed delicious new tastes.

Back at the hotel we slumped in chairs for the rest of the evening to watch television showing Peyton Place, and the Val Doonican show, an incongruous mix thousands of miles from home.

## 30<sup>th</sup> November

'Hakuna matata,' smiled the receptionist at the garage, 'It's Swahili for don't worry and enjoy life'

We had expressed impatience for the car to be fixed. The end was in sight, we'd had a taste of luxury which left us with little enthusiasm for the rest of our journey, and our irritation showed. The reminder to relax was timely.

We arranged a service for the car, but first they gave it an unrequested and through clean inside and out, making our lives a great deal more comfortable. We were glad Ross had taken the trouble to empty the back seat and leave everything in our hotel room. The oil seal in the gear box was renewed and the oil filter changed while we sat in the manager's office. The manager and his wife gave us a lift back to the city centre.

Lakshman wasn't to be found in his office, so we had lunch outside a café next to a sprawling acacia tree. Soon conversation became impossible as hundreds of weaver birds descended on the tree to check on their dangling nests. The noise they made was deafening, so we didn't linger. Ross paid the bill and we wandered off to pick up a flavour of Nairobi and use my recovering legs a little. I wasn't ready or well enough and although we had time for sightseeing, one of our few chances evaporated like all the other opportunities throughout our trip. We needed every reserve of time, strength and money for the journey without distractions.

That evening Lakshman's father accompanied us to the garage, and on arrival marched in with us, looking as if he was going to cause trouble. Once he had satisfied himself that the work was being done properly he left, and fortunately the manager didn't look at all perturbed by this onslaught. Extensive work was done on the car for the princely sum of ten pounds. This was obviously cut-price as a special favour, and we suspected had more than a little to do with Mr Mistry's visit.

We shopped for flowers to give Mrs. Mistry, finding that unlike chocolates flowers made a splendid gift. We settled on a huge bunch of pink and white orchids which would have cost a mortgage in Britain.

'Two mangoes, please,' I ordered in the fruiterer next-door.

'And what are those black wrinkly fruit?' I asked.

We were offered a taste. It was passion fruit, a new one on us, juicy and full of seeds. We bought four.

The flowers were admired, and saying a fond farewell to the Mistry family we went on our way. My health was returning after three days of recuperation, and Ross couldn't wait to get going again. We found Nairobi to be the grandest and most civilised of cities on our journey. Lakshman had shown us the wealthier side of the city, but the people also appeared to be better fed and dressed than other places we'd visited.

We left Nairobi feeling stronger than when we arrived, but still travel-weary and anxious to reach our goal. The doorman saluted us for the last time after lunch and Ross pulled out of the car park, both of us still hungry for the luxury of hotel accommodation we were leaving behind.

Immediately south of the city the Athi plains drew us in and we passed through a fence into Nairobi National Park, Kenya's first. Looking back across grasslands I watched a regal giraffe strolling across our tracks with its outline against the disappearing skyscrapers of the city behind us. Ross drove slowly and we rediscovered game-spotting. More giraffe nibbling the top of an acacia tree watched us watching them. Three sturdy zebra thundered away from the road and abruptly stopped to turn and look accusingly at us for disturbing their grazing. Few other cars on the road ruptured the peaceful scene. We felt back on track with our eyes on the road ahead.

While the roar of our vehicle in motion ensured our safety, stopping for any length of time was not advisable. The story of a Dutch couple who chose to spend the night in the park served as a warning. Elephants came to investigate their car in the darkness, turning it over with their tusks and trunks with curiosity. Two hyenas followed and scratched at the doors sensing injury and fear, wanting to exercise their vicious jaws. A ranger found the unhappy pair the next morning alive but badly shaken in a vehicle damaged beyond repair.

Darkness gathered as we approached a herd of matriarchs with their young. The elephants stood stolidly on the road swishing their tails, and the two largest turned to fix us with warning stares demanding we kept our distance. Aunts and sisters surrounded the littlest, and with slow deliberation they turned off the road, unhurried but cooperative, towards a startling sunset. Tail-end Charlotte waved her trunk gently in our direction, as appreciation of us keeping our distance or as a warning, perhaps both. Their swaggering rears ambled westwards for fifty yards before Ross turned the engine back on. Charmed and delighted we headed out of the park now wary of inadvertently crashing into other animals on the road.

The risk of a puncture in the park didn't bear thinking about now the night was falling. Lions and hyenas would be on the prowl and we needed to get away. There was no clear delineation for the southern boundary so we drove until late evening just in case, long after our last game sighting.

# CHAPTER FIFTEEN

## *The Last Lap*

1st December

Under a sky of scattered white feathers the road through Kenya continued in excellent condition and we soon reached the border to enter Tanzania, the penultimate country of our travels. The feathers flew under the climbing sun's rays. Magnificent scenery past snow-capped Mount Kilimanjaro under a flawless blue sky with flat-topped trees and grazing impala in the foreground will stay forever in our minds' eye. A black and white picture taken with a cheap camera would have been an insult so we didn't regret our lack of film. The experience could be remembered with many a pictorial advertisement for the highlights of East Africa which would stir our memories every time with 'Do you remember when…?' The iconic vision of East Africa tried to hold on to us but lingering wasn't an option, our focus had never wavered and the miles had to be put behind us. We rolled on.

'We'll get to Chingola in no time on these roads,' I said looking forward to arriving. The track wasn't surfaced but had been well-maintained.

'Good old British administration!' said Ross. 'But we still have two thousand miles to go, be careful not to talk too soon.'

The road took us south through Arusha and on to Dodoma. Henry Morton Stanley had passed through this town nearly one hundred years earlier on his Great Trans-Africa Journey. We'd already crossed the route he took in his search for Livingstone, and would cross a third before we got to Iringa, the one he took for the 'Edwin Pasha relief expedition'.

Across the plain a gleam of light reflecting off metal made me focus on a lone figure standing erect and motionless beside a dozen long-horned cattle.

'I wonder who that is,' I said, pointing.

He didn't stir once as we got close and his noble fine-featured Maasai face regarded us in mild defiance. We stopped to say hello to make some contact with the proud warrior but he stood mutely staring at us, disdainful as he perched on one leg with the resting foot wedged against the other long sinewy thigh. Thin bony-backed cows raised their long-horned heads to stare, then shuffled back with a puff of dust to graze some more. White egrets disturbed by the cattle's movements fluttered up for a few seconds before resuming their meal of ticks from the animals' hides.

The upright spear we'd seen from afar catching the sun's reflection helped to balance the eternal length of him. A maroon 'kanga' swathed around his body kept the full strength of the elements off his lithe frame. Ear lobes stretched by beads almost reached his shoulders and a stiff queue came down from his coiffure to rest on the top of his spine. It had been reddened with ochre and fat to keep every lock of hair in place. Above his bare feet were bead anklets matching the ones around his head and neck. Like a highly-paid model every inch of him spoke perfection and he knew it. Sharp eyes flickered to keep watch over his herd, us strangers, and the horizon.

'Hello,' said Ross, stopping the car and expecting the usual friendliness of Africans on the road.

He studiously ignored us, and we left him as we found him.

My mind wandered back to childhood geography lessons and poring over an old text book which described their daily diet of blood mixed with curdled milk; of their leaping vertically to great heights from a standing position; of living in long low windowless huts called manyattas and their fierce war-like tendencies which kept them from ever being enslaved. I imagined that way of life had gone, but this Maasai warrior could have stepped out of those fingered pages. Once over the surprise of finding a tribal culture still alive and well, we looked out for a settlement or other members of the tribe, but he stood alone on the vast plain.

'It looks like the Maasai are still living the way they always have,' said Ross, 'I wonder if that includes drinking blood.'

'It must be hard for them to see how life is changing around them. The towns must be quite a culture shock.' I said, feeling sorry for them.

What had been the most revered and feared tribe in Africa a hundred years earlier now lived trying to hang on to their warrior values in the changing world of East Africa in 1970.

Apart from in some widely-spaced towns and villages we saw few people in this huge but sparsely populated country. A full tank of petrol plus the contents of the jerry cans kept our stops to a minimum and we had little opportunity to test our welcome from the Tanzanians as we sped along. Compared to other countries we'd crossed in our trip the relative civilisation in East Africa encouraged an aloofness and distance. We remembered the giggling friendliness of the Congolese pygmies when we struggled with mud and breakdowns. A lack of adversity kept us from being thrown in with people along the better roads.

The long strip of track which led us southwards joined another running west to the coast, and southeast to our destination. This arterial stretch through Tanzania from Dar-Es-Salaam on the coast to land-locked Zambia was known as the 'Hell Run'. It had become notorious for atrocious conditions caused by the pounding from huge trucks that drove its length. Although the road was much below the standard of those in Kenya, the weather conditions favoured us and the car managed it with ease, averaging nearly 700 miles per day, but with a bit of cheating.

A new road was being built, and seeing a pristine paved surface, we sneaked on to it while disregarding the no-entry signs and putting the miles behind us at a satisfying speed. We were soon to be thwarted however, and the first time it happened nearly had us catapulting down a steep bank.

'My God, that was a close shave,' Ross gasped with his foot still pressed hard on the brake after his emergency stop. 'So that's why there's 'No Entry' signs.'

Neither of us had been wearing seat belts so I had been thrown against the dashboard and Ross braced himself against the steering wheel.

In Britain wearing seat belts was still optional in 1970. The manual advised: -

*Develop the habit of wearing your seat belt whenever you use the car, on short local journeys as well as longer trips.*

*Keep the belts properly adjusted so that they are not slack. When not in use, make sure there are no loops hanging loose which might get shut in the door and damaged.*

The belts dangled in an annoying way and the 'loops' could easily catch a foot as you stepped out of the car. So instead of a dignified exit you were left struggling for balance and in danger of falling flat on your face. As often as not we tucked them behind our seats out of the way.

Seriously shaken but glad to be alive with the car intact we sat still for five minutes to recover from the shock and assess the damage. The bridges connecting the road had not yet been built, and since we should not have been there in the first place there were no road signs to warn us. We'd been lucky and Ross released the handbrake with his right hand to reverse away from our brush with disaster. We had to backtrack for several miles on the empty road until we found a track leading on to the old lumpy highway. Back on the 'Hell Run' we passed the point of the bridge-less chasm and after an hour of bumps and the strain of rough driving Ross grew impatient.

Undeterred by recent experience we made another guess to where we could link up with the new road again. Our seat belts were buckled around us, I clung tight to the side of my seat and our eyes were fixed on the road ahead for missing bridges at a more controlled pace than before. Several times we repeated this pattern of good stretch, bad stretch and once a construction crew warned us off with angry waves and shouts. Chastened, Ross stuck to the old road again for another couple of hours before risking it again. We liked to think our dangerous gambling approach speeded our journey and saved us from at least some of the lumpiest patches.

Four years earlier Times Magazine described the old road as follows: -

*The Great North Road that connects it (Zambia) —sort of—with Tanzania. Winding for more than 1,000 miles through rain forests, game plains and mountain ranges, the road may well be the world's worst international highway. Its dizzy hairpin turns were scraped out and levelled (often with dragged thorn bushes) by African tribesmen working off their tax debts. Along its flat stretches, the road is little more than a trail of treacherous sand or soap-slick mud. Black, blinding rains and eerie mists make it all but impassable from October to May, and the right-of-way is often usurped by two-ton rhinos, herds of elephant and lions basking in the sun. (Time magazine Fri Feb 25th 1966)*

The condition of the road didn't compare to what we'd experienced in Cameroon and the Congo, not to mention the Sahara, so we wondered what the fuss was about. Heavy rains we supposed must make a difference.

Once the last jerry can had been emptied petrol became difficult to find again and twice we almost ran out, but we completed two thousand miles in three hard-pressed days. Towns we passed through went by without a thought; we just needed to put the mileage behind us, finish our journey and get to Zambia. Arusha, Iringa, Mbeya and finally the border post at Tunduma became markers along our way. School children streamed out in one of these towns. The girls wearing royal blue and white dresses cradled books in their arms as they do worldwide. The boys strode along in white shirts with blue ties and grey shorts, regardless of their age. Some looked like grown men with thighs straining the seams of their shorts, and shaved chins above white collars. The younger children waved and cheered at us.

Entering Nakonde at the Zambian border a new excitement grew. We had reached the country of our destination. It was number thirteen, lucky for some. Never had we been asked to pay a bribe, a report often cited by others. We found Africans respond well to strength, a smile, a show of confidence, and patience, and somehow we had managed to find the right combination between us. A readiness to laugh also helped. Along our way we'd often been asked for 'presents,' usually expressed as 'Give me...' We found 'no' to be an acceptable answer, but we usually offered some token.

The car carried us into the land we'd call home for three years.

'What sort of house do you think they'll give us?' I asked.

Without the benefit of the Company induction in London we had no idea what to expect. Our standard of comfort had dropped so low we daren't raise our hopes too high, and remembered the complaints of the Swiss couple in Nairobi. We considered the humble dwellings at the roadside.

'We only had two rooms in Edinburgh, so we're not accustomed to much luxury. The company will provide furniture for us and it'll be a lot better than living in the car.' Ross replied. 'There'll be a garden too, I know that much.'

We sat quietly wondering.

'Dave and Sandra haven't complained,' he added.

This was a hopeful thought as we knew our friends expectations would be the same as our own. Since July when they began a new life in Kitwe, their up-beat letters never hinted at housing inadequacies.

All that remained was to drive through a few more towns and we would be there to find out the answer to my question. Our wheels could stop rolling and we could gather some moss. The bittersweet feeling of an ambition hard fought and finally achieved flooded over us. I felt emotional and tears welled up, possibly from relief.

Fighting an inclination to keep driving just to get there, which would mean arriving in the small hours, common sense prevailed and we parked for the night just past Serenje. I had difficulty in falling asleep. One morning back in London I had also been restless. I had arisen early and tuned Granny's ancient wireless to the new Radio One. Mungo Jerry was singing…

*'In the summertime when the weather is high*
*You can chase right up and touch the sky…'*

It made me think about our future in Africa. Some distant cousins lived in Salisbury, Southern Rhodesia. Their Christmas letters every year sometimes included photos. Against a backdrop of stripy lawns bordered by flowering bushes, groups of bronzed children in shorts and summer dresses smiled at the camera. Returning from school in the dark and cold to see those images made a deep impression, and I'd dreamed of being with them in their enchanted existence. It had looked like a land of perpetual summertime and holidays, and soon we would be living just a few hundred miles north of them.

Doves cooed, an early truck rumbled along the road a few yards away, and I opened my eyes to a pink glow rising on the skyline. Expectation of the day snapped me wide awake. Giving a fresh mosquito bite a cautious rub I looked in the gloom to my right. Ross had also woken before the light.

'It's only five o'clock,' he said. 'Shall we just go?'

'Yes, let's get there!' I replied. So we set off immediately with the enticing prospect of a bed for the night. I reached behind for the water bottle and we forced ourselves to drink the disgusting chlorinated liquid knowing this would be our last day to suffer it.

'Would you like something to eat?'

The thought of our habitual banana sandwich for a final breakfast in the car held no interest. Better things lay ahead and we did without.

Finding a quiet spot, Ross stopped for a call of nature. Morning sunshine dappled on grass under the trees, and a dove cooed insistently. I positioned myself so that a termite mound blocked the view of me from the road, without going too close to the mound itself which could be occupied and teeming with insects. As I checked for snakes and any other undesirables some scarlet flowers caught my eye. Their petals curved together from yellow bases, and the stamens stretched out beneath. They were Flame Lilies, the national flower of Zambia growing wild in the clearing. Gathering them would become one of our rituals on the run-up to Christmas every year, but for now that could wait.

The road junction at Kapiri Mposhi went left to the mining town of Kabwe, formerly Broken Hill, and on to Lusaka the capital. But for the first time in eight weeks our destination was not south and we turned right. We were getting closer to the place we'd be calling home for at least three years.

White people were staring at us.

We kept travelling up the straight road with a new Copperbelt life ahead. A good surface made driving easy, and showed the region's wealth, the riches of the mines which brought us here. I looked back at the staring people and saw glossy hair and neat clothes. Wives who would have plenty of time on their hands to comb and groom and attend to life's comforts while their husbands earned good money for skills not much found amongst Zambians.

We'd become accustomed to stares, and used to not having life's comforts, but hadn't seen so many white faces since leaving Europe nearly eight weeks before. I felt a self-consciousness seep through me reminiscent of the misunderstandings in Algeria, and pulled out a comb to tug at hair made dull and brittle from sun, dust, and a limited diet. I looked to my right at the wild curly mass of my husband's hair. It could no longer pass as a fashion statement, even in 1970, and his hollowed eyes told the rest of the story.

Twelve thousand miles lay behind us. We'd seen terrible terrain in the least stable countries on the planet. Our hunger for fresh sights and experiences lingered on, but a new hunger gnawed. An appetite for home-making, settling down, and starting a new life needed to be satisfied. With the end in sight our adrenaline was ebbing away. We had to stop and do some nesting.

Dense bush on either side blocked any views of the flat landscape. Barefoot men looked back at us with curiosity before they turned into gaps between dust-laden spindly trees. Women followed with lumpy bundles on their heads, poised and ever-patient to follow nimble-footed up the narrow path to their settlements. Eyes met fleeting eyes and on we drove.

Battered Peugeots used as taxis accounted for much of the traffic. The vehicles' ground clearance hung dangerously low under the weight of passengers crammed inside, their mysterious luggage piled high on the roof racks and bound by ropes. One had stopped at the roadside and two men stepped back from a gush of steam emanating from under a bonnet open wide like a hippo's yawn. Twelve passengers, mainly women and children, scattered around the verge in sullen groups.

I looked again at the occupants of the other cars who had made me uneasy. They drove Ford Cortinas, Capris and Anglias interspersed with an occasional sporty Triumph or MG, all shipped over from Britain free of tax and driven up from Cape Town. They turned to gawp and point at us on their Saturday drive out with the family.

It wasn't only the Mobil advertising stickers that set us apart in our ruined car. We were approaching Ndola and a large community of British expatriates, the biggest we'd come across in our journey through Africa and these people looked like we did before we left home. Our downward transformation had been so slow we hadn't noticed. Using river water to wash our clothes had given them a grey look, and smoothing them down with a flat hand could never disguise the lack of an iron. We had taken on the rough look of homeless people who don't sleep in a proper bed, and they had spotted it. With a few exceptions, inadequate funds made beds an unaffordable comfort. If it hadn't been for the advertising stickers, the Mobil sponsorship put on in Kampala, our budget would not have stretched to get us this far.

It wasn't yet eight o'clock, so to kill time and avoid arriving too early at our friends' house we stopped at a roadside café on the outskirts of Kitwe, a mining town thirty miles south of Chingola.

'Sit at a table and you'll be served,' said the waitress with a toss of her back-combed blonde hair.

Metal tables and chairs, the clattering of plates being stacked behind the counter and low morning voices struck a familiar note, but no freshly ground aromas graced the echoing establishment. Lonely plates of flat lemon flan behind a finger-marked glass screen made no false promises. We restricted our order to coffee and scraped noisy chairs from an empty table. A disappointing first sip betrayed the blandness of chicory, and tinned evaporated milk from a chipped jug cloyed if you put in too much. Only the smell of bacon enticed until we saw the waitress carrying it to a table by the window. Undercooked and over-fatty alongside a triangle of fried bread it lost its appeal. The legacies of colonialism are many.

'Good morning, Tony. Have you just come off night shift?' She chattered as she set down the tray.

Tony glanced at the expanse of leg revealed under her mini-skirt and grunted before getting stuck-in to his greasy breakfast. He wore an open-necked khaki shirt tucked into belted shorts which stopped a few inches above long stockings and sturdy shoes. Looking like the ones Scotsmen wear with a kilt I wondered at the suitability of such robust socks in an African country. His strong accent betrayed the same South-African origins as the waitress.

We sipped hot liquid and looked around. A large Zambian woman sat down at a table near us and unfastened the ties in the cloth securing the baby on her back. Self-contained in the way of African mothers she showed no haste in her movements. The child now on her lap reached with chubby hands for the condiments and paper napkins on the table. She restrained him with her left arm and fumbled under her wrap with her right hand. Releasing an ample breast from her clothing she then reached for the sugar bowl and dipped a dark nipple into the white crystals making sure it was well covered. She offered this confection to the infant and he responded with enthusiasm allowing her to sit back placidly to slurp her own drink in peace.

'I'm glad I don't take sugar!' I whispered.

'Me too,' answered Ross.

We drew into the Copperbelt town of Kitwe, the last town before Chingola, early in the morning of the 4th December, and my eyes were agog for clues to a new life. Our friends Dave and Sandra lived here and we planned to pay them a visit. We looked for a phone box, but found none. Although we hadn't been in contact for the duration of our trip, we could rely on them to welcome us, and we'd continue to Chingola if they weren't at home. They had left on the mail ship in July so already had four months of expatriate life experience under their belts.

We found Kantanta Street in a leafy part of Kitwe. '*Posopo lo Mbwa*' said the sign on the gate with a picture of a black dog baring vicious teeth. A black Labrador puppy wagged its way towards us and accompanied us up to the front door of a comfortable-looking Mine house. The single-storey building sat in a large square plot surrounded by flowering trees and bushes. Such luxury. My hopes rose for the standard of our own accommodation.

The door opened and there stood our old friend Sandra with a vacant expression on her face.

'Yes?' she said. 'Can I help you?'

'Hello!' we cried, 'we're here at last!'

She stared at us searching our faces without recognition and Ross spoke again. 'We finally got here! I hope it's not too early for you!'

'Hello, you made it,' she became flustered. 'How are you? You look great! Come on in, it's good to see you!' She voiced platitudes to cover her bewilderment.

We should have kept looking for a phone box to warn her. Sandra admitted much later that she hadn't recognised us until Ross spoke.

It wouldn't be possible to do what we'd done for eight weeks combined with sleeping in the car and a poor diet without suffering the consequences, even with youth on our side. Ross had lost two stone in weight that he couldn't afford. I was thinner too and our general health had suffered. My hair had not seen conditioner for weeks and split ends stuck out like straw; Ross needed a hair-cut; dark half-circles cast shadows under our eyes; and our clothes had seen better days. Like true friends they sheltered us from the 'Company' for a few days and tried to build some of our strength back before Ross presented himself for work. By the time we drove into Chingola the stares from other Europeans had become less obvious.

The journey had taken two months in which time we'd covered twelve thousand miles. This amounted to triple the predicted distance measured with a wheel and over double the revised estimate. Our change of route to encompass East Africa had made the biggest difference, but diversions and side-tracks also added significant mileage.

We'd set off from London with three hundred and twenty pounds and on arrival in Chingola there were ten pounds left. Of that money two hundred and sixty pounds had been spent on petrol, ferry crossings and the car; and the other fifty pounds spent on food, accommodation and the occasional cold beer. My swollen legs still bore scars from infected mosquito bites and Ross had never fully rid himself of the stomach bug he'd had since his initial bout in the Sahara. Our record of the journey amounted to a rather boring log book wearily completed after exhausting days, and seven poor-quality black and white photo negatives. For years afterwards we lost our taste for bananas, and the fan belt failure was our only one in a life-time of driving.

The car, five months old at our time of arrival, was in a very sorry state and no longer the golden dream on wheels, but it was a tribute to the manufacturers that it made the journey at all. It had never been designed for such abuse. We had completed a route that we'd been warned over and over again would be impossible and the real golden dream had become a part of us. The enduring memory of people rich and poor who befriended and helped us on our way has never left us. We'd never have made it without them.

For eight weeks we'd been totally occupied with our own problems and we'd given little thought for the inevitable tensions and worries for those left behind. My parents had bought a large map of Africa, and as our letters were delivered my father compared notes with Ross's parents to plot our journey in red marker pen. When we finally sent a telegram announcing our arrival on the fourth of December, he was so overjoyed and relieved that he found a large Union Jack in the loft and stuck it on a pole in the middle of their small front lawn in Colinton Road for all to see. The passengers on the busy bus route must have thought him very patriotic!

We visited the local Society for the Prevention of Cruelty to Animals in Kitwe to get a guard-dog as advised by all our new acquaintances. Robberies and house break-ins were a problem.

'Oooh, look at those tiny kittens!' I exclaimed.

We approached a cage where two pieces of playful fluff clung to the wire.

'Shall we take one of these as well as the dog?' I pleaded, falling in love with the tiny creatures.

We had to wait for the dog but took one of the kittens away with us. We'd liked the name of Chergui's brother in Tamanrasset, and used his name for our new pet, Sassi. He did what all kittens do and climbed everything there was to climb, including Ross's leg. Sassi could sit comfortably in the palm of my hand so his tiny scratches went unnoticed.

My illness in Nairobi demonstrated how run-down I'd become, but Ross I am sure did not allow himself to become ill and was still running on adrenaline. Once settled in our own house in Chingola, number fourteen Eleventh Street, and the day he started work he finally succumbed and became so ill I could have lost him.

Three days after we took our kitten with us to Chingola, and as he donned his newly issued work khakis, Ross noticed signs of an infection in his leg from the almost invisible kitten-scratches. On his first day at work he hobbled into the Mine offices. His new boss sent him straight to the hospital and the doctor signed Ross off work before he'd even started. Two days later he pulled up the cotton of his shorts to show me red poison lines creeping upwards from under his long thick sock. He went back to the hospital. The first course of antibiotics hadn't worked and blood samples had to be sent to South Africa in order to prescribe the right one. The doctor was worried. He prescribed complete rest until the infection subsided.

It turned out to be 'cat-scratch fever' which is not normally dangerous in temperate climates. But in Zambia and in a patient whose immune system has been compromised by a demanding journey it became life-threatening until the right antibiotic could be found.

Taking time off work in the first week of starting a new job was not the way to impress management in normal circumstances. His growing reputation for having completed such a challenging journey soon mitigated any damage and we found ourselves telling and retelling tales from our journey to an audience who understood Africa. This is what embedded them into our memory and decades later we finally have them down on paper. We'd driven down a narrow corridor in time between the Biafran war in Nigeria and the explosion of Idi Amin's blood-soaked regime in Uganda; between the Congo Crisis and tribal warfare in Rwanda; following the dominance, cruelties and paternalism of colonialism into the stumbling perilous first steps of emerging independent African nations.

It had been a long and a dusty road and the swallows overtook us, but we still arrived before the ship.

# *Acknowlegements*

I would like to thank every kind stranger who helped us on this journey, and hope they have found the same kindness in their own travels.

I would also like to thank the following people for helping me to bring our story to life: -

The Paphos Writers Group; Val Day; Bryan Drake; Eddy Rafter; Anne Jennings-Brown; Ian Dey; Nigel Pearson; and most of all Ross who has been with me every step of the way, prepared the maps and turned his hand to drawing.